"When you're facing a maze, it's not only crucial to know to get out; you also need to know the way to get in. For many beginning students, Greek is indeed a 'foreign language'—the letters look strange; the pronunciation sounds strange; and just when you think you're getting the hang of it, somebody tells you that you are at a dead end. Chad Thornhill has provided an excellent guide through the maze of beginning Greek that will not leave you lost in the middle with no clear way out. Written in clear, easy-to-follow prose, this book is an excellent step-by-step guide to begin to learn the language of the New Testament. I commend this to every student who would like to finally stop saying 'It's all Greek to me!'"

Ben Witherington III, Jean R. Amos Professor of New Testament
for Doctoral Studies, Asbury Theological Seminary;
doctoral faculty emeritus, St. Andrews University, Scotland

"Many who have never taken courses in Greek feel they lack the skills to interpret the New Testament competently. For many the only thing more challenging than interpreting the New Testament without a working knowledge of Greek is actually learning Greek. Few people have hundreds of hours to memorize the thousands of words and grammatical forms that are the focal points of traditional courses in Greek. But without such an investment, how can students move beyond dependence on English translations? A. Chadwick Thornhill's *Greek for Everyone* bridges this gap. *Greek for Everyone* solves the vocabulary problem by focusing on the use of interlinear tools and deciphering grammatical terms and concepts. The result is a readable resource for self-study that orients readers to the impact of the Greek language for interpretation, one that evades the sorts of obstacles that discourage Bible students."

Michael Heiser, scholar in residence, Logos Bible Software

"In *Greek for Everyone* we have a great introduction to the Greek of the New Testament. What makes this book distinctive is that it is written especially for those who need help understanding language and grammar, things that most other grammars assume readers already know.

Professor Thornhill provides helpful, transparent explanations of the grammar of the Greek New Testament. From participles to prepositions, from nouns to verbs, *Greek for Everyone* keeps it simple and clear. Students will love it."

Craig A. Evans, John Bisagno Distinguished Professor
of Christian Origins and dean of the School
of Christian Thought, Houston Baptist University

"Dr. Chad Thornhill has done us a tremendous service in this useful book. By distilling his experience teaching Greek, he has given us a wonderful resource with a multitude of applications: pastors who have let their Greek slide or simply need a refresher, professors who would like to glean from another teacher of the language, students who could benefit from additional encouragement and insight as they grapple with Greek, and lay people who may not have had an opportunity to study the language formally but who would love nothing more than to grow in their understanding of the New Testament. There is something here for everyone. I can't recommend this resource highly enough!"

Todd Wilson, senior pastor, Calvary Memorial Church;
cofounder and chairman of the Center for Pastor Theologians

GREEK FOR EVERYONE

GREEK FOR EVERYONE

INTRODUCTORY GREEK FOR BIBLE STUDY AND APPLICATION

A. CHADWICK THORNHILL

BakerBooks
a division of Baker Publishing Group
Grand Rapids, Michigan

Published by Baker Books
a division of Baker Publishing Group
P.O. Box 6287, Grand Rapids, MI 49516-6287
www.bakerbooks.com

Printed in the United States of America

Library of Congress Cataloging-in-Publication Data
Names: Thornhill, A. Chadwick, 1983– author.
Title: Greek for everyone : introductory Greek for Bible study and application / A. Chadwick Thornhill.
Description: Grand Rapids, MI : Baker Books, 2016. | Includes bibliographical references, appendices, and index.
Identifiers: LCCN 2016009299 | ISBN 9780801018916 (pbk.)
Subjects: LCSH: Greek language, Biblical—Self-instruction. | Greek language, Biblical—Grammar—Problems, exercises, etc.
Classification: LCC PA817 .T56 2016 | DDC 487/.4—dc23
LC record available at http://lccn.loc.gov/2016009299

Unless otherwise noted, all translations are the author's.

16 17 18 19 20 21 22   7 6 5 4 3 2 1

For my parents,
Bobby and Darlene,
who have invested so much in me

Contents

Contents

Preface

If you've ever wondered why our Bible translations differ (sometimes drastically), why pastors, theologians, and scholars differ on how to interpret the Gospels or the writings of Paul, what reading the original words of the New Testament might reveal, or how to better study the New Testament in order to better teach, preach, or live its message, this book was written for you. Studying the New Testament in Greek opens up a world of interpretation not possible without it. A colleague of mine often says it's like going from black-and-white television to high-definition. This book will not make you a master of the Greek language, but it will enable you to understand its basics, interact with quality commentaries and research on the New Testament, and gain more confidence in rightly interpreting the Bible.

The resources available today for learning Greek and Hebrew are immense and incredibly helpful. With that in mind, I have written this book to focus solely on issues of morphology (how words are formed), grammar (how meaning is structured), syntax (how words and phrases are arranged), structural analysis (how ideas interact with one another), and introductory exegetical (i.e., interpretive) matters. The goal is to understand how language as a whole works, and in particular the Greek language, and to apply our findings to Scripture. Through this book we will not become experts in Greek, but we will become better students of the New Testament.

This book is dedicated to all of the students who have put up with my instruction in Greek grammar for nearly a decade now. Their interactions have helped to shape how I understand, teach, and appreciate the language of the New Testament. My goal for this book is to equip the reader with a working knowledge of Greek. This will not be equivalent to the experience most students receive in an undergraduate, seminary, or graduate program in Greek, where the emphasis is on memorizing numerous vocabulary words, conjugations, and declensions and translating large portions of the New Testament. Rather, this book aims to equip those who do not undertake that process. While other, more intensive approaches may result in a more extensive understanding of the language and more efficient interaction with texts, this approach will seek to equip the reader with the *skills* to work through a passage exegetically, knowing how to get the lay of the textual land and understand what features to give the most attention.

I would be remiss, of course, not to thank also my own Greek professors. First, Dr. Ben Gutierrez introduced me with his usual passion to Greek in his introductory grammar courses many years ago and helped instill in me a desire to continue growing in my knowledge of New Testament Greek. Also, Dr. Jim Freerksen greatly influenced me through his instruction and his modeling the patience, persistence, and humility needed for those seeking to both learn and teach the Scriptures to others.

Drs. Wayne Stacy and Daniel Steffen have my gratitude for their thorough and insightful comments and remarks on a rough draft of this text. Their input was invaluable, and the book is better off because of their thoroughness.

One final note: I have generally opted not to include endnotes in the initial chapters of this work in order to make it as accessible as possible to the reader. This may give the regrettable impression that everything herein is the result of my own work. This is certainly not the case. I would like to acknowledge the important conversation partners on whom I have relied in writing this work. First, Logos Bible Software, which I highly recommend, was invaluable in searching for examples and looking at usage patterns. I rely in most places on the *Lexham Greek-English Interlinear New Testament* for interlinear presentations (with modifications in places), and the text of the Greek New Testament is taken from the *Novum Testamentum Graece*, Nestle-Aland, 28th edition. Second, I highly recommend the works of A. T. Robertson (*A Grammar of the Greek New Testament in Light of Historical Research*), William Mounce (*Basics of Biblical Greek*), Rodney Decker (*Reading Koine Greek*), Daniel Wallace (*Greek Grammar beyond the Basics*), Stanley Porter (*Idioms of the Greek New Testament*), Constantine Campbell (*Basics of Verbal Aspect in Biblical Greek*), and Steven Runge (*Discourse Grammar of the Greek New Testament*).[1] I have reviewed other works on occasion, but these resources were ever at my side and are a must for anyone who is interested in taking their study of New Testament Greek further than what is offered in this (very) introductory book.

I pray both that this book faithfully represents the language of the New Testament and that it might be used "to equip the saints for the work of ministry" (Eph. 4:12).

Abbreviations

General

acc.	accusative	neut.	neuter
chap(s).	chapter(s)	nom.	nominative
dat.	dative	pl.	plural
fem.	feminine	sg.	singular
gen.	genitive	voc.	vocative
masc.	masculine		

Bible Editions and Versions

AMP	The Amplified Bible
CEV	Contemporary English Version
ESV	English Standard Version
GNT	Good News Translation
GW	GOD'S WORD Translation
HCSB	Holman Christian Standard Bible
KJV	King James Version
LEB	Lexham English Bible
LXX	Septuagint
MSG	The Message
NA[28]	*Novum Testamentum Graece*, Nestle-Aland, 28th edition

NASB   New American Standard Bible
NCV   New Century Version
NET   The NET Bible (New English Translation)
NIrV   New International Reader's Version
NIV   New International Version
NKJV   New King James Version
NLT   New Living Translation
RSV   Revised Standard Version
TLB   The Living Bible
TNIV   Today's New International Version
UBS⁵   *The Greek New Testament*, United Bible Societies, 5th edition

Secondary Sources

BDAG   Frederick W. Danker, Walter Bauer, William F. Arndt, and F. Wilbur Gingrich, *A Greek-English Lexicon of the New Testament and Other Early Christian Literature*, 3rd ed. (Chicago: University of Chicago Press, 2000)

Liddell-Scott   Henry George Liddell, Robert Scott, and Henry Stuart Jones, *A Greek-English Lexicon*, 9th ed. with rev. supplement (Oxford: Clarendon, 1996)

Louw-Nida   Johannes P. Louw and Eugene A. Nida, eds., *Greek-English Lexicon of the New Testament: Based on Semantic Domains*, 2nd ed. (New York: United Bible Societies, 1989)

LTW   Douglas Mangum, ed., *Lexham Theological Wordbook* (Bellingham, WA: Lexham, 2014)

Lust   J. Lust, E. Eynikel, and K. Hauspie, eds., *Greek-English Lexicon of the Septuagint*, rev. ed. (Stuttgart: Deutsche Bibelgesellschaft, 2003)

NIDNTTE   Moisés Silva, ed., *New International Dictionary of New Testament Theology and Exegesis*, 2nd ed., 5 vols. (Grand Rapids: Zondervan, 2014)

1

Language Learning, Koine Greek, and the Greek Alphabet

Learning a new language is like learning to dance. There are rules that govern one's participation in the activity. In dancing, the elements of rhythm, space, and motion come together to create something beautiful. Should one not follow the rules appropriately, moving too fast or slow, moving the wrong way or the wrong foot, the results become disastrous. You could go from tango to disco in one fell swoop!

Language, like dance, has its own rules. Instead of coordinating our movements to the music, we bring together different elements to create meaning, things such as lexical (think "dictionary") data, grammar, and syntax. But in order to understand what is being said, we must understand the parts to understand the whole, just like trying to learn a new dance. Like a zoom lens, our approach in this book will take that journey by first, after our preliminaries, thinking about the whole of how language works before examining the parts that make up a sentence, and then zooming back out to see how the whole looks different with these parts understood.

1

How to Learn a New Language

In my first-semester Greek classes, my students often look for shortcuts as they navigate the maze of learning a new language (and a "dead" language at that!). Eventually they catch on and realize that shortcuts do not exist in the world of language learning. Repetition and memorization are the initial building blocks of the adventure, and apart from those practices, little progress can be made. There are some important strategies, however, that can help along the way. As I coach you through this journey, I would like to pass on to you these same time-tested principles.

Study in increments. Students quickly discover that cramming for a language exam does not work well. Just as a good meal deserves to be savored, learning a language requires a slow-paced, methodical approach. I often ask my students, "How do you eat an elephant?" to which the only proper response is "One bite at a time!" Greek will feel like an elephant on your plate at times, so approaching this feast in small, manageable bites is a necessity.

Master vocabulary. One of the most important building blocks in learning a language is mastering the vocabulary. Here, again, where memorization is so important, shortcuts will prove ineffective, and a manageable approach is essential. Through this book we will work to learn some of the most common vocabulary in the New Testament in order to make our study of the text more efficient. Keeping up with the vocabulary is a must!

Learn in a group. Learning in general takes place more effectively when a group of learners collaborate. When you are ready to quit, they will be there for encouragement. When a new concept or term isn't sticking, they may have some memorization techniques to help you. If possible, working through this book with other like-minded individuals will be to your advantage.

Don't take shortcuts! I've mentioned several times now that there are no shortcuts in language learning. This doesn't mean that they haven't been tried, but rather it means that they have been found wanting. Time and repetition are vital for language to stick. You may be able to cram for a vocabulary quiz, but a few weeks, months, and years from now, that information will not be retained. Time and repetition (both in this book and afterward) will ensure the effort you put into learning will continue to pay dividends down the road.

Make sure you understand the material before moving on to the next chapter. Going back to our meal analogy, even if it were possible to eat the elephant in one sitting, the aftermath would not be pretty. No matter how savory a meal might be, if you overindulge, there will be consequences. In the same vein, your brain can take only so much new information at one time before it shuts off. As we move through the material, make sure that you understand each chapter and its concepts before moving on to the next. Allow the concepts to simmer and soak into your brain. Language learning, to be effective, must be a marathon, not a sprint.

Use multiple senses. The more senses you employ in language learning, the more quickly your brain will absorb the information. This means that reading (visual), writing (physical), and saying (audial) the letters, words, phrases, and sentences that we explore will contribute to better retention. I've found that the last element (saying) intimidates students the most, but just remember that you will never do what you do not try. Even if the sounds come out weird or wrong at first, keep practicing until you get it right.

Start using your Greek for reading the New Testament. One of the best motivating factors for persevering in your Greek studies is to start looking at the New Testament. All sorts of great resources (which we will discuss later) are available to make the Greek New Testament accessible to new readers of Greek. The more you use Greek in your own study, whether for sermon preparation, academic study, or personal enrichment, the more likely you are to keep using it in the months and years ahead.

What Is Koine?

Language itself is never static, always evolving through usage. We often laugh at the new words added to the dictionary each year that seem unnecessary (like "hashtag," "selfie," and "tweep" in 2014), but this practice recognizes that culture, and language with it, is constantly in flux. You may notice, as will be illustrated through this book, that the words and forms that are used most frequently in most languages are often the most irregular, breaking the normal patterns of usage. For example, most verbs in English do not change their form significantly when their subject changes (e.g., I run, you run, he runs). Common verbs, such as a stative verb like "is," however, are often irregular (e.g., I am, you are, he is). With usage comes accommodation and alteration.

The language of the New Testament is known as Koine (i.e., "common") Greek. As the Greek language spread across the ancient world as a result of Alexander the Great's conquests, the language encountered other dialects and went through various metamorphoses. The Koine period, spanning from about 330 BCE to 330 CE, represents the height of ancient empires, when the entire Mediterranean region was united under a single rule and language. Koine, as a common dialect, was less polished than its earlier, classical predecessor, a result of the spread of the language. Koine, in general, adopted shorter, less complex sentences than classical Greek, and implicit features in classical Greek became explicit (and thus easier to recognize for the masses) in Koine. Even within Koine, however, there were more and less polished forms of the dialect, as found when comparing, for example, the Greek of Mark against the refined Greek of Luke-Acts. Thus, when we examine exegetical features related to grammar, we must take care to do this in the context of the writing we are studying and avoid making sweeping claims that may or may not be true of the style of each author of the New Testament.

The other benefit of learning Koine is that, while grammatical differences exist between them, much of what is learned about the New Testament applies also to the Greek Old Testament (the Septuagint [LXX], the Greek translation of the Old Testament) and the writings of many of the early church fathers. Investing in learning this language can pay dividends beyond just our study of the New Testament.

Table 1. Greek Alphabet and Pronunciation

Letter Name	Upper-case	Lower-case	Translit-eration	Pronunciation	Alternate Pronunciation
Alpha	A	α	*a*	"a" as in "father"	
Beta	B	β	*b*	"v" as in "vet"	"b" as in "book"
Gamma	Γ	γ	*g*	"g" as in "go"	
Delta	Δ	δ	*d*	"th" as in "the"	"d" as in "dog"
Epsilon	E	ε	*e*	"e" as in "bet"	
Zeta	Z	ζ	*z*	"dz" as in "gadzooks"	
Eta	H	η	*ē*	"i" as in "ski"	"a" as in "ape"
Theta	Θ	θ	*th*	"th" as in "theater"	
Iota	I	ι	*i*	"i" as in "ski"	"i" as in "igloo" (short), "i" as in "ski" (long)
Kappa	K	κ	*k*	"k" as in "kettle"	
Lambda	Λ	λ	*l*	"l" as in "love"	
Mu	M	μ	*m*	"m" as in "mother"	
Nu	N	ν	*n*	"n" as in "nose"	
Xi	Ξ	ξ	*x*	"x" as in "oxen"	
Omicron	O	ο	*o*	"o" as in "oval"	"o" as in "hot"
Pi	Π	π	*p*	"p" as in "party"	
Rho	P	ρ	*r*	"r" as in "race"	
Sigma	Σ	σ, ς	*s*	"s" as in "snake"	
Tau	T	τ	*t*	"t" as in "tour"	
Upsilon	Y	υ	*u, y*	"u" as in "flu" or "i" as in "ski"	
Phi	Φ	φ	*ph*	"ph" as in "phone"	
Chi	X	χ	*ch*	"ch" as in "loch"	
Psi	Ψ	ψ	*ps*	"ps" as in "psychology"	
Omega	Ω	ω	*ō*	"o" as in "oval"	

Alphabet, Pronunciation, and Punctuation

We won't get far learning Greek if we don't know the alphabet and how to pronounce it. In table 1 you will find the letter names, upper-case symbols (found in our earliest manuscripts, without accents or punctuation marks—more on that below and in chap. 15), the lowercase symbols (which we will use and are found in our printed Greek New Testaments), the transliteration values (which we use when writing Greek in English characters), and the pronunciations. While varying pronunciation systems are employed by Greek scholars, we will use the one that likely best approximates how Koine Greek was spoken in the ancient world. (The final column of the table also provides a version of the Erasmian pronunciation scheme, which is the traditional pronunciation system many teachers and scholars favor.)

We have a few more bits of information to cover before we are ready to start reading Greek. First, we have seven vowels in Koine Greek (α, ε, η, ι, ο, υ, ω) and seventeen consonants. **Sigma** is represented by two symbols, one occurring at the beginning of or within a word (σ, such as in σῶμα), and one occurring only at the end of a word (ς, such as in λόγος).

Second, you may also notice that **upsilon** (υ) has two different transliteration values, a *u* occurring when it is paired with another vowel (forming a diphthong, such as εὐθύς) and a *y* when it occurs on its own (such as ὑπέρ).

Third, like English, Greek employs what are known as **diphthongs**, which are vowel combinations that make a single sound together. Table 2 lists the proper diphthongs in Koine Greek.

The improper diphthong, which is not pronounced, occurs when an **iota** (ι) is placed below an alpha (α), eta (η), or omega (ω). This iota subscript (such as under the alpha [α] at the end of καρδίᾳ) is not pronounced, but it does often impact the meaning of a word, so be aware of it.

Fourth, **gamma** (γ), when preceding another guttural consonant (like gamma [γ], kappa [κ], chi [χ], or xi [ξ]), will make an "n" sound, as in the word ἄγγελος, which we would pronounce as "angelos" rather than "aggelos."

Fifth, there are also **accents** and **breathing marks** in Greek. **Accents** were added to help nonnative speakers recognize when to make changes in their vocal inflections when pronouncing words. They occur only

Table 2. Diphthongs

αι	"ai" as in "air"
ει	"ei" as in "receive"
οι	"oi" as in "oil"
υι	"ui" as in "suite"
αυ	"av" as in "avoid"
ευ	"ev" as in "ever"
ου	"ou" as in "soup"

over vowels and diphthongs. The **acute** accent (ά) points upward, the **grave** accent (ὰ) points downward (to the grave!), and the **circumflex** accent (ᾶ) is curved. **Breathing marks** occur only at the beginning of a word and usually over a vowel or diphthong, and they can affect both the pronunciation and the meaning of a word. The **smooth** breathing mark (ἀ) is unpronounced and is the most common. The **rough** breathing mark (ἁ) is pronounced with an "h" sound.

Finally (and by now you are saying, "There is more?"), our Greek New Testament also contains "uninspired" **punctuation**. As we mentioned in passing earlier, our earliest manuscripts were written in uppercase characters and contained no punctuation. Punctuation, like accent marks, was added later to aid in reading. Our four punctuation marks are the **comma** (,), which looks like an English comma; the **period** (.), which looks like an English period; the **semicolon** (·), which looks like a "floating" period; and the **question mark** (;), which looks like an English semicolon.

Let's Read!

In just one chapter you are now already ready to start reading Greek (never mind that we will have no idea yet what any of this means). Feel free to brag to your friends! But seriously, let's work at practicing some of what we just covered.

Let's sound out the word below (you can reference the chart above, but be sure to memorize the alphabet and its sounds as soon as possible).

λόγος

For good measure, let's break it into syllables.

λό   γος

Okay, let's put it back together now and then transliterate it.

λόγος   *logos*

Curious about this word? λόγος means "word," "message," or "account." We are familiar with this from John 1:1, where we read, "In the beginning was the Word [λόγος]."

Okay, now let's try a few words together. Sound out each letter, and then put the sounds together for each word. You may even want to write it down on a piece of paper or index card as you say it.

εὐλογήσαι σε κύριος

Let's separate the syllables again to make it easier.

εὐ λο γή σαι   σε   κύ ρι ος

Now again together and transliterated.

εὐλογήσαι σε κύριος   *eulogēsai se kyrios*

Curious what this means? This comes from the Septuagint of Numbers 6:24 in the passage known as the priestly blessing. We might translate this as "May the Lord bless you."

εὐλογήσαι	σε	κύριος
May he bless	you	(the) Lord

(How did we know that σε was the object of our verb and κύριος the subject? More on that ahead.)

All right, one last thing to practice before we move on (and remember, make sure you have this chapter well in hand before moving on to the next). Write out the following passage on a sheet of paper, and practice pronouncing each word aloud. It may take some practice, but keep trying even if it doesn't come naturally at first (remember, you can transliterate it as well if it will help with the pronunciation).

Πάτερ, ἁγιασθήτω τὸ ὄνομά σου· ἐλθέτω ἡ βασιλεία σου·
τὸν ἄρτον ἡμῶν τὸν ἐπιούσιον δίδου ἡμῖν τὸ καθ' ἡμέραν·
καὶ ἄφες ἡμῖν τὰς ἁμαρτίας ἡμῶν, καὶ γὰρ αὐτοὶ ἀφίομεν
    παντὶ ὀφείλοντι ἡμῖν·
καὶ μὴ εἰσενέγκῃς ἡμᾶς εἰς πειρασμόν.

Father, may your name be revered; may your kingdom come;
give to us each day our daily bread;
and forgive us our sins, for we ourselves are also forgiving
    everyone indebted to us;
and do not lead us into temptation. (Luke 11:2–4)

2

The Big Picture of Language

Most grammars would take us at this point straight into the details of Greek forms (probably nouns or verbs of some variety). Our focus in this book is learning Greek in order to become better students of Scripture rather than students of Greek. While most introductions to Greek explain the forms and functions of the language (and necessarily so), few do so specifically in conjunction with developing Bible study skills. Since that is the interest for those who want to know enough Greek to understand the New Testament, it will be helpful for us to approach exploring Greek with that end in mind. Our aim is thus to balance the "what" of language and the "so what" of Bible study. Furthermore, too often in the process of exegesis, we focus solely on the various parts of a passage (primarily words and phrases) and never step back and look at the big-picture meaning of a text. This happens as well in examining grammar. Our starting point will thus be to think about how language works in the first place.

What Does It Mean?

I often assign exegetical papers to my students in order to examine just how well they can deploy the tools they have been given to analyze a passage. Too often I find a sentence as follows: "This verb is a second aorist, active, indicative, third person, singular and means 'he went.'" Now, from our vantage point that might seem like an impressive array of information, especially since we may not yet know what half of those words mean. The problem, however, is that the student has dumped a good bit of grammatical information in front of us without asking why it is relevant or how it helps us to better understand the text. Grammar is essential for understanding any passage, but just knowing how to recognize the form of a word and to parse it (i.e., to identify all of its grammatical features) does not equal exegesis.

Here is where the big picture is important. We will begin and end our journey with the big picture in mind. If all we gain from studying Greek is the ability to identify grammatical features, we haven't gained much at all. If, however, our understanding of grammatical features enables us to better understand the meaning of a passage, then we have gained much.

So what do we mean when we talk about the "big picture" of language? Essentially this: *words do not have meaning.* "Preposterous!" you might say. And I am, of course, exaggerating (a little). For example, "cat" for most English speakers invokes the image of a four-legged feline. But it could also, in a certain context, refer to a "cool guy" (especially as it relates to jazz musicians) or even be an abbreviation or acronym for some other, even more obscure meaning. Or take the word "ball." The initial image is probably of some sort of spherical object, like a soccer ball or baseball. But it may also refer to the count against a batter (e.g., "three balls and two strikes") or a formal event. So how do we know what meaning a word takes? Context. Words have ranges of meaning, which we sometimes refer to as their "semantic domain," but the context determines which meaning is intended in a given passage. Thus what we must examine in exegesis are the words themselves (lexical information), their relationships to one another (grammar/syntax), and the context in which they occur (literary analysis).

11

If we were to map out a sentence visually using zeros instead of words, we would end up with something like figure 2.1 (just humor me for now). We will even throw in some punctuation for good measure.

Fig. 2.1

0 0 0 0 0 0 0 0 . 0 0 0 0 , 0 0 0 0 0 , 0 0 0 . 0 0 0 0 0 0 .

When we operate on the word level, as important as it is, we neglect to examine how these bits of data are related.

Levels of Meaning

In the above examples, however, we were primarily dealing with meaning at the level of the word ("What does this word mean around these other words?"). Grammar also helps us to distinguish how groups of words, which we call **clauses** and **phrases**, relate to one another. We will talk about these items in more detail in the next chapter, but for now we should think of clauses and phrases as groups of words that have defined parameters in terms of what words are "in" and what words are "out."

Within a clause or phrase (which I will simply call a "group of words" or GW, for now), there are defined relationships between the words. Each word in the GW has a role to play in relationship with the other words in the GW. If we return to our diagram, we might think of it now more like this:

Fig. 2.2

(0000) (0000.) (0000,) (00000,) (000.) (000000.)

We now can see more clearly defined boundaries in our "text." Our words carry meaning, yes, but as a part of a larger unit. Rarely do words stand on their own, grammatically unrelated to anything around them. It is within these GWs that we can better understand how individual words function. Their relationships with other words are what ultimately give them their meaning.

But there are other levels to consider. Our GWs combine to make sentences, complex arrays of words that deliver information to the reader. Some sentences may have only one or two GWs present in them. Others may have many (Paul is, perhaps, most famous for his run-on sentences, something that would make the average English teacher shudder and the ancient Greek teacher elated). So ultimately our words take their meaning from the GW, and the GW (composed of its words) from the sentence.

Fig. 2.3

We see, then, that words are not isolated entities that have meaning independent of their relationships to other words. Rather, there is a complex web of relationships between the words themselves, the GWs, and the sentences that they create. If we think that this is where our journey of structure ends, with our sentences tied in their nice, neat packages, we would be mistaken. Beyond the sentence level, we have a larger unit at work, where sentences join together. Bible scholars often refer to this as a "pericope" ("a cutting"), what we might think of in English as a paragraph or a section. So our sentences join together, formed by our words and GWs, to create a larger set of meaning. In a narrative, we might think of these sections as a scene, clearly delineated by certain discourse features, such as a change in location, characters, or theme. Our sentences thus belong to a bigger picture as well.

Fig. 2.4

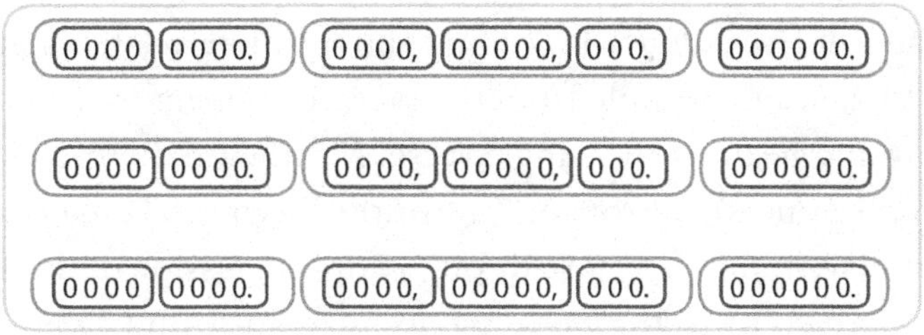

Okay, so now we have exhausted the level of relationship between words, GWs, sentences, and units, right? Not quite. A good writer, regardless of genre, knits together their work into a cohesive whole. So our units themselves also are a part of something bigger, which we might call the book level. We could possibly even expand our diagram further, but hopefully the point is well made. When we think about what a word means, we must think ultimately about its range of meaning and its contexts. To visualize this another way, we can arrange the structure as follows:

Fig. 2.5

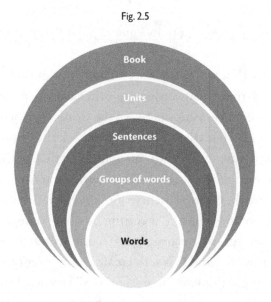

The Big Picture in the Gospel of Matthew

I have outlined some principles above concerning how we should think about these different units of meaning and their interrelationship. It may help to look at an example from the New Testament in the Gospel of Matthew and begin with a single verse. Matthew 5:17 reads, "Do not think that I came to destroy the Law or the Prophets; I did not come to destroy but to fulfill." To move through our progression outlined above, we may have come to this verse by doing a word study, for example, on the Greek word for "Law" (νόμος; *nomos*). To understand what is being said about the Law here, however, requires that we look beyond the word to the larger context.

We may notice here that nothing in the immediate context (such as a conjunction of some kind) grammatically indicates that a new section begins with Matthew 5:17. There is nothing here that seems to prompt Jesus's comments—no accusations from the scribes or Pharisees, no question from the disciples, and no introductory comment by Jesus. The comment comes within the context of the Sermon on the Mount, which begins in Matthew 5:1 and does not end until Matthew 7:28 (LEB), where we are told, "And it happened when Jesus finished these words, the crowds were amazed at his teaching." From Matthew 5:1 to 7:27, we find one, long, dense section of teachings from Jesus occurring in roughly twenty blocks of material. If we step out a bit further, we will find that the Sermon on the Mount is one of five blocks of discourse (5:1–7:27; 10:1–42; 13:1–52; 18:1–35; 24:1–25:46) in Matthew's Gospel that serve as a macrostructure for the whole Gospel. That Matthew intends this to serve as some organizing structure is made even clearer in that each discourse ends with a closing phrase noting the end of the section of teaching (7:28; 11:1; 13:53; 19:1; 26:1). The events of Matthew's narrative are thus hung around these large teaching units, and each of the units, containing various instructions, parables, and so on, is intended to be read both *as a unit* and as a part of the Gospel of Matthew as a literary whole. It is possible that Matthew has structured these teachings in five discourses to portray Jesus as a "new Moses," organizing the material in comparable fashion to the five books of Moses (Genesis–Deuteronomy). The possibility is strengthened by the events of Matthew 2–4, which Matthew arranges in similar fashion to Moses's story (threat of death by a tyrant king, fleeing for safety, coming out of Egypt, passing through the water [i.e., being baptized], and being tempted in the wilderness). If Matthew's structure intentionally presents Jesus as a new Moses (which it likely seems to do), then Jesus going up to the mountain to give his teachings in chapter 5 further follows the narrative pattern of Moses.

When we come across the word "Law" in Matthew 5:17, and Jesus's instruction "Do not think that I came to destroy the Law or the Prophets; I did not come to destroy but to fulfill," having this larger structure in mind will both further illuminate this section and prompt us to ask better questions about what is being said as we consider its meaning and significance. As we consider, for example, what Jesus means by "fulfilling" the Law instead of "destroying" it, this larger structure should inform our considerations.[1] And having this larger structure of Matthew's five discourses in mind adds greater significance to the end of the book as well, in the Great Commission. Here Matthew presents Jesus's instructions to the disciples—to teach new followers "to obey everything that I commanded you" (28:20).

I have dealt only very briefly here with this example from Matthew's Gospel. Hopefully, however, I have demonstrated the importance of stepping back and getting a fuller sense of the place of a passage in the context of a book. In doing so, we seek to pay attention to the author's own structural cues and the significance that this structure conveys to us. As we talk about language, grammar, meaning, and in particular how all of this fits together in Greek, it is this bigger picture that we need to keep in mind throughout our discussion. Word studies are necessary. Grammar is necessary. Syntax is necessary. But ultimately we will be working toward thinking about how all of these elements fit together to create something big. And Scripture, indeed, is big, and it is worth stepping back to look at the big picture.

3

Phrases, Clauses, and Conjunctions

As we begin to examine the way words, groups of words, sentences, and discourses interact, we will start on the intermediate level, looking at clauses, phrases, and conjunctions. As we examine these elements, a few definitions will be necessary before we can explore how these elements function in New Testament Greek.

A **sentence** is a structured group of words consisting at least of a subject and a predicate.

A **subject** is the "what" or "who" that a sentence is about.

A **predicate** is basically the rest of the sentence. It consists of a verb (stated or implied) and expresses something about the subject.

> NOTE: In this chapter we will be looking at various Greek parts of speech with which you are not yet familiar (e.g., prepositions, participles, infinitives, conjunctions, etc.). Our purpose in this chapter is to see how phrases and clauses work together to create meaning. We will address in later chapters how to identify and recognize these words using various methods and resources.

Phrases

A grammatical **phrase** is a group of words within a sentence that lacks a subject-predicate structure. Phrases are thus by nature grammatically **dependent**, meaning that they do not express a complete (i.e., subject-predicate) thought and must rely on other units of meaning to express it.

Prepositional Phrases

Prepositional phrases are introduced by, you guessed it, a preposition. A **preposition** is a word that specifies a relationship between a word in the sentence and another word (usually another noun or pronoun, though other words may be used as well). For example, in the statement "The boy climbed **onto the bus**," "onto" is the preposition and introduces the prepositional phrase "**onto** the bus." Here "the bus" is the **object of the preposition,** or the word that the preposition specifies. The relationship being specified here is *what* the boy climbed onto.

In Greek, the structure of prepositional phrases is very similar to English in that the preposition precedes its object. One unique feature of Greek prepositions is that they can take a range of meaning (e.g., διά [*dia*] can mean "through" or "because of," among other things). Often in Greek what narrows the meaning of the preposition is the case of the noun (which we will address in chaps. 6–8). For now, just realize that in Greek we must pay close attention to the object of the preposition to determine its meaning.

Since prepositional phrases are dependent, they always modify some other idea. They cannot form a complete thought (i.e., subject-predicate), and thus they give us more information about something else in the sentence.

Let's look at a few examples. One of the key prepositional phrases in Paul's writings is the phrase "in Christ." In fact, it is used almost exclusively by Paul in the New Testament. The phrase occurs twice in Romans 8:1–2. Let's read through the Greek aloud before we note the preposition.

Rom. 8:1

Οὐδὲν	ἄρα		νῦν	κατάκριμα	τοῖς	ἐν	Χριστῷ	Ἰησοῦ.
no	therefore	*(there is)*	now	condemnation	to those	in	Christ	Jesus

Therefore there is now no condemnation to those in Christ Jesus.

Our prepositional phrase here is ἐν Χριστῷ Ἰησοῦ (*en Christō Iēsou*). The phrase is introduced by the preposition ἐν, and the object of the preposition is Χριστῷ Ἰησοῦ. Notice the phrase occurs again in Romans 8:2, along with an additional prepositional phrase. Our phrase here specifies more information about the "those" who are not under condemnation, telling us it is a specific "those" in mind.

Rom. 8:2

ὁ	γὰρ	νόμος	τοῦ	πνεύματος	τῆς	ζωῆς	ἐν	Χριστῷ	Ἰησοῦ
the	for	law	of the	Spirit	of (the)	life	in	Christ	Jesus

For the law of the Spirit of life in Christ Jesus

ἠλευθέρωσέν	σε	ἀπὸ	τοῦ	νόμου	τῆς	ἁμαρτίας	καὶ	τοῦ	θανάτου.
has freed	you	from	the	law	of (the)	sin	and	of (the)	death.

has freed you from the law of sin and death.

We have repeated here the same phrase as in verse 1 (ἐν Χριστῷ Ἰησοῦ) with the additional prepositional phrase ἀπὸ τοῦ νόμου τῆς ἁμαρτίας καὶ τοῦ θανάτου (*apo tou nomou tēs hamartias kai tou thanatou*). Our preposition here (ἀπό) again introduces the phrase, and the object of our phrase is τοῦ νόμου ("the law"). This phrase is modified by two nouns; τῆς ἁμαρτίας ("[the] sin") and τοῦ θανάτου ("[the] death"), which are connected together by the conjunction καί ("and"; more on that below). Our phrase here specifies what "you" have been freed from, that is, from the law of sin and of death.

We will cover prepositions in more detail in chapter 8. For now, focus your attention on the way prepositions function to specify a relationship between a word in the sentence and the object(s) of the preposition. Remember also that prepositional phrases are dependent phrases, meaning that they give us additional information but do not form a complete thought.

Participial Phrases

Participles are verbal adjectives, meaning that they contain characteristics of both verbs (describing an action or state) and adjectives (describing a noun/pronoun). As such, even when functioning like an adjective, they carry verbal notions as well. As we saw with prepositional phrases, participial phrases will usually begin with the participle as the first word in the phrase. Participial phrases tend to be more complex than either prepositional (see above) or infinitival (see below) phrases. For now our focus is on recognizing the place of the participial phrase, which is grammatically dependent (i.e., it does not express a complete thought).

Since participles function like adjectives and verbs, we will take a look at an example that illustrates each function. In the sentence "**Having studied hard**, Karen felt prepared for the exam," "**Having studied**" represents our participle. Where two (or more) words (including helping verbs) are required in English to build participial phrases, in Greek all of this information is contained in the participle's form. On the adjectival end of the spectrum, in the sentence "The boy **singing** on the stage is my son," "**singing**" is our participle, and here it is modifying "boy," telling us more about that noun.

In Greek, participial phrases are structured similarly to English, but the participles themselves are far more complex than their English counterparts. This is because Greek participles encode a great deal of information within the form of the participle itself. Interpreting participles is tricky business (which we will explore in chap. 13). For now we are again highlighting how participial phrases structurally work in conjunction with other groups of words in the New Testament. A few examples will help to illustrate our point.

Matt. 8:1

Καταβάντος δὲ αὐτοῦ ἀπὸ τοῦ ὄρους ἠκολούθησαν αὐτῷ ὄχλοι Πολλοί.
after came down now   he   from the mountain   they came   to him crowds many

Now after he came down from the mountain many crowds came to him.

Our participle in this sentence is Καταβάντος (*katabantos*), which introduces the participial phrase. Our phrase contains the participle, its subject (αὐτοῦ), and a prepositional phrase (ἀπὸ τοῦ ὄρους). We would consider this a "temporal" participial phrase since it tells us about the time in which the main verb (ἠκολούθησαν) occurs. Note again that this phrase is dependent; it cannot stand alone and needs the verb of the main clause.

John 4:10

καὶ ἔδωκεν ἄν σοι ὕδωρ ζῶν
and he would give to you water living

and he would give to you living water

Our participle in this sentence is ζῶν (*zōn*), which makes up the entire participial phrase here. We would consider this an adjectival participle because it is modifying the noun ὕδωρ (*hydōr*), telling us more about the "water." Though containing verbal qualities, the participle cannot stand on its own but rather provides additional information about another element in the sentence.

Infinitive Phrases

Infinitive phrases are, much like participial phrases, flexible phrases with wide-ranging possibilities for meaning. An **infinitive** is a verbal noun, containing properties of both nouns (person, place, thing, etc.) and verbs (describes an action or state). As we saw with participles, some infinitive phrases will emphasize the noun end of the spectrum, and others the verbal end. In the sentence "The family wanted **to travel** to Europe," the infinitive "**to travel**" completes the main verb in the sentence, "wanted." In the sentence "**To fear** is a natural human emotion," the infinitive ("**to fear**") acts as the subject of the sentence. In both examples, the infinitive phrase is a dependent phrase, meaning that it cannot express a complete thought on its own.

In Greek, infinitive phrases function comparably to English infinitive phrases, but they are structured differently. While the form of the Greek infinitive is much simpler than that of the Greek participle, there are a number of syntactical issues with the infinitive that must be taken into account. We will address these issues in chapter 12, but for now our goal is to see how the infinitive phrase fits into the structure of the Greek sentence.

Matt. 5:17

Μὴ νομίσητε ὅτι ἦλθον **καταλῦσαι** τὸν νόμον ἢ τοὺς προφήτας
not you should that I came to destroy the Law or the Prophets
think
Do not think that I came to destroy the Law or the Prophets

Our infinitive in this sentence is καταλῦσαι (*katalysai*), which introduces the infinitival phrase. Here the infinitive phrase expresses the content of what Jesus's hearers should not think about why he came. The Law and the Prophets (τὸν νόμον ἢ τοὺς προφήτας) act as the object of the infinitive, the things that are not to be abolished or destroyed. The entire phrase is dependent and connects to the rest of the sentence in order to fill in the details of what Jesus expects his hearers to reject.

Phil. 1:21

Ἐμοὶ γὰρ **τὸ ζῆν** Χριστὸς καὶ **τὸ ἀποθανεῖν** κέρδος.
to me for to live (is) Christ and to die is gain
For to me to live is Christ and to die is gain.

Our sentence here has two infinitives, τὸ ζῆν (*to zēn*) and τὸ ἀποθανεῖν (*to apothanein*). Both are acting as the subject of a stative verb, which is implicit in the sentence (more on verbs in chaps. 5 and 9–11). Though containing verbal qualities, the phrases are still dependent.

Clauses

Though sometimes the words "phrase" and "clause" are used interchangeably, we will maintain a distinction between them. A **clause** is a group of words containing a subject and a predicate in which the predicate contains a finite verb. Thus the major difference between a clause and a phrase is that clauses contain a verb that can create a complete thought, while phrases, though they may contain verbals (i.e., participles and infinitives), do not contain a finite verb.

Clauses may, however, be either independent or dependent. An **independent clause** contains a finite verb and expresses a complete thought, meaning that it can stand alone with no further required elements. A **dependent clause**, however, though containing a finite verb, stands in a subordinate relationship to other elements in the sentence. Thus it requires connection to an independent clause to be grammatically correct.

For example, in the sentence "John raised his hand because he knew the answer," we have two clauses. The first clause ("John raised his hand") is an independent clause. If we removed the second half of the sentence, this clause would function just fine on its own. The second clause, however, since it is introduced by "because," stands in a subordinate relationship to the first clause. If we were to remove the first clause, the second could not stand on its own because it expresses an incomplete idea. To explore this further, we will look at examples of these clauses from the New Testament.

Independent Clauses

Independent clauses usually contain the main thought in a passage. There are different kinds of independent clauses, in terms of both function and form. Independent clauses may contain statements, questions, or commands. One of the challenges with English translations is that ideas that are *dependent* in Greek are frequently made *independent* in the English translation in order to better conform to English grammar and style. As we learn about the different kinds of verbal forms in later chapters, we will see how the form of the verb relates to its function in the sentence in terms of its independence or dependence. For now our goal is simply to understand these different grammatical levels of thought. An example will help to illustrate.

Matthew 28:19–20 is famously known as the Great Commission. Our translations don't always make clear, however, exactly what is being commissioned here. I've highlighted the verbal forms in the passage below.

πορευθέντες ... **μαθητεύσατε** ... βαπτίζοντες ... διδάσκοντες ...

go ... **make disciples** ... baptizing ... teaching ...

We have one independent clause in this passage, which contains the verb μαθητεύσατε (*mathēteusate*; "make disciples"). We know this by the kind of verb we have (more on that later). The other phrases in the passage are participial phrases, meaning that they are dependent on the command to "make disciples," so our main idea here is to "make disciples."

Dependent Clauses

Dependent clauses usually do not contain the main thought in a passage but rather contain supporting information related to the main thought. The primary way in which dependent clauses are introduced in the New Testament is either by a relative pronoun (a word such as "who" or "which"; we will discuss them in chap. 8) or a subordinating conjunction, which is a word that introduces a clause and creates a subordinate relationship (words such as "that," "because," "although," etc.; see below). Likewise, participles and infinitives are usually contained within dependent clauses. Since we will attend to the forms involved in dependent clauses later, our focus here again is simply on distinguishing between these different levels of thought.

Greek tends to pile on dependent clauses more than English does, which is why this often creates problems for translators. One classic example of this phenomenon is Ephesians 1:3–14. This long stretch of verses contains but one independent clause ("Blessed is the God and Father of our Lord Jesus Christ") and a string of dependent clauses that follow it, consisting of relative-pronoun clauses, participial phrases, infinitival phrases, and prepositional phrases. Since all of these clauses and phrases are grammatically dependent, it creates a large run-on sentence, which English translators tend to avoid. Structurally, since our independent clause comes first, we might say that everything that follows it supports Paul's declaration that God is "blessed" or "praised."

To return to the Great Commission discussed above, we recognize a number of dependent phrases here.

πορευθέντες ... μαθητεύσατε ... βαπτίζοντες ... διδάσκοντες ...
go ...   make disciples ...   baptizing ...   teaching ...

The dependent phrases here have two separate functions. The first participial phrase, "go" (πορευθέντες; *poreuthentes*), piggybacks on "make disciples" and acts like the imperative "make disciples," but it is secondary to it. The following two participial phrases, "baptizing" (βαπτίζοντες; *baptizontes*) and "teaching" (διδάσκοντες; *didaskontes*), are likewise dependent and specify how the making of disciples is to occur (i.e., by baptizing and teaching them). Again our main concern here is to note that paying attention to the structure of the passage gives us insight into the main and supporting ideas.

Conjunctions

One of the ways Greek sometimes distinguishes between independent and dependent clauses is by the conjunction used to introduce the clause. A **conjunction** is a word that connects words and constructions together. Many independent clauses in the Greek New Testament are introduced by a **coordinating conjunction**, which is a word that joins together two equal clauses (i.e., one is not subordinate to the other) that both contain a finite verb, such as what we call "indicative" or "imperative" verbs (more on these later). In Greek, our main coordinating conjunctions are καί (*kai*; "and," "now," "even"), δέ (*de*; "and," "now," "but"), γάρ (*gar*; "for"), ἀλλά (*alla*; "but"), and οὖν (*oun*; "therefore"). (Note: Some conjunctions like δέ, γάρ, and οὖν are "postpositive," meaning they appear second in the clause they introduce though they are translated first.) Thus when we see a finite verb with a coordinating conjunction, we will often find that our clause is independent. Though each conjunction performs a coordinating function, these conjunctions operate in differing ways.

καί—connects ideas that are usually in continuity with one another

δέ—marks some development or new information

γάρ—explanatory, giving offline or supplemental information

ἀλλά—offers a contrast with a previous idea

οὖν—notes development or conclusion with close connection to what has preceded

Many dependent clauses in the Greek New Testament are introduced by a **subordinating conjunction**, which is a word that joins together two unequal clauses (i.e., one is subordinate to the other) that contain a finite verb, such as a subjunctive verb (more to come on this). In Greek, our main subordinating conjunctions are ὅτι (*hoti*; "that," "because"), ἵνα (*hina*; "in order that," "so that"), εἰ (*ei*; "if"), ἐάν (*ean*; "if"), and ὅτε (*hote*; "when"). Clauses that follow these conjunctions will be grammatically dependent, supporting some other element in the sentence. Like their independent counterparts, though all introducing dependent clauses, these conjunctions have varying functions.

ὅτι—introduces a causal idea ("because") or specifies the content of something (e.g., "I know *that* . . .")

ἵνα—indicates a purpose for or a result of an action

εἰ, ἐάν—present a conditional idea ("if . . . then")

ὅτε—indicates the timing of an action

Summary

Before beginning our journey, we have taken this ten-thousand-foot view of the structure of Greek sentences in order to gain an understanding of the topography and the key landmarks we will find along the way. Having done so allows us to see how words and ideas fit together grammatically before we look at the various individual parts. As we suggested in chapter 2, understanding the structure of ideas is important in working toward understanding the meaning. In using language, we tend to structure our ideas for emphasis. This allows us to see the main ideas over against the supporting ideas. In doing so, we get a better sense of how much emphasis to assign to various phrases and clauses as we study and interpret the New Testament.

As we move through later chapters, we will explore some of the grammatical elements that contribute to independent and dependent thoughts in Greek. Our goal is to give a well-rounded, functional understanding of the language so such an understanding can be applied to studying the New Testament. But first, we will need to deal with how we can even tell all of these different kinds of words apart.

Words to Memorize

Though we are not taking a traditional-grammar approach, it will be helpful for us to learn some of the frequently reccurring words in the New Testament. Below are a few we encountered in this chapter that should be memorized.

ἀλλά	but, and, yet	καί	and, now, also, yet, then
γάρ	for, because		
δέ	and, but, now	ὅτε	when, as long as
ἐάν	if, when	ὅτι	that, because
εἰ	if, because, that	οὖν	therefore, thus, indeed, but
ἵνα	in order that, so that, that		

4

Resources for Navigating the Greek New Testament

Imagine that someone drove you to a city you had never visited before, handed you a map, and asked you to find a particular location. Depending on your general familiarity with the city, road systems, and so on, it would take you a bit of time to get acclimated, but you could most likely eventually find your way to the destination. Now imagine that they took you to a city in China, handed you a map written in Chinese, and asked you to find your way around. It's unlikely you would have much success. You would be better off finding a bilingual guide who could give you some pointers. The map would be rather useless.

Trying to navigate Greek offers a similar challenge. If you were given the Greek New Testament at this point and told to navigate, you'd likely feel like you were lost in Beijing. Fortunately there are some very helpful bilingual guides who can help us find our way around. Our goal in this chapter is to find out what resources are available to help us understand what we encounter when we open a Greek New Testament. But first, we need to talk a bit about the nature of Koine Greek.

An Inflected Language?

Greek is a highly inflected language. When I tell my first-year students this, they usually think I mean that Greek is an *infected* language. **Inflection** refers to the change of the form of the word to indicate a change in some component of meaning. English is also an inflected language, but it is not highly, or even consistently, inflected. For example, if I am describing several animals known as a "dog," I change the form of the word by adding an *s* to indicate the plural form of the word (i.e., "dogs"). Pronouns in English are also inflected, changing their form to indicate a change in **person** (the relationship between the author and the subject of the verb) or in **number** (whether singular or plural), as we see in "I," "you," "he, she, it," and so on. We see an example of the inconsistent inflection found in English in the second-person plural form of the pronoun ("you"), which is identical to the second-person singular form.

In Greek, most of our grammatical forms are inflected, and some of them are inflected in very complex ways. Nouns, adjectives, articles, pronouns, verbs, participles, and infinitives undergo some form of inflection in Greek. We will not attempt to memorize all of the different forms for these words as we would in a traditional-grammar approach, but we will attempt to have some recognition of these different parts of speech. Rather than memorizing endings to produce some reading fluency, we will instead utilize the resources available to help us understand the forms and functions of the words we will encounter in the Greek New Testament.

For example, a common noun in the Greek New Testament is λόγος (*logos*; "word"). This particular form of the word is its lexical form, or the form we would find when we went to look it up in a dictionary (or lexicon). But λόγος takes many other forms (seven others, to be exact). It can appear as λόγου, λόγῳ, λόγον, λόγοι, λόγων, λόγοις, or λόγους. Each of these forms indicates some particular grammatical information about the role the word is playing in the sentence. They all share the same possible range of meaning since they come from the same lexical form, but they perform different functions in a sentence. Understanding that most Greek words are inflected is incredibly important as we work to understand how words, phrases, clauses, sentences, and passages connect together.

Tools for the Journey

An ever-expanding plethora of resources is now available for Bible study. This is particularly true for language study. Whereas decades ago language study without a full course of grammatical study was extremely cumbersome, today print and electronic aids abound. We will not be able to cover here all of the resources available, but we will attempt to highlight the most important and significant resources.

Interlinear Bibles

The first and most efficient step in examining the Greek text is to use an interlinear New Testament. An interlinear will display the Greek text along with a rough English translation below or beside each Greek word. This allows the reader to see which English word or words were derived from the Greek terms. Some interlinears will also display the concordance number for each word so the words can be looked up in a concordance. Numerous interlinears are available on the book market. There are also a number of electronic resources available. Bible software programs, such as Logos, BibleWorks, or Accordance, include various kinds of interlinear New Testaments. While these software programs are extremely valuable for Bible study, they are also expensive. A number of free interlinears are also available online. Some recommended websites can be found below.

https://net.bible.org/
http://www.studylight.org/desk/interlinear.cgi
http://www.scripture4all.org/OnlineInterlinear/Greek_Index.htm
http://www.biblestudytools.com/interlinear-bible/

A typical interlinear will look something like the example below. Here the first line contains the inflected Greek text, as you would find it in the Greek New Testament. The second line shows the lexical form of the inflected words, allowing you to look up the term for further word study. The third line gives a rough English translation of the text. The fourth line contains the *Strong's Concordance* number, which is also useful for word studies. This thus allows us to examine the Greek text with English equivalents nearby and information for further study readily available.

John 1:1

Ἐν	ἀρχῇ	ἦν	ὁ	λόγος,	καὶ	ὁ	λόγος	ἦν	πρὸς	τὸν	θεόν
ἐν	ἀρχή	εἰμί	ὁ	λόγος	καί	ὁ	λόγος	εἰμί	πρός	ὁ	θεός
in	the beginning	was	the	word	and	the	word	was	with	—	God
1722	746	2258	3588	3056	2532	3588	3056	2258	4314	3588	2316

Lexicons

Once you've found the words behind our English translations, you may be curious what they mean. An interlinear will give the basic meaning of the word, but there is much more to meaning than that. Words rarely have a single meaning; rather, they have a range of meanings, which grammarians frequently call a word's "semantic domain" (which we discussed briefly in chap. 2). A lexicon will give a full-orbed picture of the meaning of a word. The standard lexicons for New Testament Greek are Bauer and Danker's *A Greek-English Lexicon of the New Testament and Other Early Christian Literature* and Louw and Nida's *Greek-English Lexicon of the New Testament: Based on Semantic Domains.*[1] While these are two of the most complete lexical aids available, they can also be expensive. These resources are often included or available in the Bible study software I mentioned earlier. There are, however, some online resources available that, though not as comprehensive, still give a good sense of the meaning of a word. I recommend the following sites:

http://www.biblestudytools.com/lexicons/greek/nas/
http://www.tlg.uci.edu/lsj/#eid=1&context=lsj
http://www.studylight.org/lexicons/greek/
http://www.perseus.tufts.edu/hopper/resolveform?redirect=true
https://www.teknia.com/greek-dictionary

In order to look up a lexical entry, you will need to search by the lexical form of the word, which our interlinear above so readily provides for us. As mentioned for λόγος, no matter what form the word takes in a particular sentence, its lexical form will always remain the same. Using an interlinear that provides that information for you will make locating the word in a lexicon that much easier. I will discuss the process of studying individual words later, but for now you know what resources are available to help you when you are ready.

Analytical Lexicons / Parsing Aids

Knowing the meaning of a word is certainly a significant part of studying a passage. Too often our study ends at the word level. In order to understand how a word is related to the words around it, we have to analyze the form of the word. We frequently refer to this as "parsing" the word. We will discuss the significance of these grammatical components later. The most helpful resources for identifying this information are found in the various Bible study software available. This information can also be found in print in an analytical lexicon. These print versions can, however, be time consuming to use, and their electronic counterparts are recommended instead. When Bible study software is not an option, there are a number of websites that make this information accessible, some through search features and others simply by clicking on the word in a passage to get the information:

http://www.greekbible.com/index.php
https://unbound.biola.edu/index.cfm?method=greekSearch.show
   SearchForm
https://net.bible.org/

The information gained for parsing a word can be a bit overwhelming or confusing at first. Our tour through the basics of Greek grammar in the chapters ahead will both help us to better navigate the associated terminology and also serve as a reference point for future study.

Concordances

When you've discovered the meaning(s) for a word, you may be curious to see how that word is used in other places in the New Testament. This requires the use of a software program or website that contains a search feature, or a concordance. The most widely used concordance is the *Strong's Exhaustive Concordance of the Bible*.[2] This can be accessed through a number of websites for free, and two recommended sites are below:

> http://biblehub.com/strongs.htm
> http://www.blueletterbible.org/lang/lexicon/Lexicon.cfm?Strongs
>   =G25&t=NASB

We will examine the proper use of concordances later on when we discuss word studies. For now it is sufficient to know what role they play in our examination of the Greek text.

Grammar Resources

Finally, there are also helpful grammatical resources available for studying a passage. These will become more useful once we understand some of the terminology associated with Greek grammar. They will shed additional light on what is going on in a text and alert us to interpretive problems where commentators disagree on how to take certain constructions and phrases. A helpful resource is the *New Linguistic and Exegetical Key to the Greek New Testament* by Rogers and Rogers, which gives the reader an overview of the lexical and grammatical issues for each verse in the New Testament.[3] Though not exhaustive, it is a good place to start. Exegetical commentaries will also be very useful as we analyze a passage. It is always recommended that you do your own study first before consulting the commentaries, but commentaries are indispensable in exegetical study. Some particularly helpful commentary series for studying the Greek New Testament are the New International Commentary on the New Testament (NICNT; Eerdmans), the New International Greek Testament Commentary (NIGTC; Eerdmans), the Baker Exegetical Commentary on the New Testament (BECNT), the Exegetical Guide to the Greek New Testament (EGGNT; B&H Academic), and the Baylor Handbook on the Greek New Testament (BHGNT; Baylor University Press).

We now have the lay of the land and better understand what bilingual guides are available to us so we can make sense of our map of this unknown place and unknown language. As we embark on our study of the forms and functions found in Greek grammar, we will continue to illustrate our examples and summarize the key features that bear the most importance for studying the biblical text. Our bags are packed. Our guides are ready. It's time to begin the journey!

5

Introduction to Greek Verbs
and Nominals

Greek Verbs and Verbals

Verbs are the movers and shakers of language. Virtually everything in a sentence revolves around the verb. Verbs act as the hub of the sentence to which all of the other spokes of words connect. A **verb** is a word that describes an action or a state of being. In English, as in Greek, verbs have various components that combine to make up their meaning.

The **person** of a verb specifies the relationship between the author/speaker and the subject of the verb. In a **first-person** verb, the author and subject are one and the same ("I am writing"). In a **second-person** verb, the author/speaker is addressing another ("You are reading"). In a **third-person** verb, the author/speaker is speaking about someone or something else ("This book is great!").

Verbs also have **number**, indicating whether one or more subjects are performing the verb. In English, number is more explicitly expressed through the subject (e.g., man and men, chair and chairs, sheep and sheep) but is indicated inconsistently through verbal inflection.

Voice refers to the relationship between the subject of the verb and the action. There are four major ways we speak about voice in Koine Greek. **Active** voice, which is the most common voice used, occurs when the subject performs the action of the verb ("John kicks the ball"). In the **passive** voice, which is the second most common, the subject receives the action of the verb ("John was hit by the ball"). Third, the **middle** voice is used to express some self-interest by the subject in the verb. There are various ways this occurs, but one example is the **reflexive middle**, where the subject does and receives the action ("He is dressing himself"). In Greek, we also have what some grammarians call **deponent** voice, which is when the form of the verb looks passive or middle but has an active meaning.[1] We will look at examples of all these variations as we explore our verbal forms.

> **NOTE:** Often when a passive-voice verb occurs, an "agent" who performs the action of the verb is specified. Three different kinds of agency are commonly found with Greek passive verbs: direct, intermediate, and impersonal. **Direct agency**, which indicates the ultimate agent of an action (e.g., "by God"), usually occurs with the preposition ὑπό + a genitive-case noun (more on that in chap. 7). We find **intermediate agency**, when a secondary agent performs an action (e.g., "through the church"), present when we have the preposition διά + a genitive-case noun. Finally, Greek also expresses **impersonal agency**, which usually occurs when an object acts as the agent (e.g., "by fire"), through a dative-case noun with or without the preposition ἐν.

Tense is another important component of verbs. We tend to think of tense in English as the time in which the verb occurs (past, present, or future). English is slightly more complex than this, but that is our basic notion. In Greek, tense is a bit more complex. There is actually quite the debate raging among Greek grammarians as to how to define tense (indeed, someone has to debate these things!). In general terms, tense in Greek involves the *combination* of **time** and **verbal aspect**.

Time in the Greek verb refers to *when* the action occurs. The time of a verb can essentially be either past, present, or future, just as in English. We cannot equate our tenses in Greek with their time, however. In Greek, the tense of the verb (particularly in the indicative) may convey aspect and time, with the aspect generally being the primary factor and time a secondary one (so "past time" verbs can sometimes be present tense, etc.). The time of the verb is thus often largely developed from contextual features rather than from the verb itself, though certain verbal tenses (such as the imperfect or future) tend to have a fairly solid pattern of time reference.

While we understand the basic concept of time with verbs from English, aspect is likely a new category. **Aspect** refers to the *viewpoint* adopted by the author/speaker in relation to an action or state. There are three types of verbal aspect in Greek, which we will refer to with the names "aoristic," "imperfective," and "perfective." **Aoristic aspect** (which some grammarians refer to as "perfective aspect") views the action as a whole, from a distant perspective. It is sometimes referred to as the "unmarked" form of aspect, meaning that it is a way of describing an action without any special emphasis. **Imperfective aspect** views the action in process, or from an up-close perspective. This is sometimes thought of as an ongoing or "in the middle of" kind of viewpoint. **Perfective aspect** (which some grammarians refer to as "stative aspect") either specifies a state of being or indicates a completed action with an emphasis on the results of the action. We will explore this more as we talk about our various tenses in Greek.

Finally, Greek verbs also have **mood**. While we think of the word "mood" typically as one's demeanor, mood in language refers to the relationship of the action to reality. Our most frequent mood in Greek is the **indicative mood**, which makes an assertion about reality ("Today is Tuesday"). Assertions in the indicative can be either true or false (so if you are reading this on a Tuesday, it is true; otherwise, it is not). In contrast to the indicative mood, the other moods in Greek describe potential actions. The **imperative mood** is used to direct someone's action and is referred to as the mood of command ("Finish reading this chapter," which you may or may not do). The **subjunctive mood** describes an action that, though it may be actual now, is offered in terms of potential or possibility ("You should finish reading this chapter"). These represent our primary moods in Koine Greek.

This chapter has given us an overview of the terrain for our Greek verbs. Before we move ahead, let's recap our newly learned terminology:

Verb—a word that describes an action or a state of being

Person—the relationship between the author/speaker and the subject of the verb

Number—the number of actors connected to the subject

Voice—the relationship between the subject of the verb and the action

Tense—the form of the verb that encodes aspect (and possibly time)

Time—when the action occurs

Aspect—the viewpoint adopted to describe the action

Mood—the relationship of the verb to reality

So how do we recognize all of these different moving parts in our Greek verbs? Greek encodes all of this information in the actual verb itself, which means that our verbs can get pretty complicated. The basic way Greek verbs disclose this information to us is through the form of the verb and its affixes. **Affixes** are elements added to a word that affect its meaning. In Greek we have two major types of affixes: prefixes and suffixes. As you might have guessed, **prefixes** are added to the front of the word, and **suffixes** are added to the end of the word.

Take the verb λέγω (*legō*), for example, which means "I speak." By changing the suffix, we can specify a different person and/or number for the subject of the verb (see table 1).

Notice that the stem or root of our verb (λέγ-) has not changed, which is where we get the range of meaning of our word ("speak"), but our ending has changed, which is where we derive the person and number of the verb.

Table 1. Present Active Indicative

1st, sg.	λέγω	"I speak."
2nd, sg.	λέγεις	"You [sg.] speak."
3rd, sg.	λέγει	"He/she/it speaks."
1st, pl.	λέγομεν	"We speak."
2nd, pl.	λέγετε	"You [pl.] speak."
3rd, pl.	λέγουσι(ν)[a]	"They speak."

[a]Some forms contain what is referred to as a "movable nu" on the end of the word. In general, this letter is placed on the word when the word that follows begins with a vowel or a diphthong. The absence or presence of the nu does not change the meaning of the word.

Table 2. Imperfect Active Indicative

1st, sg.	ἔλεγον	"I was speaking."
2nd, sg.	ἔλεγες	"You [sg.] were speaking."
3rd, sg.	ἔλεγε(ν)	"He/she/it was speaking."
1st, pl.	ἐλέγομεν	"We were speaking."
2nd, pl.	ἐλέγετε	"You [pl.] were speaking."
3rd, pl.	ἔλεγον	"They were speaking."

Furthermore, if we add a certain prefix to the word (ἔλεγ-), we change its tense ("was speaking"). As you might guess, we can then apply person/number suffixes to specify the subject of the verb in this tense as well.

You can see, then, that structurally, Greek verbs are very different from English verbs. Where English verbs tend to add helping words to specify things such as person, number, tense, voice, and mood, in Greek these are encoded in the form of the verb itself by either changing the form or adding affixes. As we explore all of the verbal forms, we will examine this more closely. For now, this framework for understanding how Greek verbs are formed and function will also help us with understanding Greek nominals.

Greek Nominals

While verbs are the movers and shakers of our sentences, nominals are the moved and the shaken. These important words fill in the details surrounding our verbs. We may define a **nominal** as a word that names an entity. I've chosen here to speak of nominals rather than nouns since Greek pronouns, adjectives, and even articles can fill this role. These words also function sometimes in ways very similar to Greek nouns, so exploring some of these foundational concepts will be helpful before we look at these parts of speech on their own.

Like verbs, nominals in Greek encode various kinds of information. First, nominals often contain grammatical gender. **Gender** in grammar refers more to the kind of endings a word takes than to biological gender, though these obviously sometimes overlap. For example, the word for "heart" in Greek is καρδία, which is a grammatically feminine noun. This does not mean that the Greeks thought of the heart as having feminine properties, but rather that the word takes a feminine ending. For the word for "woman" (γυνή), however, we would expect its gender to indicate both grammatical and biological gender. In Greek, there are three different kinds of grammatical gender: masculine, feminine, and neuter. This means that many of the words that can take different genders (such as adjectives) can have up to three different forms that correspond to the three grammatical genders.

As we saw with verbs, **number** in nominals indicates whether a single (singular) entity or two or more (plural) entities are in mind.

Probably the most important concept for Greek nominals is that of case. In Greek, the term **case** refers to the encoding of a specific grammatical function (or range of functions) within a nominal ending. In other words, the case of a nominal tells us what it is doing in a sentence or how it relates to the words around it. There are five cases in Greek, which we will attend to in the next two chapters.

As you may have noticed when we described the gender of Greek nouns, there are a number of forms of endings to deal with. This concept is connected to noun **declension**, which refers to the grouping of words that share similar kinds of endings. Greek has three declensions, which we will examine in the next chapter.

Finally, an important concept with nominals is that of grammatical agreement. **Grammatical agreement** refers to the necessity of nominals that are related to one another to conform to a particular pattern in order to alert the reader to the connection between the words. For example, with Greek adjectives, the agreement of the adjective in gender, number, and case tells us which noun the adjective is modifying.

Let's take a moment again to review these terms before we look at an example of the forms of a Greek nominal.

Gender—the kind of endings a nominal takes

Number—whether a nominal indicates one entity or two or more entities

Case—the range of grammatical functions indicated by a nominal ending

Declension—a grouping of words that share the same or similar patterns of endings

Grammatical agreement—the conformity of nominals to a particular form (gender, number, and case) that confirms the relationships between those words

As in the last chapter, an illustration will be helpful. Though we have not talked about what the cases mean yet, I will simply use the

Table 3. First-Declension Nouns

nominative singular	καρδία
genitive singular	καρδίας
dative singular	καρδίᾳ
accusative singular	καρδίαν
nominative plural	καρδίαι
genitive plural	καρδιῶν
dative plural	καρδίαις
accusative plural	καρδίας

case names to show how the endings of nominals are utilized. Since we already mentioned καρδία earlier in the chapter, we will revisit that term again. Table 3 shows the different forms that καρδία may take.

You will notice, then, that a change in endings for a noun (which καρδία is) indicate either a change in grammatical case (nom., gen., dat., or acc.) or a change in number (sg. or pl.). We have thus introduced the essential concepts involved with nominals. Now it is time to explore Greek cases and their functions.

6

Nominative, Accusative, and Vocative Cases

By way of reminder, as we look at Greek cases, we are examining how Greek nominals use their case endings to specify the grammatical function of the word in the sentence. The two most commonly used cases in the Greek New Testament are the nominative and accusative cases, which we will explore in this chapter along with the least-used case in the New Testament, the vocative case.

The Nominative Case

The **nominative case** is often referred to as the "naming" case, meaning that it functions to designate something in the sentence. Most commonly what the nominative designates is the **subject** of the sentence. In English, we recognize the subject by the word order of a sentence. So in the sentence, "John kicks the ball," we know the subject because it is first and the direct object because it follows the verb. If we rearrange the word order to "The ball kicks John," we have altered the meaning of the sentence. In Greek, the case endings determine which word is the subject and which is the object, so we can usually alter the word order without affecting the meaning. Table 1 gives examples of nominative-case nouns in each of the three declensions (i.e., major patterns of endings).[1]

Table 1. The Nominative Case

First Declension	Second Declension	Third Declension
"writing, Scripture"	"word"	"flesh"
γραφή—nom. sg.	λόγος—nom. sg.	σάρξ—nom. sg.
γραφαί—nom. pl.	λόγοι—nom. pl.	σάρκες—nom. pl.

Notice that each of these forms is in the nominative case, but the endings differ somewhat drastically. In a typical-grammar approach, you would work to memorize all of the endings for the various declensions in Greek and all (or most) of their variations. In our approach, however, we are more concerned with focusing on understanding what these terms and forms mean in their contexts than with acquiring proficiency in recognizing the forms. It would be worthwhile to pause for a moment to remind ourselves of how to go about identifying what grammatical information is encoded in a particular word by means of an analytical lexicon or parsing aid (cf. chap. 4).

NOTE: Our general progression will be from identifying a particular word in our interlinear text, to identifying its meaning through a lexical tool, to finding its grammatical information through an analytical lexicon or parsing tool, and finally to studying its grammatical force through scholarly works such as commentaries, books, and journal articles. While we will not repeat the process here, we will illustrate its results, both here and throughout our examination of these various parts of speech.

Let's take a look at each of these words in a sentence in one of its nominative-case forms.

Rom. 10:11

λέγει	γὰρ	ἡ	γραφή
λέγω	γάρ	ὁ	γραφή
says	for	the	Scripture
3004	1063	3588	1124

Our interlinear of Romans 10:11 here gives (1) the inflected Greek words, (2) their lexical (dictionary) form, (3) a literal translation, and (4) the *Strong's Concordance* number. In order to identify the grammatical information for each word, we would also need to turn to an analytical lexicon or a parsing tool. If we inputted or located γραφή, we would find that this word is a *noun* (part of speech), *nominative* (case), *singular* (number), and *feminine* (gender). We would also note upon further inspection that it agrees with λέγει, since that verb is *third person* and *singular*. Thus we conclude here that γραφή is the subject of the verb, and we would then understand the statement to mean "For the Scripture says/is saying."

We should stop here to recognize again that clearly Greek does not always (or even usually) follow the word order we expect in English. English sentences fairly strictly follow the subject-verb-object pattern since English relies on word order (lacking a case system) to determine which words are playing which roles. In Greek, word order is much more fluid (though there are constraints in certain situations) than in English. This is all the more reason to pay careful attention to the case endings since they alert us to the role a word plays in a sentence.

Next, let's look at a use of σάρξ in the nominative case.

Gal. 5:17

ἡ	γὰρ	σάρξ	ἐπιθυμεῖ	κατὰ	τοῦ	πνεύματος
ὁ	γάρ	σάρξ	ἐπιθυμέω	κατά	ὁ	πνεῦμα
the	for	flesh	desires	against	the	Spirit
3588	1063	4561	1937	2596	3588	4151

Here we see the interlinear version of Galatians 5:17. As we gather the grammatical information for σάρξ here, through either an analytical lexicon or a parsing tool, we will find it is a *noun, nominative, singular,* and *feminine.* It shares the same grammatical information as γραφή above, though that word is in the first declension and σάρξ is in the third. Here again the noun agrees with the verb (ἐπιθυμεῖ; *third person, singular*), showing us again it is the subject of the sentence ("For the flesh desires/is desiring against the Spirit").

In our final example, from John 1:1, we will note an additional use of the nominative case.

John 1:1

καὶ	θεὸς	ἦν	ὁ	λόγος
καί	θεός	εἰμί	ὁ	λόγος
and	God	was	the	Word
2532	2316	2258	3588	3056

Here we find λόγος, which the parsing tools will tell us is a *noun, masculine, nominative,* and *singular.* The verb, ἦν, is *third person* and *singular.* It seems we have a match here for a subject again. However, if we examine θεός as well, we will find that it too is a *noun, masculine, nominative,* and *singular.* Both nouns are candidates for the subject of the verb. So which is it?

Here a grammatical cue comes from the **article** (more on this in chap. 8), ὁ, which precedes λόγος. The article here functions to mark the subject of our verb ("The Word was . . ."). What, then, is θεός doing? Here θεός is functioning as the predicate nominative, another way in which the nominative case can function. A **predicate nominative** is a nominal that is joined to a subject nominative by a stative verb, which is what ἦν (from εἰμί) is here. Thus our sentence reads "and the Word was God."

ADVANCED INFORMATION: So how do we know whether a nominative is functioning as a subject nominative or a predicate nominative in these situations? There are three basic rules to guide our thinking here. First, if there is a pronoun present, it will be the subject nominative. Second, if there is an article present, it will mark the subject nominative (as in the example above). Third, if there is a proper name present, it will be the subject.

Though the nominative case functions in other, less common ways, two important but less-common functions of the nominative case that we will look at briefly are the nominative absolute and the nominative for vocative.

The **nominative absolute** is found when a nominative-case word occurs apart from any verbs. We find this most commonly in the opening sections of the Epistles. So in Galatians 1:1, where Paul writes Παῦλος ἀπόστολος ("Paul, an apostle"), the noun here is disconnected from any verb and serves simply as a salutation. We would not call these nominatives "subjects" since there is no verb present. Rather, they stand alone as a "from" line in the epistle, identifying its author. Technically speaking, the second nominative, ἀπόστολος, functions as a **nominative of simple apposition**, meaning that it redefines the first noun, Παῦλος. We know this because the two nouns have the same gender, number, and case and do not stand in a subject-predicate relationship.

The **nominative for vocative** occurs when a nominative-case noun is functioning in place of the vocative case. Since we will be addressing the vocative case later, we will save our explanation for then. For now recognize that nominative-case nouns can occasionally function like the vocative case.

This covers the major uses of the nominative case. Remember, *the nominative case most commonly functions to mark the subject*, but we will see these other somewhat common functions (and especially the predicate nominative function) from time to time as well. We now turn our attention to the second case to be examined in this chapter.

The Accusative Case

The **accusative case** can be described as functioning to limit the action of a verb. As we will see, this can be done in a number of ways in the accusative, but the most common way the accusative limits the verb is by functioning as the **direct object**. In other words, the accusative as direct object expresses the extent to which an action operates. In the sentence "John is reading the book," the action of reading is limited to "the book." Table 2 gives examples of accusative-case nouns in each of the three declensions.

Table 2. The Accusative Case

First Declension	Second Declension	Third Declension
"prophet"	"man, human"	"woman, wife"
προφήτην—acc. sg.	ἄνθρωπον—acc. sg.	γυναῖκα—acc. sg.
προφήτας—acc. pl.	ἀνθρώπους—acc. pl.	γυναῖκας—acc. pl.

Let's take a look at each of these words in a sentence in one of its accusative-case forms.

Eph. 5:25

Οἱ	ἄνδρες,	ἀγαπᾶτε	τὰς	γυναῖκας
ὁ	ἀνήρ	ἀγαπάω	ὁ	γυνή
—	husbands	love	your	wives
3588	435	25	3588	1135

In locating the noun γυναῖκας here, we notice it is paired with an article (τάς; more on that in chap. 8). Upon examining the form via an analytical lexicon or other parsing tool, we find γυναῖκας is a *noun, feminine, accusative,* and *plural.* If we were to look up ἄνδρες, we would find it is a *noun, masculine, nominative,* and *plural,* acting here as a "vocative of address," though also clarifying the subject ("you") of the verb "love," and making γυναῖκας, since it is accusative, the direct object. Thus our sentence reads, "Husbands love your wives." (If you are wondering where the "your" came from in our translation, it is inferred from the definite article τάς. More on that in chap. 8.)

As with the nominative case, however, accusative nouns perform a range of functions, though the direct object is the most common one. We sometimes find accusatives functioning in a **double accusative** construction. We find an example of this construction in James 5:10.

48

James 5:10

ὑπόδειγμα	λάβετε	...	τοὺς	προφήτας
ὑπόδειγμα	λαμβάνω		ὁ	προφήτης
[as an] example	take		the	prophets
5262	2983		3588	4396

The two accusatives here are ὑπόδειγμα (*noun, neuter, accusative*, and *singular*) and προφήτας (*noun, masculine, accusative*, and *plural*). This represents a **double accusative of object and complement**, where προφήτας is the actual object of the verb ("take the prophets"; we know it is the object because of the article), and ὑπόδειγμα complements or supplements the object ("take the prophets *as an* example").

A second kind of double accusative construction is the **double accusative of person and thing**, of which we find an example in Luke 11:46.

Luke 11:46

φορτίζετε	τοὺς	ἀνθρώπους	φορτία
φορτίζω	ὁ	ἄνθρωπος	φορτίον
you load	—	people	[with] burdens
5412	3588	444	5413

The two accusatives here are ἀνθρώπους (*noun, masculine, accusative,* and *plural*) and φορτία (*noun, neuter, accusative,* and *plural*). In the person-thing double accusative, the person (here "people") receives the thing (here "burdens") even though they are not in a subject-object relationship.

Finally, an accusative nominal, like all of the cases, may also function in simple apposition to another nominal. In a **simple apposition** construction, an accusative noun will redescribe a previously mentioned accusative noun. So in Acts 16:31, where Luke writes, "Believe in the Lord Jesus" (πίστευσον ἐπὶ τὸν κύριον Ἰησοῦν), Ἰησοῦν ("Jesus") is redescribing the first accusative, κύριον ("Lord"). All of the cases can function in this manner of simple apposition.

There are other, less common functions of the accusative case, but this gives us a good survey of the basic uses. Remember, *the accusative case most commonly functions to mark the direct object*, but we will see these other somewhat common functions from time to time as well. We now turn our attention to the final case to be examined in this chapter.

The Vocative Case

The **vocative case** is the least common of the five Koine Greek cases and is known as the case of direct address. It is typically used to address a person in dialogue. Thus, in Matthew 19:16, when Jesus is approached and asked, "What good thing must I do to gain eternal life?" the inquirer first addresses Jesus as διδάσκαλε ("teacher") with a vocative-case noun. This is the basic function of the vocative case.

Your Turn

I have outlined the most-common functions of the nominative, accusative, and vocative cases. Now it is your turn to test out your newfound knowledge. Examine the bolded words in the sentence below. Using an analytical lexicon or parsing tool (see chap. 4), identify the grammatical information for each word. Once you have identified the gender, number, and case, using the categories described above, determine how each of these words is functioning. After you have made a decision about the case and function, check your answers in the key in appendix 1.

1 John 1:9

ἐὰν	ὁμολογῶμεν	τὰς	**ἁμαρτίας**	ἡμῶν,	**πιστός**	ἐστιν	καὶ	**δίκαιος**
ἐάν	ὁμολογέω	ὁ	ἁμαρτία	ἐγώ	πιστός	εἰμί	καί	δίκαιος
if	we confess	—	sins	our	faithful	he is	and	just
1437	3670	3588	266	2257	4103	2076	2532	1342

Words to Memorize

As we work to develop a baseline vocabulary, below are some additional words you will find helpful to memorize.

ἄνθρωπος	human, man	λόγος	word, statement
γραφή	writing, Scripture	προφήτης	prophet,
γυνή	woman, wife		proclaimer
θεός	God, god	σάρξ	flesh, body
λαμβάνω	to take, to receive		

7

Genitive and Dative Cases

Our English translations usually render nominatives and accusatives in a fairly straightforward manner since they are generally less flexible in their case functions. This is not true, however, of the genitive and dative cases, which are far more flexible and can take on greater nuances. The range of functions for both of these cases is fairly broad. We will look in this chapter only at the most frequent functions in order to illustrate their most common uses.

The Genitive Case

The **genitive case** is the most flexible of all of the Greek noun cases. The genitive case essentially limits a noun being modified with regard to some qualitative aspect. In other words, the genitive narrows the description of the noun that it modifies, which is referred to as the **head noun**. In English, for example, "The house of my parents" narrows the meaning of "house" (the head noun) to a specific house ("of my parents," the genitive idea present). In English, the genitive case is often rendered with the word "of," though we will see that the flexibility of the case extends well beyond this one word. Table 1 gives examples of common genitive-case noun forms in each of the three declensions.

Table 1. The Genitive Case

First Declension	Second Declension	Third Declension
"sin"	"Christ, Anointed One"	"faith, trust"
ἀμαρτίας—gen. sg.	Χριστοῦ—gen. sg.	πίστεως—gen. sg.
ἀμαρτιῶν—gen. pl.	N/A	N/A

Col. 1:1

Παῦλος	ἀπόστολος	Χριστοῦ	Ἰησοῦ
Παῦλος	ἀπόστολος	Χριστός	Ἰησοῦς
Paul	an apostle	of Christ	Jesus
3972	652	5547	2424

In Colossians 1:1, we find an example of the **genitive of source**. The first two nouns (Παῦλος and ἀπόστολος) are *masculine, nominative,* and *singular,* with Παῦλος acting as a nominative absolute and ἀπόστολος acting as a nominative of simple apposition (two concepts we discussed in the previous chapter). These are followed by two *genitive nouns* (Χριστοῦ and Ἰησοῦ), which are both *masculine* and *singular.* If we consider Χριστοῦ as a genitive of source, this would signify that Paul, as a "sent messenger" (ἀπόστολος), was commissioned by none other than Christ himself. The second genitive (Ἰησοῦ) is functioning in simple apposition to Χριστοῦ. Notice then we consider ἀπόστολος to be the head noun and Χριστοῦ to be the genitive that describes it.

Rom. 1:1

Παῦλος	δοῦλος	Χριστοῦ	Ἰησοῦ
Παῦλος	δοῦλος	Χριστός	Ἰησοῦς
Paul	a slave	of Christ	Jesus
3972	1401	5547	2424

Romans 1:1 illustrates two other potential uses of the genitive case: the **genitive of possession** and **genitive of subordination**. Here, in a

construction similar to that of Colossians 1:1 above, Paul writes he is a "slave of Christ Jesus." Notice again that the four nouns here parallel the four examined above. We would likely not consider this a genitive of source, however, because δοῦλος does not carry the idea of sending. Rather a **genitive of possession** ("a slave *belonging to* Christ Jesus") or a **genitive of subordination** ("a slave *under the authority of* Christ Jesus") would make a better fit.

John 21:15

Σίμων	Ἰωάννου
Σίμων	Ἰωάννης
Simon	[son] of John
4613	2491

Another common function of the genitive is the **genitive of relationship**, which we see in John 21:15 above. Here we see the proper noun Ἰωάννου (*masculine, genitive,* and *singular*) appended to the proper noun Σίμων (*masculine, vocative,* and *singular*), indicating a relationship between these two persons, here of a father (Ἰωάννου) to a son (Σίμων).

Rom. 6:6

τὸ	σῶμα	τῆς	ἁμαρτίας
ὁ	σῶμα	ὁ	ἁμαρτία
the	body	of	sin
3588	4983	3588	266

An example of the **attributive genitive** occurs in Romans 6:6. Here Paul speaks of τὸ σῶμα τῆς ἁμαρτίας ("the sinful body"). The head noun, σῶμα (*neuter, nominative,* and *singular*), is modified by the genitive noun ἁμαρτίας (*feminine* and *singular*), much like an adjective would modify a noun. For this reason some refer to the attributive genitive as the **adjectival genitive**. (Note it is also possible to see this as a genitive of subordination, since Paul personifies sin in Romans. This would mean "the body under Sin's authority" or something of the like.)

Rom. 3:22

διά	πίστεως	Ἰησοῦ	Χριστοῦ
διά	πίστις	Ἰησοῦς	Χριστός
through	faith	in Jesus	Christ
1223	4102	2424	5547

While most of these examples have been fairly straightforward, in many instances the genitive-case function is unclear. Sometimes this is a matter of slight significance, but in other situations, very important interpretive questions rest on how the genitive case is interpreted. A perennially debated example of this is found in Romans 3:22. Here Paul speaks of "the righteousness of God" (a phrase with its own interpretive questions) coming through the πίστεως Ἰησοῦ Χριστοῦ (all three nouns are *genitive* and *singular*; πίστεως is *feminine*, while Ἰησοῦ and Χριστοῦ are *masculine*). Most of the debate around this verse has been whether Ἰησοῦ should be taken as a **subjective genitive** ("the faith[fulness] of Jesus Christ") or an **objective genitive** ("faith in Jesus Christ"). In the subjective genitive, the genitive noun acts as the subject of the head noun (so the faith[fulness] that Jesus Christ performs), while in the objective genitive, the genitive noun acts as the object of the head noun (the faith that is directed toward Jesus Christ). These are obviously dramatically different interpretations, and thus heavily debated by New Testament scholars.

Rom. 1:5

ὑπακοὴν	πίστεως
ὑπακοή	πίστις
[the] obedience	of faith
5218	4102

Another important example of the controversial ambiguity of the genitive case occurs in Romans 1:5. Here the head noun ὑπακοήν (*feminine*, *accusative*, and *singular*) is modified by the genitive noun πίστεως (*feminine* and *singular*). Numerous suggestions have been offered for how to understand the relationship between these two nouns. Some suggest we have a **genitive of apposition,** which means the genitive re-describes the head noun ("the obedience *that is* faith"). Others suggest it should be taken as a **genitive of source** ("the obedience *that comes from* faith") or an **attributive genitive** ("faithful obedience"). Others still suggest this is a **genitive of production,** which is similar to the notion of source ("the obedience *that is produced by* faith").

As you can see here, these options do impact how the phrase, and thus the passage and book, are understood. And these decisions rest (at least to some extent) on understanding the relationship between the genitive noun and its head noun. The genitive case has other nuances, but this gives us a good overview of the variety of ways it can be taken. This also should encourage us to review genitives, especially exegetically significant ones, very carefully as we study a passage and seek to understand its message. We will see the dative case contains flexibility similar to that of the genitive case, though not to the extent that we find in the genitive.

The Dative Case

The **dative case** is quite flexible in terms of its functions. In general, the dative specifies a relationship between two words. Frequently in English, the dative will be rendered with a preposition such as "in," "by," "to," or "with." This illustrates the range of possibilities with the dative. As in previous sections, our goal here is not to memorize all of the possible forms of the dative. Rather, with our tools handy

Table 2. The Dative Case

First Declension	Second Declension	Third Declension
"poor, poverty"	"he/she/it, them"	"water"
πτωχείᾳ—dat. sg.	αὐτῷ—dat. sg.	ὕδατι—dat. sg.
N/A	αὐτοῖς—dat. pl.	ὕδασι(ν)[a]—dat. pl.

[a]The nu that appears at the end of some forms and appears in parentheses here may or may not appear on the word in all instances. Its absence or presence does not change its meaning, but it does affect how the form is recognized.

to recognize the dative case, our goal is to understand what it means when we are studying a passage. To do so we will again review a few examples of the most common dative functions.

John 10:28

κἀγὼ	δίδωμι	αὐτοῖς	ζωὴν	αἰώνιον
κἀγώ	δίδωμι	αὐτός	ζωή	αἰώνιος
and I	give	to them	life	eternal
2504	1325	846	2222	166

Many grammars will define the dative case as the case that marks the indirect object, since that is a very frequent function of the case. We see an example of this in John 10:28. Here "eternal life" (ζωὴν αἰώνιον), which is in the accusative case, is the direct object of the verb "give," which has "I" (nominative case) as its subject. Notice the pronoun (more on those in the next chapter) αὐτοῖς, then, is *masculine, dative*, and *plural*. Since "eternal life" is the thing being given, the indirect object identifies who is receiving the direct object. We call this the **dative of indirect object**. This is typically translated with the preposition "to," and thus this sentence would be rendered "and I give eternal life to them."

Matt. 23:31

μαρτυρεῖτε	ἑαυτοῖς
μαρτυρέω	ἑαυτοῦ
you testify	against yourselves
3140	1438

Similar to the dative of indirect object, the **dative of interest** indicates self-interest in the action being described and can express either an advantageous or a disadvantageous situation. In Matthew 23:31, we see an example of the disadvantage connotation. The negative idea of the verb is connected here to the pronoun ἑαυτοῖς (*masculine, dative*, and *plural*), and thus the idea is "you testify against yourselves," with the "against" being inferred from the dative case of the pronoun.

Luke 3:16

ἐγὼ	...	ὕδατι	βαπτίζω	ὑμᾶς
ἐγώ		ὕδωρ	βαπτίζω	σύ
I		in water	baptize	you
1473		5204	907	5209

In Luke 3:16, we find another common use of the dative, one that expresses either **sphere** or **location**. Sometimes this function specifies the realm in which something happens (such as "in Christ" or "in the heavenlies"), while other times it refers to a physical location, as here in Luke. By examining our words, we find that the pronoun ἐγώ (*nominative* and *singular*) is the subject and the pronoun ὑμᾶς (*accusative* and *plural*) is the direct object. The dative here specifies the location in which the baptizing (or "immersing") is occurring: "in water." The notion of "in" is supplied by the dative case, so our sentence reads, "I baptize you in water."

Eph. 2:5

συνεζωοποίησεν	τῷ	Χριστῷ
συζωοποιέω	ὁ	Χριστός
he made [us] alive together with	—	Christ
4806	3588	5547

While the dative of Χριστός often carries a spherical notion in Paul's Letters, in Ephesians 2:5, we more likely find what is referred to as the **dative of association**. The verb συνεζωοποίησεν gives us this indication since it is what is known as a **compound verb** (a verb that has a prepositional prefix), and the preposition σύν often indicates association or accompaniment. Thus here, rather than Paul saying believers were made alive "in Christ," he indicates believers were made alive "together with Christ," taken from the combination of the compound verb and the dative case.

Heb. 11:27

Πίστει	κατέλιπεν	Αἴγυπτον
πίστις	καταλείπω	Αἴγυπτος
by faith	he left	Egypt
4102	2641	125

Another fairly common use of this case is the **dative of means**. Hebrews 11:27 illustrates this usage. Here the author states that Moses (who in context is the referent) left "Egypt" (Αἴγυπτον; *noun, feminine, accusative,* and *singular*) "by faith" (πίστει; *noun, feminine, dative,* and *singular*). The dative case here likely indicates that it was "by means of" his "faith" or "trust" in God that Moses was able to embark on the journey.

2 Cor. 8:9

ἵνα	ὑμεῖς	τῇ	ἐκείνου	πτωχείᾳ	πλουτήσητε
ἵνα	σύ	ὁ	ἐκεῖνος	πτωχεία	πλουτέω
in order that	you	because of	his	poverty	may become rich
2443	5210	3588	1565	4432	4147

The final function we wish to consider here is known as the **dative of cause**. Second Corinthians 8:9 illustrates this usage. Here Paul writes that the Corinthians (the "you" subject expressed by ὑμεῖς) may become rich "because of his [Jesus's] poverty." The pronoun ἐκείνου here is in the genitive case and likely indicates possession. The dative noun πτωχείᾳ (*feminine* and *singular*) here likely indicates cause (though other options are possible). Thus the basis or ground for their becoming rich is the poverty of Christ.

As with the genitive, the nuances of the dative case should be carefully considered since the meaning of a passage is connected to how the dative is understood. These concepts are also important because we find Greek cases in nouns, adjectives, pronouns, articles, and even participles. There is thus both grammatical and exegetical significance found in the Greek case system.

We have looked at how we identify the grammatical components of the words we find in our interlinear text through the various tools suggested. We have now also explored the very important matter of Greek cases. Next we turn our attention to a few other parts of speech that are both common and significant for our understanding of the New Testament in its original language.

Your Turn

I have outlined the most-common functions of the genitive and dative cases. Now it is your turn. Examine the bolded words in the sentence below. Using an analytical lexicon or parsing tool (see chap. 4), identify the grammatical information for each word. Once you have identified the gender, number, and case, using the categories described above, determine how each of these words is functioning. After you have made a decision about the case and function, check your answers in the key in appendix 1.

Col. 1:3

Εὐχαριστοῦμεν	τῷ	**θεῷ**	**πατρὶ**	τοῦ	**κυρίου**	**ἡμῶν**	**Ἰησοῦ**	**Χριστοῦ**
εὐχαριστέω	ὁ	θεός	πατήρ	ὁ	κύριος	ἐγώ	Ἰησοῦς	Χριστός
we give thanks	to	God	the Father	of	Lord	our	Jesus	Christ
2168	3588	2316	3962	3588	2962	2257	2424	5547

Words to Memorize

ἁμαρτία	sin	πίστις	faith, trust,
ἀπόστολος	apostle, emissary		faithfulness
αὐτός	he, she, it; self,	σῶμα	body
	same	ὕδωρ	water
δοῦλος	slave, servant	Χριστός	Christ, Anointed
Ἰησοῦς	Jesus		One

8

Articles, Pronouns, Adjectives, and Prepositions

This chapter may seem like a bit of a hodgepodge of random parts of speech. All of these words pull the important freight of sentence meaning, so we want to be sure to examine each one with some care. We are growing accustomed to the idea that there are varying functions of and degrees of nuances within these different kinds of words. As before, we will not seek to exhaust them all here; rather we will work to understand the most common functions of these terms, beginning with the extremely important Greek article.

The Article

The **article** (ὁ, ἡ, τό, and their derivate forms; sometimes referred to as the "definite article") in Greek is a bit more complex than what we think of in English with our roughly equivalent word "the." The Greek article does not always act the way the English article typically does. The

English article makes a word definite ("*the* house" specifies a certain house). The article in Greek can particularize another word, but it can also refer to a category of items or act as a function marker, meaning that it tells us that another word, such as a participle, is behaving in a certain way. Our aim here will be to gain an overall sense of how the article functions in Greek.

John 1:17

ὁ	νόμος	διὰ	Μωϋσέως	ἐδόθη,
ὁ	νόμος	διά	Μωϋσῆς	δίδωμι
the	law	through	Moses	was given
3588	3551	1223	3475	1325

ἡ	χάρις	καὶ	ἡ	ἀλήθεια	διὰ	Ἰησοῦ	Χριστοῦ	ἐγένετο.
ὁ	χάρις	καί	ὁ	ἀλήθεια	διά	Ἰησοῦς	Χριστός	γίνομαι
—	grace	and	—	truth	through	Jesus	Christ	came
3588	5485	2532	3588	225	1223	2424	5547	1096

The article is most frequently used to reference a **particular** nominal or a **category** of a nominal. For example, in John 1:17 above, the article is used three times to reference a particular item, though, because of English limitations, it is typically only translated with the first. Notice that the articles here and the nouns they accompany agree in gender, number, and case (ὁ and νόμος are *masculine, nominative,* and *singular*; ἡ and χάρις are *feminine, nominative,* and *singular*; ἡ and ἀλήθεια are *feminine, nominative,* and *singular*). In English, however, only ὁ νόμος is translated with the article ("the law"), since abstract nouns like "grace" and "truth" are not made definite in English. The untranslated articles point out in Greek, however, that John has a particular "grace" and "truth" in mind, namely, God's "grace" and "truth" revealed through Jesus. In Matthew 12:35, however, it is not a specific "good person" (ὁ ἀγαθὸς ἄνθρωπος) or "evil person" (ὁ πονηρὸς ἄνθρωπος) that is in mind but rather the categories of good and evil people.

These are the main overarching classifications for the two most basic ways the article is used in Greek. Note again that there are times when the article is present in Greek but is not translated in English. This does not mean the article serves no purpose in Greek, but rather that English has no suitable way in which to render it. We see this further illustrated when the article is paired with a proper name (such as in John 1:19 [τοῦ Ἰωάννου], which we wouldn't translate as "the John"). Many time we will find the presence of the article can be translated well with "the," but we should recognize that even when it cannot, it is not a useless word in Greek. The article's most basic function is thus again better thought of as signifying a particular idea or a category rather than something definite per se. Ultimately, the context of the passage being considered must determine how the article is being used.

The article can also act as a **substantive**, meaning that it functions equivalently to what we would call a "pronoun." Since we are getting a bit ahead of ourselves by mentioning this (given that we have not discussed pronouns yet), we will speak broadly here. Sometimes the article will appear by itself without an agreeing noun and look out of place. In these instances the article is usually acting like a pronoun. Depending on the context, the article may be used as a **personal pronoun** ("he, she, it, they"), a **relative pronoun** ("who, which"), or a **possessive pronoun** ("his, her, their"). We find an example in John 4:32.

John 4:32

ὁ	δὲ	εἶπεν	αὐτοῖς
ὁ	δέ	εἶπον	αὐτός
he	but	said	to them
3588	1161	2036	846

Here the subject of our sentence is the article ὁ (*masculine, nominative*, and *singular*). Rather than being translated as "the," here it acts as a pronoun and thus fills the grammatical role of the subject. In the context, the article refers to Jesus, so the appropriate translation for the article here would be the English masculine pronoun "he" ("but he said to them"). Notice here the article has no noun, adjective, or other word to accompany it, and thus the pronoun function seems fairly clear.

The **substantiver** use of the article occurs when the article makes a word that isn't a noun act as though it were one. The article can perform this function when accompanying an adjective, participle, infinitive, or adverb, and in various other constructions. In Mark 1:24, Jesus is referred to as ὁ ἅγιος τοῦ θεοῦ ("the Holy One of God"). The article ὁ here accompanies the adjective ἅγιος. Both are *masculine, nominative,* and *singular.* While adjectives typically modify a noun, when they lack an agreeing noun they function substantivally (more on this below). The presence of the article signifies here that the adjective ἅγιος is acting as a noun, and thus when we translate the word here, we supply the word "One" to give it a substantival force in English.

Last, but not least, the article often acts as a **function marker**, meaning that its presence signifies that another word or group of words is behaving in a particular manner. In this function it may inform us of the kind of adjectival or participial construction we observe, identify the subject nominative in a subject–predicate nominative construction, or provide us with some other grammatical information. As we suggested above, the article serves some important roles with the adjective (which we will see below) as well as with participles, is used with irregular (or indeclinable) nouns to signify their case, frequently marks the subject of a verb, and has various other functions as well. We will not explore these in detail here since we will address them as we look at other parts of speech, but this function-marking feature of the article is an important one.

Pronouns

A **pronoun** is a word that takes the place of a noun. Several kinds of pronouns are used in the Greek New Testament. Our goal in this section is to examine five of the more common pronouns used. In doing so, we will again not seek to examine or memorize all of the various forms and endings for these words since our tools can help us to identity their grammatical information. Rather, we will focus on what they do.

The **personal pronoun** is the most common of the Greek pronouns. It takes three sets of forms: first person (ἐγώ [sg.]; ἡμεῖς [pl.]), second person (σύ [sg.]; ὑμεῖς [pl.]), and third person (αὐτός [masc.]; αὐτή [fem.]; αὐτό [neut.]). Each of these forms occurs in each of the four major cases (nom., gen., dat., acc.). The personal pronoun is used to take the place of a noun. The word that it replaces is called the **antecedent**, and the pronoun will usually agree with its antecedent in gender and number, while the pronoun's case will be determined by its function in the sentence.

Matt. 1:21

αὐτὸς	γὰρ	σώσει	τὸν	λαὸν	αὐτοῦ
αὐτός	γάρ	σῴζω	ὁ	λαός	αὐτός
he	because	will save	—	people	his
846	1063	4982	3588	2992	846

The above example illustrates the most common use of the personal pronoun. The first pronoun, αὐτός, is *masculine, nominative, and singular*. It thus stands as the subject of the sentence. Because it is redundant (the verb already has an implied subject within it), possibly some emphasis or special attention is intended. This applies to the nominative of the personal pronoun in general, though especially for αὐτός. The pronoun here stands in place of the noun Ἰησοῦς. Since they agree in gender and number, the connection between the pronoun and its antecedent is clear.

The second pronoun in this example is αὐτοῦ, which is *masculine, genitive,* and *singular*. It too stands in place of the noun Ἰησοῦς, though it, because it is genitive, is functioning to show possession ("*his* people"). The majority of instances of personal pronouns in the New Testament fall along the lines of these two instances.

Two special considerations are necessary for the third-person form of the pronoun (αὐτός; αὐτή; αὐτό). We have already alluded to the first above, which is the **intensive** function of the third-person pronoun. Though all nominative pronouns possibly have some degree of special emphasis, the intensive use of αὐτός occurs when the nominative form of the word is paired (1) with a noun that has an agreeing article or (2) with a proper name or (3) is used with a first- or second-person verb. In these constructions it emphasizes the identity of the subject it accompanies and is typically translated with a form of "-self" (e.g., "himself," "herself," etc.).

1 Thess. 4:16

ὅτι	αὐτὸς	ὁ	κύριος	... καταβήσεται
ὅτι	αὐτός	ὁ	κύριος	καταβαίνω
for	himself	the	Lord	will descend
3754	846	3588	2962	2597

The pronoun here agrees with the noun κύριος (*masculine, nominative, singular*), which also has an agreeing article (ὁ). The noun κύριος is the subject of the verb, and the pronoun αὐτός brings additional emphasis to the noun. It is the Lord himself, in his very person, who will descend.

The second special function of αὐτός is the **identifying adjective** function. In this use, the pronoun agrees with a noun, and the pronoun is preceded by an article. When this occurs, the pronoun takes on the meaning "same." In 1 Corinthians 12:4–5, Paul speaks of "the same Spirit" (τὸ ... αὐτὸ πνεῦμα) and "the same Lord" (ὁ αὐτὸς κύριος). Both of these constructions illustrate this use of αὐτός.

Another very common pronoun in Greek is the **demonstrative pronoun**. The demonstrative acts as a pointer and sometimes places special emphasis on its antecedent in some way. The demonstrative has two forms: the near demonstrative (οὗτος [masc.]; αὕτη [fem.]; τοῦτο [neut.]), which identifies something in close proximity, and the far demonstrative (ἐκεῖνος [masc.]; ἐκείνη [fem.]; ἐκεῖνο [neut.]), which identifies something at a distance. Sometimes the significance of the proximity of the demonstrative is weakened, and so in some instances it is treated like the personal pronoun.

In Matthew 9:3, when some of the scribes say οὗτος βλασφημεῖ ("this [man] is blaspheming"), the near demonstrative likely indicates spatial proximity, since Jesus was in the same area as them. In 1 Corinthians 9:25, Paul contrasts the motivation of the Corinthian believers with that of athletic competitors, stating that "those" (ἐκεῖνοι; i.e., the athletes) train for a perishable crown. The demonstrative here indicates conceptual distance rather than spatial distance.

The **relative pronoun** (ὅς, ἥ, ὅ) is also fairly common in the New Testament. You may notice the forms are very similar to those of the article, so the two are sometimes confused by new students of Greek. The relative pronoun usually follows its antecedent, which it will agree with in gender and number. The case of the pronoun is usually determined by its function in the relative clause that it introduces (you may recall our discussion of dependent clauses in chap. 3). The relative pronoun is thus a bit unusual since it introduces a clause and refers to an antecedent, rather than referring to an antecedent only.

Acts 4:10

Ἰησοῦ	Χριστοῦ	τοῦ	Ναζωραίου	ὅν	ὑμεῖς	ἐσταυρώσατε
Ἰησοῦς	Χριστός	ὁ	Ναζωραῖος	ὅς	σύ	σταυρόω
of Jesus	Christ	the	Nazarene	whom	you	crucified
2424	5547	3588	3480	3739	5210	4717

Acts 4:10 above provides an example of the typical relative pronoun function. The relative-pronoun clause, introduced by the pronoun ὅν (*masculine, accusative, singular*), has Ἰησοῦ (*masculine, genitive, singular*) as its antecedent. The pronoun and the noun agree in gender and number, but the pronoun is in the accusative case because it functions as the direct object of the verb ἐσταυρώσατε in the relative-pronoun clause. Though sometimes relative pronouns do not follow this rule (a phenomenon referred to as "attraction"), most of the time they do.

Less common is the **interrogative pronoun** (τίς [masc./fem.]; τί [neut.]), which introduces a question (normally "Who?" or "What?"). This is seen in Mark 8:27, where Jesus asks:

Mark 8:27

τίνα	με	λέγουσιν	οἱ	ἄνθρωποι	εἶναι;
τίς	ἐγώ	λέγω	ὁ	ἄνθρωπος	εἰμί
who	I	say	—	[do] people	am
5101	3165	3004	3588	444	1511

The pronoun τίνα (*masculine, accusative, singular*) functions both to introduce the question and substantivally ("Who are people saying I am?").

Finally, and also less common, there is the **indefinite pronoun** (τις [masc./fem.]; τι [neut.]), which introduces a member of a group or class without specifying the class itself. It is usually translated as "someone" or "a certain person." The indefinite pronoun can function substantivally (i.e., act like a noun) or adjectivally (i.e., modify a noun). We find this pronoun just a few verses down, in Mark 8:34.

Mark 8:34

εἴ	τις	θέλει	ὀπίσω	μου	ἀκολουθεῖν
εἰ	τίς	θέλω	ὀπίσω	ἐγώ	ἀκολουθέω
if	anyone	wants	after	me	to follow
1487	5100	2309	3694	3450	190

The indefinite pronoun here likely represents humanity in general ("if any person") and thus universalizes Jesus's instructions.

Adjectives

An **adjective** is a word that modifies or qualifies a nominal. Adjectives aren't usually the actors in sentences but rather are the costumes that dress up the actors. Greek adjectives can perform three different kinds of functions.

The **attributive** adjective function modifies or qualifies a nominal, which is the function we most commonly think of when we hear the term "adjective" in English. The attributive function must have an agreeing noun (gender, case, and number) that it modifies. Usually either the adjective or the noun and the adjective will have an article (which will also agree).

In the phrase ὁ πατὴρ ὁ οὐράνιος (Matt. 23:9), the articles, the noun πατήρ ("father"), and the adjective οὐράνιος ("heavenly") are all *masculine*, *nominative*, and *singular*. The adjective here is attributive because it has an agreeing noun and an article ("the heavenly Father"). There are different ways in which the attributive adjective and the noun can be arranged, but the basic meaning of the construction remains the same.

The **predicate** function of the adjective places the adjective in relationship with another noun via a stative verb ("to be"), which may be either present or implied. Like the attributive adjective, the predicate adjective must have an agreeing noun, but the predicate adjective will never have an article, though its accompanying noun may. The Beatitudes in Matthew's Gospel use a series of predicate adjectives throughout the passage. In Matthew 5:5, we find the predicate construction μακάριοι οἱ πραεῖς. The adjective (μακάριοι; "blessed"), article (οἱ), and adjective (πραεῖς; "meek") are all *masculine*, *nominative*, and *plural*. Since the adjective πραεῖς has the article and μακάριοι does not, μακάριοι fits the bill as a predicate adjective, and thus we insert a stative verb to complete the thought: "Blessed are the meek."

The **substantival** function of the adjective is perhaps the easiest to recognize since it involves the adjective with no agreeing noun. Usually a substantival adjective requires supplying a noun in translation in accordance with the adjective's gender (i.e., "man," "woman," or "thing/one"). One of the more interesting examples of a substantival adjective is found in the Lord's Prayer of Matthew 6. The prayer closes (6:13) by asking for deliverance from τοῦ πονηροῦ. This is a *masculine* (or *neuter*), *genitive*, *singular* form of the adjective πονηρός ("evil") with an agreeing article. Since this is an abstract word, it could mean to deliver from "evil" or from "the evil one." Commentators are divided as to which meaning is best intended by the phrase.

Prepositions

The final part of speech to address in this chapter is the preposition. A **preposition** is a word that introduces a prepositional phrase and indicates a relationship between a noun and another word in the sentence (usually another noun or a verb). Unlike most parts of speech in Greek, prepositions are not inflected, meaning that they do not change their form. Like most Greek words, however, prepositions have a range of meanings; thus, a single preposition can take a variety of possible meanings in various contexts and constructions. Prepositions introduce a prepositional phrase, which will at least contain the noun associated with the preposition.

Some prepositions take different meanings depending on the case of the noun with which the preposition is used. Thus, the preposition διά may mean "through" when used with a genitive-case noun but "because of" with an accusative noun. The meanings of Greek prepositions are reflected in the case functions (chaps. 6 and 7), but prepositions narrow the possibilities considerably. Thus they are both functionally helpful and considerably important for understanding the text. The below chart illustrates the spatial nature of many Greek prepositions. In the chart, arrows indicate directional movement and lines indicate nonmovement. This is intended to represent some of the

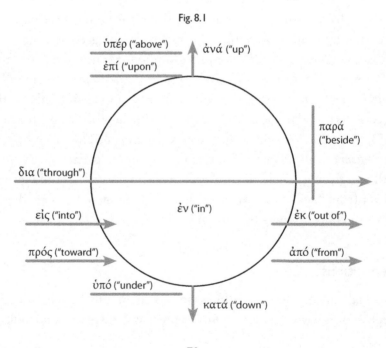

Fig. 8.1

concepts associated with these prepositions, but note again that their meanings are not limited to what is reflected below.

When we consider the meaning of a preposition, (1) the case of the associated noun must be taken into account along with (2) the lexical meaning(s) of the preposition and (3) the context of the passage. These three items together will help to clarify the use of the preposition in most situations, though there may be multiple options to consider in other instances.

Prepositions may also be affixed to the front of a verb to create a compound verb. Sometimes the meaning of the compound verb takes the literal meanings of the preposition and the verb. This is illustrated with the verb ἐξέρχομαι ("to go out"), which is a combination of the preposition ἐκ ("out") and the verb ἔρχομαι ("to go"). A verb like ἀναγινώσκω ("to read"), however, does not take a straightforward meaning from the combination of the two words since ἀνά means "up" and γινώσκω means "to know."

Your Turn

I have outlined the most-common functions of the article, the major pronouns, adjectives, and prepositions. Now it is your turn to apply what you have learned. Examine the bolded words in the sentence below. Using an analytical lexicon or parsing tool (see chap. 4), identify the grammatical information for each word. Once you have identified the part of speech and grammatical information, using the categories described above and a Greek lexicon, determine how each of these words is functioning. After you have made a decision about the form and function, check your answers in the key in appendix 1.

Matt. 26:18

ὑπάγετε	εἰς	τὴν	πόλιν	πρὸς	τὸν	δεῖνα	καὶ	εἴπατε	αὐτῷ
ὑπάγω	εἰς	ὁ	πόλις	πρός	ὁ	δεῖνα	καί	εἶπον	αὐτός
go	into	the	city	to	a	certain man	and	tell	him
5217	1519	3588	4172	4314	3588	1170	2532	2036	846

Words to Memorize

ἅγιος, -η, -ον	holy, saint	κύριος	a lord, Lord
ἀνά	(acc.) up	ὁ, ἡ, τό	the, this one, who
ἀπό	(gen.) from	ὅς, ἥ, ὅ	who, which
διά	(gen.) through; (acc.) on account of	οὗτος, αὕτη, τοῦτο	this; he, she, it
ἐγώ	I	παρά	(gen.) from; (dat.) with; (acc.) beside
εἰς	(acc.) into		
ἐκ, ἐξ	(gen.) out of, from	πατήρ	father
ἐκεῖνος, ἐκείνη, ἐκεῖνο	that; he, she, it	πρός	to, toward, with
		σύ	you (sg.)
		τίς, τί	who, what
ἐν	(dat.) in	τις, τι	someone, a certain one
ἐπί	(gen.) over, on, at the time of; (dat.) on the basis of; (acc.) on, to, against		
		ὑμεῖς	you (pl.)
		ὑπέρ	(gen.) for; (acc.) above
ἡμεῖς	we	ὑπό	(gen.) by; (acc.) under
κατά	(gen.) down from, against; (acc.) according to, throughout, during		

9

(Independent) Indicative-Mood Verbs

We have already covered quite a bit of ground in examining the language of the New Testament. We have focused in the previous chapters on those elements necessary for understanding and studying the New Testament in Greek. We have not aimed to gain reading proficiency but rather are working to establish the ability to use various tools to study the text in Greek. As we move into the world of the Greek verb and Greek verbals, we will maintain that approach. While there is value in learning the forms and gaining reading proficiency, we will focus on the functional aspects of the language. It is important, however, that we retain the concepts we introduced in chapter 5 as we approach this study. If those details are foggy, it would be helpful here to go back and review.

In this chapter we will explore the indicative mood of the Greek verb. The **indicative mood** is the mood of reality, or, perhaps better, the mood used to make an assertion about reality (after all, you can tell a lie in the indicative mood). In general, the indicative maintains a **declarative** force, meaning that it makes statements. It can be used to ask questions, set forth conditions, or issue commands (though rarely). Most indicative verbs occur in **independent** clauses, though the conjunction that introduces them ultimately determines this. Thus if an indicative verb is introduced by a dependent conjunction like ὅτι, it will be grammatically dependent (see discussion of conjunctions in chap. 3).

The indicative mood is the most common mood in the New Testament and also contains the largest number of tenses. In the sections below we will briefly examine each tense and look at an example of some of its key usages.

Present Indicative

The **present indicative** is marked by *imperfective aspect*, meaning that it portrays the action of the verb from an up-close perspective. In light of this, the present indicative often indicates present time as well, but not always. Most commonly, the present emphasizes either the ongoing or repeated nature of an action.

John 4:22

ὑμεῖς	προσκυνεῖτε	ὃ	οὐκ	οἴδατε
σύ	προσκυνέω	ὅς	οὐ	οἶδα
you	worship	what	[you do] not	know
5210	4352	3739	3756	1492

In John 4:22, Jesus says to the Samaritan woman, "you [Samaritans] are worshiping what you do not know." The verb προσκυνεῖτε is a *present*, *active*, *indicative*, *second person*, and *plural* verb. The present tense here indicates the ongoing or **in-progress** activity among the Samaritans.

Matt. 17:15

πολλάκις	γὰρ	πίπτει
πολλάκις	γάρ	πίπτω
often	for	he falls
4178	1063	4098

An example of the present showing **repetition** occurs in Matthew 17:15. Here the father of the demon-possessed man says his son is "often falling" into fire and water. The verb πίπτει is *present, active, indicative, third person*, and *singular*. Combined with the adverb here, πολλάκις, the present indicates this occurred on numerous occasions.

John 3:8

τὸ	πνεῦμα	ὅπου	θέλει	πνεῖ
ὁ	πνεῦμα	ὅπου	θέλω	πνέω
the	wind	wherever	it wishes	blows
3588	4151	3699	2309	4154

The present is also used to describe **timeless, universal actions**, such as the one expressed in John 3:8 above. Here the verb θέλει (*present, active, indicative, 3rd person*, and *singular*) expresses a principle that extends beyond a pattern of repetition to something that is enduringly true.

Mark 5:22

πίπτει	πρὸς	τοὺς	πόδας	αὐτοῦ
πίπτω	πρός	ὁ	πούς	αὐτός
he fell down	at	—	feet	his
4098	4314	3588	4228	846

The final major use of the present indicative is perhaps the most controversial. This is the so-called **historical present**, where the present indicative is used for a past action. These verbs primarily occur in narratives, and scholars are divided as to the significance of the occurrence. In general, though, this use of the present intends to bring special attention to the verb. We see an example of this in Mark 5:22, where Mark says that Jairus was "falling down at his feet" (πίπτει; *present, active, indicative, 3rd person, singular*). The present here is likely not intended to show in-progress, repeated, or timeless action. Rather, the tense is used to bring added attention to the action. Most translations will not render these verbs any differently than a simple-past verb ("he fell"; cf. NIV, NASB, ESV). The author likely intends to highlight or foreground the action, though, and thus the significance or highlighting is normally recognized only in the Greek text.

Imperfect Indicative

The **imperfect indicative** is also marked by *imperfective aspect* (i.e., an up-close perspective). It thus functions similarly to the present tense, though it typically has a past-time reference in mind. The imperfect is most commonly used in narrative texts, with the overwhelming majority (nearly 90 percent) of uses found in the Gospels and Acts. The imperfect signifies this past-time association with the augment, or the past-time morpheme ε, which is added as a prefix to the verbal stem (e.g., ἐ + λέγ = ἔλεγ-). In terms of its aspect, the imperfect indicative typically seeks to highlight the action in some manner, either by viewing it as in progress or emphasizing its duration in some way.

Matt. 8:24

αὐτὸς	δὲ	ἐκάθευδεν
αὐτός	δέ	καθεύδω
he himself	but	was asleep
846	1161	2518

In Matthew 8:24, the imperfect of the verb καθεύδω (*imperfect, active, indicative, 3rd person*, and *singular*) is used to highlight the fact that Jesus was sleeping while the storm was going on, or what we might call an **in-progress** activity. The imperfect here gives offline or side-note information, highlighting the remarkable nature of Jesus's sleeping during the turbulence of the storm. It thus adds both vividness and intensity to the narrative.

John 5:16

ἐδίωκον	οἱ	Ἰουδαῖοι	τὸν	Ἰησοῦν
διώκω	ὁ	Ἰουδαῖος	ὁ	Ἰησοῦς
began persecuting	the	Jews	—	Jesus
1377	3588	2453	3588	2424

Sometimes the imperfect tense emphasizes the **beginning of an ongoing** or **in-progress action**. John 5:16 illustrates such a use. Here the imperfect (ἐδίωκον; *imperfect, active, indicative, 3rd person,* and *plural*) highlights that the persecution of the Jewish leadership against Jesus began as a result of his healing the sick on the Sabbath. This thus focuses on the beginning of the action while also hinting at the continuation of the persecution.

Luke 2:41

Καὶ	ἐπορεύοντο	οἱ	γονεῖς	αὐτοῦ	κατ'	ἔτος	εἰς	Ἰερουσαλὴμ
καί	πορεύομαι	ὁ	γονεύς	αὐτός	κατά	ἔτος	εἰς	Ἰερουσαλήμ
and	went	—	parents	his	every	year	to	Jerusalem
2532	4198	3588	1118	846	2596	2094	1519	2419

Like the present, the imperfect is sometimes used to indicate the periodic **repetition** of an action. In this function the action is not necessarily in progress or ongoing but rather is repeated with some degree of frequency. In Luke 2:41, Luke states Jesus's parents "were going" (ἐπορεύοντο; *imperfect, deponent, indicative, 3rd person,* and *plural*) to Jerusalem every year. The prepositional phrase "every year" (κατ' ἔτος) clarifies the frequency of the travel.

Matt. 3:14

ὁ	δὲ	Ἰωάννης	διεκώλυεν	αὐτὸν
ὁ	δέ	Ἰωάννης	διακωλύω	αὐτός
—	but	John	tried to prevent	him
3588	1161	2491	1254	846

Finally, another common use of the imperfect is to show **attempted action**. Matthew 3:14 illustrates this function. Here John the Baptist was "*trying* to prevent" (διεκώλυεν; *imperfect, active, indicative, 3rd person,* and *singular*) Jesus from being baptized by him (John). The imperfect here signifies the action was attempted, but the context clearly shows John gave in to Jesus's request.

Aorist Indicative

The **aorist indicative** is marked by *aoristic aspect*, meaning that it portrays the aspect from a distant or zoomed-out perspective. It is sometimes referred to as the "unmarked" tense, meaning that it is the way to describe an action without special emphasis on the nature of the action. It does not necessarily imply once-for-all action, as has sometimes been suggested. Since the aorist frequently occurs in narratives, it often, though not always, has a past-time connotation. Some actions that do not usually express duration (such as "to find" or "to receive") naturally fit better into the aorist category though they may have present-time associations. We are thus on safer ground to think of the aorist as the summary tense rather than as necessarily a past-time tense, though the majority of its uses will fall into that category. Like the imperfect, the aorist is constructed with the augment plus the verbal stem (ἐ + ποιε- = ἐποιη), though it uses either a suffix (-σα or -σε; ἐποίησα) or an altered stem (often called a "second aorist"; e.g., εἶπον for λέγω) in its formation. Since we are relying on our tools to identify the form of the word, we are less concerned with its formation than with its significance.

Mark 4:39

καὶ ...	ἐπετίμησεν	τῷ	ἀνέμῳ	καὶ	εἶπεν	τῇ	θαλάσσῃ ...
καί	ἐπιτιμάω	ὁ	ἄνεμος	καί	εἶπον	ὁ	θάλασσα
and	rebuked	the	wind	and	said	to the	sea
2532	2008	3588	417	2532	2036	3588	2281

καὶ	ἐκόπασεν	ὁ	ἄνεμος	καὶ	ἐγένετο	γαλήνη	μεγάλη.
καί	κοπάζω	ὁ	ἄνεμος	καί	γίνομαι	γαλήνη	μέγας
and	abated	the	wind	and	there was	calm	a great
2532	2869	3588	417	2532	1096	1055	3173

The aorist is quite commonly used in narrative passages to **move along the events** of the story. This is an example of the **summary** nature of the aorist verb. In Mark 4:39, four *aorist, active, indicative, third person*, and *singular* verbs (ἐπετίμησεν, εἶπεν, ἐκόπασεν, and ἐγένετο) are used to portray the sequence of events. The verbs move the story forward but do not emphasize the nature of the actions, instead portraying them in summary fashion.

Matt. 9:27

ἠκολούθησαν	[αὐτῷ]	δύο	τυφλοὶ
ἀκολουθέω	αὐτός	δύο	τυφλός
followed	him	two	blind men
190	846	1417	5185

Sometimes aorist verbs signify the **beginning of an action**, such as in Matthew 9:27.[1] Here the *aorist* verb ἠκολούθησαν (*active, indicative, 3rd person*, and *plural*), marks the beginning of the action but does not emphasize its duration as the imperfect tense would.

James 1:11

ἀνέτειλεν	γὰρ	ὁ	ἥλιος	...	καὶ	ἐξήρανεν	τὸν	χόρτον
ἀνατέλλω	γάρ	ὁ	ἥλιος		καί	ξηραίνω	ὁ	χόρτος
rises	for	the	sun		and	dries up	the	grass
393	1063	3588	2246		2532	3583	3588	5528

Aorist verbs can also occasionally describe a **timeless, universal action**, much like the present indicative. In James 1:11, several *aorist, active, indicative* verbs are used (ἀνέτειλεν and ἐξήρανεν above) to describe a timeless event portrayed from a zoomed-out perspective. This is different from the present portrayal of timeless, universal action in that it does not emphasize the pattern of repetition.

John 13:31

νῦν	ἐδοξάσθη	ὁ	υἱὸς	τοῦ	ἀνθρώπου
νῦν	δοξάζω	ὁ	υἱός	ὁ	ἄνθρωπος
now	is glorified	the	Son	of	Man
3568	1392	3588	5207	3588	444

Sometimes the aorist tense portrays a **present action viewed from a distant perspective.** Such an occurrence is found in John 13:31, where

Jesus states that the Son of Man "is now glorified" (ἐδοξάσθη; *aorist*, *passive*, *indicative*, *3rd person*, and *singular*). The present force of this aorist verb is indicated by the adverb νῦν ("now"), but the verb does not emphasize duration or progression as would the present tense; rather, it presents the present-time action in summary form.

Future Indicative

The **future indicative** occurs less frequently than the other tenses examined so far, though it is still fairly common in the New Testament. Similar to the aorist, the future indicative portrays an aoristic (i.e., summary or zoomed-out) perspective on an action, but one that is future in time. The future indicative is formed by adding a sigma (σ) to the end of the verbal stem (e.g., ἀκου- + σ = ἀκούσ-).

John 16:13

τὸ	πνεῦμα	τῆς	ἀληθείας,	ὁδηγήσει	ὑμᾶς
ὁ	πνεῦμα	ὁ	ἀλήθεια	ὁδηγέω	σύ
the	Spirit	of	truth	he will guide	you
3588	4151	3588	225	3594	5209

The most common function of the future indicative presents a **summary of a future event**. In John 16:13, Jesus tells the disciples that when the Spirit comes, "he will guide" (ὁδηγήσει; *future, active, indicative, 3rd person*, and *singular*) them. The future here does not emphasize the process or duration of the action but rather portrays it from a zoomed-out perspective and in future time.

Matt. 22:37

ἀγαπήσεις	κύριον	τὸν	θεόν	σου
ἀγαπάω	κύριος	ὁ	θεός	σύ
you shall love	the Lord	—	God	your
25	2962	3588	2316	4675

The future indicative may also be used to **issue a command**. Matthew 22:37 contains an example of such a use. Here the *future indicative* verb ἀγαπήσεις (*active*, *2nd person*, and *singular*) does not present a prediction or description of a future event but rather gives a directive for behavior. This is one of several ways that commands can be issued in New Testament Greek.

Rom. 5:7

μόλις	γὰρ	ὑπὲρ	δικαίου	τις	ἀποθανεῖται
μόλις	γάρ	ὑπέρ	δίκαιος	τίς	ἀποθνῄσκω
only rarely	for	on behalf of	a righteous person	someone	will die
3433	1063	5228	1342	5100	599

Finally, on rare occasions the future indicative is used to present a **timeless, universal action from a future perspective.** In Romans 5:7, Paul writes that only rarely someone "will die" (ἀποθανεῖται; *future, middle, indicative, 3rd person,* and *singular*) for a righteous person. The future verb here refers not to a specific event or scenario but to a general principle, cast in future time and from a zoomed-out perspective.

Perfect Indicative

There is considerable debate among Greek grammarians concerning how to define the **perfect indicative.** There is agreement, however, that the perfect tense often involves a *completed action* or a *state* that is given additional focus (what we have called "perfective aspect"). It is often considered the most marked of the tenses, or the tense that stands out as most prominent (along with the pluperfect). In other words, perfect verbs often either contain additional *emphasis* or *intensification* or *focus* on a resulting state from a past activity. The perfect tense is formed with two significant morphological changes (see table 11 in appendix 2). The first is the reduplication of the verbal stem, in which the first letter of the stem is doubled (γε + γράφ- = γέγραφ-) or the beginning vowel of the stem is doubled and subsequently lengthened (α + ἀγαπά- = ἠγάπη-). Notice for αγαπα-, which is what is known as a "contract verb," the vowel at the end of the stem also lengthens, which occurs in other tenses, like the aorist, as well. The second morphological change is the suffix, -κα, which is normally attached to the end of the word (e.g., ἠγάπηκα). We will look below at the most common uses of the perfect indicative.

1 Cor. 15:4

καὶ	ὅτι	ἐγήγερται	τῇ	ἡμέρᾳ	τῇ	τρίτῃ
καί	ὅτι	ἐγείρω	ὁ	ἡμέρα	ὁ	τρίτος
and	that	he was raised up	on the	day	—	third
2532	3754	1453	3588	2250	3588	5154

Often the perfect **emphasizes a resultant state** or **effect** from a previous action. Such a use is likely intended in 1 Corinthians 15:4 with the *perfect passive indicative* verb ἐγήγερται (*3rd person* and *singular*). The verb describes the resurrection from the viewpoint of its completion though emphasizing the resultant state ("has been raised and still stands as raised") of the action of raising.

John 5:33

καὶ	μεμαρτύρηκεν	τῇ	ἀληθείᾳ
καί	μαρτυρέω	ὁ	ἀλήθεια
and	he has testified	to the	truth
2532	3140	3588	225

At other times, the perfect indicative **emphasizes the completion of an action.** John 5:33 expresses such a use. Here John "has testified" (μεμαρτύρηκεν; *perfect, active, indicative, 3rd person,* and *singular*) to the truth. The use of the perfect here focuses more on the completion of the event than a resultant state.

John 7:28

κἀμὲ	οἴδατε	καὶ	οἴδατε	πόθεν	εἰμί
κἀγώ	οἶδα	καί	οἶδα	πόθεν	εἰμί
me	you [both] know	and	you know	where	I am [from]
2504	1492	2532	1492	4159	1510

The perfect indicative also simply **expresses a state**, such as in John 7:28. Here two instances of the *perfect active indicative* verb οἴδατε (*2nd person* and *plural*) occur that express a state rather than place an emphasis on the completion or the results of an action. This use occurs most commonly with the verb οἶδα ("to know"), though other verbs, such as ἵστημι ("to stand") and ποιέω ("to do"), also fall into this category. These verbs, by nature of the action that they describe, are more stative in their presentation.

Pluperfect Indicative

The least frequent of these tenses is the **pluperfect indicative**. The pluperfect, like the perfect, takes on perfective aspect. Like the imperfect, however, the pluperfect is restricted to past time or "offline" information and thus focuses on results or states in force in the past or supplemental to the narrative flow. The pluperfect, like the perfect, reduplicates its stem and sometimes adds the augment ἐ to the front of the word (πε + ποιέ- = πεποιή-), which signifies past time. It also has an additional morpheme attached to the end of the stem (-κει-; πεποιήκειν). The pluperfect thus is likewise the most marked of the indicative tenses.

Luke 8:29

πολλοῖς	γὰρ	χρόνοις	συνηρπάκει	αὐτὸν
πολύς	γάρ	χρόνος	συναρπάζω	αὐτός
many	for	times	it had seized	him
4183	1063	5550	4884	846

In Luke 8:29, the *pluperfect indicative* verb συνηρπάκει (*active, 3rd person*, and *singular*) **emphasizes a resultant state** or **effect**. Here the verb in the larger context focuses less on the completion of the action than on its resulting effects. As is often typical of the pluperfect, it also presents offline information, details that fill in the background of the story but do not necessarily move the narrative forward.

John 9:22

γὰρ	συνετέθεεντο	οἱ	Ἰουδαῖοι
γάρ	συντίθημι	ὁ	Ἰουδαῖος
for	decided	the	Jews
1063	4934	3588	2453

The pluperfect also **emphasizes the completion of an action**. John 9:22 offers an example of this use. Here the *pluperfect indicative* verb συνετέθειντο (*middle, 3rd person*, and *plural*) focuses more on the completion of this decision than on its lingering effects. Here again, the pluperfect presents offline information that adds background details to the narrative and relegates the action to a more distant position in the past.

John 2:9

καὶ	οὐκ	ᾔδει	πόθεν	ἐστίν
καί	οὐ	οἶδα	πόθεν	εἰμί
and	[did] not	know	where	it was [from]
2532	3756	1492	4159	2076

Finally, and again like the perfect, the pluperfect often simply **expresses a state**. In John 2:9, the *pluperfect active indicative* verb ᾔδει (*3rd person* and *singular*) expresses a temporally distant state. Here again the information provided is offline detail.

Understanding Aspect

We have attempted to offer a brief summary of the most common uses of the indicative while highlighting the major differences between the tenses. We have sought to shed light rather than to pile on darkness, but information overload is certainly a possibility. In terms of understanding and engaging with verbal aspect in our study of Greek verbs, Constantine Campbell has offered a helpful framework for this area. Campbell suggests the following four steps for examining aspectual significance: (1) identify the aspect, (2) consider the type of action (e.g., punctiliar ["point in time"], stative ["state" or "condition"], transitive [acts upon an object])portrayed by the lexeme (i.e., a "unit of meaning"), (3) examine the context to consider the portrayal of the action (e.g., time, duration), and (4) determine which type of action is intended as a result of the combination of these factors (e.g., past progressive, iterative, stative).[2] Campbell's recommended procedure is one worth applying as we examine the significance of aspect in the Greek New Testament verbal system.

Summary

We have by no means exhausted the topic but have provided a framework for how to understand the usage of these tenses. We emphasized the prominence of verbal aspect (primary) and its relationship to the time of an action (secondary and primarily contextually determined), and we also attempted to offer some categories for the most common behaviors of indicative tenses. To summarize briefly what we have explored above, table 1 shows the basic map for how Greek verbs in the indicative mood function.

Table 1. Indicative Mood Tenses

Indicative Tense	Aspect	Time	Common Uses
Present	imperfective (in progress)	generally present	in progress; repetition; timeless, universal action; historical present
Imperfect	imperfective (in progress)	past	in progress; beginning of an in-progress action, repetition; attempted action
Aorist	aoristic (zoomed out)	generally past	summary; beginning of an action; timeless, universal action; present viewed from a distant perspective
Future	aoristic (zoomed out)	future	summary of a future event; issue a command; timeless, universal action from a future perspective
Perfect	perfective (up close)	generally present	emphasize a resultant state; emphasize the completion of an action; express a state
Pluperfect	perfective (up close)	past	emphasize a resultant state; emphasize the completion of an action; express a state

Your Turn

I have outlined the most-common functions of the indicative tenses. Now it is your turn to test out your newfound knowledge. Examine the bolded words in the sentence below. Using an analytical lexicon or parsing tool (see chap. 4), identify the grammatical information for each word. Once you have identified the tense, voice, mood, person, and number, using the categories described above, determine how each of these words is functioning. After you have made a decision about the form and function, check your answers in the key in appendix 1.

1 John 1:2

ἡ	ζωὴ	ἐφανερώθη,	καὶ	ἑωράκαμεν	καὶ	μαρτυροῦμεν
ὁ	ζωή	φανερόω	καί	ὁράω	καί	μαρτυρέω
the	life	was revealed	and	we have seen	and	testify
3588	2222	5319	2532	3708	2532	3140

Words to Memorize

ἀγαπάω	to love
ἀκούω	to hear
γίνομαι	to be, to exist (deponent)
ἐγείρω	to rise, to wake
θέλω	to wish, to desire
λέγω	to speak (aorist: εἶπον)
οἶδα	to know
πορεύομαι	to come, to go

10

(Independent) Imperative-Mood Verbs

One of the more significant moods in the Greek verbal system for the present-day Christian to carefully consider is the imperative. The **imperative mood** is the mood of command or volition. Imperatives attempt to direct the action of others and thus often, for example, provide the "so what" that follows a didactic (i.e., "teaching") section. If the last chapter seemed overwhelming (and understandably so), this chapter should provide some relief. The imperative mood in the New Testament contains only two tenses: the present and the aorist. We will examine both in what follows, along with their most common uses. As in the indicative, in general the aorist imperative views the command as a whole (zoomed out), and the present imperative views the command as in progress. Both tenses, however, take on other nuances in various contexts. Outside the indicative, it is also important to remember that aspect is central and time is never inherent to nonindicative verbs.

Present Imperative

The present imperative often presents either a general command or a command that emphasizes some aspect of duration. This may focus on the continuation of the command, the command while in progress, or the intended repetition of the command. All of these are possible emphases of the present imperative. The emphasis can be determined by examining the kind of action in view and the context of the command.

Matt. 8:22

ὁ	δὲ	Ἰησοῦς	λέγει	αὐτῷ·	ἀκολούθει	μοι
ὁ	δέ	Ἰησοῦς	λέγω	αὐτός	ἀκολουθέω	ἐγώ
—	but	Jesus	said	to him	follow	me
3588	1161	2424	3004	846	190	3427

In Matthew 8:22, we find an example of the present imperative given to **command the beginning and continuation of an action.** Here Jesus instructs the man to "begin and continue following" (ἀκολούθει; *present, active, imperative, 2nd person*, and *singular*) him. This verb in the context could also be taken as a command to **continue an action already being pursued.** In either case, the emphasis of the present aspect seems to lie on the continuation of the action.

Luke 6:35

πλὴν	ἀγαπᾶτε	τοὺς	ἐχθροὺς	ὑμῶν	καὶ	ἀγαθοποιεῖτε
πλήν	ἀγαπάω	ὁ	ἐχθρός	σύ	καί	ἀγαθοποιέω
but	love	—	enemies	your	and	do good
4133	25	3588	2190	5216	2532	15

Sometimes the present imperative is used to **command an action that is to be habitually carried out.** Luke 6:35 contains such an emphasis. Here the two *present imperatives* ἀγαπᾶτε and ἀγαθοποιεῖτε (both *active, 2nd person*, and *plural*) indicate that the actions of loving and doing are to be habitually repeated as a pattern of behavior.

2 Cor. 13:5

ἑαυτοὺς	δοκιμάζετε
ἑαυτοῦ	δοκιμάζω
yourselves	examine
1438	1381

Finally, the present imperative may also **command to keep repeating an action.** In 2 Corinthians 13:5, the *present imperative* δοκιμάζετε (*active, 2nd person,* and *plural*) expects the activity of self-examination to be periodically repeated. This is intended to be not necessarily a continuous activity but rather one to be repeated.

Aorist Imperative

The **aorist imperative** generally either presents a specific command intended for a specific context or presents a command as a whole, with no emphasis on its duration. This may mean that the command is intended as a one-time activity, but not necessarily so. Often the aorist simply does not emphasize duration or repetition, though that may still be appropriate for the command.

Matt. 3:8

ποιήσατε	οὖν	καρπὸν	ἄξιον	τῆς	μετανοίας
ποιέω	οὖν	καρπός	ἄξιος	ὁ	μετάνοια
produce	therefore	fruit	worthy	of	repentance
4160	3767	2590	514	3588	3341

The typical function of the aorist imperative is to present a **command viewed as a whole.** In Matthew 3:8, the *aorist imperative* ποιήσατε (*active, 2nd person,* and *plural*) likely does not intend to convey a onetime action but rather is simply presenting the command as a whole from a zoomed-out or summarized perspective. This does not mean that producing fruit has no duration but rather that no duration is emphasized here or perhaps that the command is **restricted for a specific context.**

Rom. 6:13

ἀλλὰ	παραστήσατε	ἑαυτοὺς	τῷ	θεῷ
ἀλλά	παρίστημι	ἑαυτοῦ	ὁ	θεός
but	present	yourselves	to	God
235	3936	1438	3588	2316

Sometimes the aorist imperative **commands to begin an action**. In Romans 6:13, the *aorist imperative* παραστήσατε (*active, 2nd person,* and *plural*) possibly conveys such a meaning. If you take a look at the text in an interlinear, you may notice the contrast of παραστήσατε here with the *present imperative* παριστάνετε (*active, 2nd person,* and *plural*) earlier in the verse, which possibly intends to draw out the differing aspects. We may interpret the contrast as "do not keep offering [παριστάνετε] your members to sin" but "offer [παραστήσατε] yourselves to God." This does not necessarily mean that the aorist imperative should be viewed as a onetime action, but rather the event as a whole is in view with possible emphasis on the beginning of the action.

Third-Person Imperatives

We offer here one final note about the imperative mood. While in English we tend to think of imperatives as second-person verbs ("you [go] study," etc.), in Greek the imperative also occurs in the third person. This can present a potentially awkward translation ("he [go] study"), so we must add a word such as "let" or "must" when translating these forms ("let him study" or "he must study"). Though second-person imperatives are more common in the Greek New Testament, third-person imperatives occur with some frequency as well.

Your Turn

I have outlined the most-common functions of the present and aorist imperatives. Now it is your turn to test out your newfound knowledge. Examine the bolded words in the sentence below. Using an analytical lexicon or parsing tool (see chap. 4), identify the grammatical information for each word. Once you have identified the tense, voice, mood, person, and number, using the categories described above, determine how each of these words is functioning. After you have made a decision about the form and function, check your answers in the key in appendix 1.

Rev. 3:19

ζήλευε	οὖν	καὶ	μετανόησον
ζηλεύω	οὖν	καί	μετανοέω
be zealous	therefore	and	repent
2206	3767	2532	3340

Words to Memorize

ἀκολουθέω	to follow
ἄξιος	worthy
ἑαυτοῦ	yourself, himself, herself, itself
ἐχθρός	enemy
καρπός	fruit
μετάνοια	repentance

11

(Dependent) Subjunctive-Mood Verbs

As we continue to move away from the indicative, it is worth remembering that we are moving away from purported descriptions of reality to volition or potential. This is where we find the subjunctive mood located. The **subjunctive mood** is often described as the mood of potential or projection. Subjunctive verbs examine an action as a potential action to consider. They can function in a number of ways. We will again examine the most common uses along with the significance of the verbal aspect of the two tenses used most commonly in the subjunctive mood. As we do, we will emphasize the primacy of verbal aspect in each tense.

Present Subjunctive

The **present subjunctive** maintains the zoomed-in or in-process perspective found in the present indicative and imperative. For the subjunctive, this usually means that the duration, process, or continuation of the action is in view when the present subjunctive is used.

Matt. 5:23

Ἐὰν	οὖν	προσφέρῃς	τὸ	δῶρόν	σου	ἐπὶ	τὸ	θυσιαστήριον
ἐάν	οὖν	προσφέρω	ὁ	δῶρον	σύ	ἐπί	ὁ	θυσιαστήριον
if	therefore	you present	—	gift	your	at	the	altar
1437	3767	4374	3588	1435	4675	1909	3588	2379

Sometimes the present subjunctive describes an action as **in progress.** In Matthew 5:23 the subjunctive here (combined with the conjunction ἐάν) indicates that potential action is in mind. The *present subjunctive* προσφέρῃς (*active, 2nd person,* and *singular*) portrays this action as in progress. The idea is "therefore, if you are in the process of presenting your gift" and remember an unreconciled relationship, stop *in the middle of the process* and go make amends.

Matt. 10:23

Ὅταν	δὲ	διώκωσιν	ὑμᾶς
ὅταν	δέ	διώκω	σύ
whenever	and	they persecute	you
3752	1161	1377	5209

The subjunctive also sometimes indicates a **repeated** frequency of action, as in Matthew 10:23. Here the *present, active, subjunctive* verb διώκωσιν (*3rd person* and *plural*) combined with the conjunction ὅταν indicates the potentiality of the action. The combination with the present tense focuses on the potential repetition of the persecution. The idea is "any time in which persecuting starts or is occurring."

Rom. 6:1

ἐπιμένωμεν	τῇ	ἁμαρτίᾳ
ἐπιμένω	ὁ	ἁμαρτία
shall we continue	in	sin
1961	3588	266

Finally, the present subjunctive can also indicate the **continuation of an action.** In Romans 6:1, Paul asks whether "we should be continuing in sin" (ἐπιμένωμεν; *present, active, subjunctive, 1st person,* and *plural*). The subjunctive verb here emphasizes the continuation of the action ("should we keep continuing"), which arises naturally out of the meaning of this verb itself.

Aorist Subjunctive

The **aorist subjunctive**, because it represents aoristic aspect, presents an action from a zoomed-out perspective. Thus aorist subjunctive verbs usually describe the action as a whole or focus on the action as a point-in-time event.

John 6:5

πόθεν	ἀγοράσωμεν	ἄρτους
πόθεν	ἀγοράζω	ἄρτος
where	can we buy	bread
4159	59	740

A typical notion presented by the aorist subjunctive is portraying the action as a **summary**. In John 6:5, the disciples ask Jesus where they "might buy" (ἀγοράσωμεν; *aorist, active, subjunctive, 1st person*, and *plural*) bread. There is no emphasis here on the process or duration of the action, but rather the question is presented with the action as a whole in view. The nature of the action itself (buying) also lends itself more to the aspect of the aorist tense.

Matt. 2:8

ἐπὰν	δὲ	εὕρητε
ἐπάν	δέ	εὑρίσκω
when	and	you have found [him]
1875	1161	2147

In addition, the aorist subjunctive may also focus on an action as happening at a **point in time**. In Matthew 2:8, King Herod instructs the wise men to inform him when they find the child (Jesus). The aorist subjunctive verb εὕρητε (*active, 2nd person*, and *plural*) could be taken to mean "at the point in time in which you find him." There is no emphasis here on the process but rather a view of the action from a distance.

Subjunctive Functions

We have developed an overview of the significance of the present and aorist subjunctives in terms of their aspectual force. We now must address the various functions of the subjunctive mood. Though the mood in general emphasizes the potential for an action or projects its possibility, there are a variety of ways in which this action might be portrayed in the subjunctive mood.

Heb. 4:14

κρατῶμεν	τῆς	ὁμολογίας
κρατέω	ὁ	ὁμολογία
let us hold fast to	our	confession
2902	3588	3671

Sometimes the subjunctive takes on the force of an imperative-mood verb and presents a **command** or an **exhortation** for a certain action. This usually occurs with subjunctive verbs in the *first-person plural*, such as κρατῶμεν (*present* and *active*) in Hebrews 4:14. These commands, often called **hortatory subjunctives**, have a softer force than the imperative mood and are more akin to an exhortation. They are typically translated with "let us."

Rom. 10:14

πῶς	δὲ	ἀκούσωσιν	χωρὶς	κηρύσσοντος;
πῶς	δέ	ἀκούω	χωρίς	κηρύσσω
how	and	will they hear about	without	one who proclaims
4459	1161	191	5565	2784

The subjunctive may also ask a **question** in either a **real** or **rhetorical** context. In Romans 10:14, the *aorist subjunctive* ἀκούσωσιν (*active, 3rd* *person*, and *plural*) portrays such a function. Here Paul asks the question rhetorically, "How will they hear without one who is proclaiming?" He answers the question in the affirmative in 10:18 (yes, they have heard, but have not believed).

Gal. 5:26

μὴ	γινώμεθα	κενόδοξοι
μή	γίνομαι	κενόδοξος
[we must] not	become	conceited
3361	1096	2755

The subjunctive can also present a negative command, or **prohibition**. Most often this is found with the combination of μή ("no, not") + an *aorist subjunctive*. We find this construction in Galatians 5:26. Here Paul commands the Galatian believers to "not become" (γινώμεθα; *present, deponent, subjunctive, 1st person*, and *plural*) conceited.

Gal. 5:16

καὶ	ἐπιθυμίαν	σαρκὸς	οὐ	μὴ	τελέσητε
καί	ἐπιθυμία	σάρξ	οὐ	μή	τελέω
and	the desire	of the flesh	[you will] never	—	carry out
2532	1939	4561	3756	3361	5055

More forceful still than the prohibitive subjunctive is the subjunctive of **emphatic negation**. This construction combines both negatives, οὐ and μή, with an aorist subjunctive. The force of the emphatic negative is "never," ruling out even the possibility of the idea presented. In Galatians 5:16, οὐ μή is combined with the *aorist subjunctive* τελέσητε (*active, 2nd person*, and *plural*) to assert that those who walk by the Spirit "will never carry out" the desire of the flesh.

Phil. 2:10–11

ἵνα	ἐν	τῷ	ὀνόματι	Ἰησοῦ	πᾶν	γόνυ	κάμψῃ	···
ἵνα	ἐν	ὁ	ὄνομα	Ἰησοῦς	πᾶς	γόνυ	κάμπτω	
so that	at	the	name	of Jesus	every	knee	should bow	
2443	1722	3588	3686	2424	3956	1119	2578	

καὶ	πᾶσα	γλῶσσα	ἐξομολογήσηται
καί	πᾶς	γλῶσσα	ἐξομολογέω
and	every	tongue	confess
2532	3956	1100	1843

In addition, the subjunctive may portray the **purpose** or **result** of an action. Philippians 2:10–11 provides an example of this function with the *aorist subjunctive* verbs κάμψῃ and ἐξομολογήσηται (both *3rd person* and *singular*). The verbs here, introduced by the conjunction ἵνα (though other conjunctions may be used with this function), indicate the purpose of God exalting Jesus. God's plan was to exalt him in order to bring all creation under his rule.

Though there are other functions we could examine, this covers the majority of the most common uses of the subjunctive mood. It is worth reiterating again that you must recognize the primacy of verbal aspect when interpreting the subjunctive mood as well as identify which function of the subjunctive is in view in the context. These two elements together will help give insight to the significance of the form in its context.

Your Turn

I have outlined the most-common functions of the present and aorist subjunctive. Now it is your turn to test out your newfound knowledge. Examine the bolded words in the sentence below. Using an analytical lexicon or parsing tool (see chap. 4), identify the grammatical information for each word. Once you have identified the tense, voice, mood, person, and number, using the categories described above, determine how each of these words is functioning. After you have made a decision about the form and function, check your answers in the key in appendix 1.

Rev. 19:7

χαίρωμεν	καὶ	ἀγαλλιῶμεν	καὶ	δώσωμεν	τὴν	δόξαν	αὐτῷ
χαίρω	καί	ἀγαλλιάω	καί	δίδωμι	ὁ	δόξα	αὐτός
let us rejoice	and	be glad	and	give	the	glory	him
5463	2532	21	2532	1325	3588	1391	846

Words to Memorize

γλῶσσα	tongue, language
δῶρον	gift
εὑρίσκω	to find
κηρύσσω	to proclaim, to preach
μή	not, lest
ὄνομα	name
οὐ, οὐκ, οὐχ	not

12

(Dependent) Greek Infinitives

The final two verbal forms we have to deal with are technically not verbs. They are both **verbals**, meaning that they can act like verbs but also take on properties of other words, such as nouns or adjectives. They will thus act like verbs in some ways but will usually be dependent or subordinate, rather than independent or mainline, ideas. The first verbal that we will address is the **infinitive**. Infinitives are verbal nouns, meaning that they take some characteristics of verbs while functioning primarily as a noun. Though infinitives are not inflected, they do sometimes appear with the neuter article, which helps to clarify an infinitive's case, and thus also its function in the sentence. Infinitives are simpler in form than verbs, possessing only *tense* and *voice*. Because infinitives emphasize aspect rather than time, they occur only in three tenses: *present, aorist*, and *perfect*. We will examine each tense and its aspect in turn before examining common functions of the infinitive.

Present Infinitive

The **present infinitive** portrays imperfective aspect, an up-close or in-process view of the action. As in the verbal moods explored above, this can be expressed in several different nuances.

Luke 15:14

καὶ	αὐτὸς	ἤρξατο	ὑστερεῖσθαι
καί	αὐτός	ἄρχω	ὑστερέω
and	he	began	to be in need
2532	846	756	5302

Sometimes the present infinitive focuses on **the beginning of an action** while adopting an up-close or in-process view of the action's progression. In Luke 15:14, in the parable of the prodigal son, the son begins "to be in need" (ὑστερεῖσθαι; *infinitive, present,* and *passive*). The infinitive here places the reader at the beginning of the action as the parable goes on to describe the son's response during this time of need.

Rom. 7:6

ὥστε	δουλεύειν	ἡμᾶς	ἐν	καινότητι	πνεύματος
ὥστε	δουλεύω	ἐγώ	ἐν	καινότης	πνεῦμα
so that	may serve	we	in	newness	of [the] Spirit
5620	1398	2248	1722	2538	4151

The present infinitive may also portray the **ongoing** nature of an action. Romans 7:6 likely contains such an emphasis. Here, Paul writes that death to sin results in "serving" (δουλεύειν; *infinitive, present,* and *active*) in the Spirit. The infinitive δουλεύειν here likely highlights the in-progress and ongoing nature of this activity.

Luke 9:29

ἐν	τῷ	προσεύχεσθαι	αὐτὸν
ἐν	ὁ	προσεύχομαι	αὐτός
as	—	was praying	he
1722	3588	4336	846

At other times the present infinitive indicates that the action of the infinitive **occurs at the same time** as the action of its associated verb. In Luke 9:29, during the transfiguration narrative, we are told Jesus's appearance changed "while he was praying" (προσεύχεσθαι; *infinitive, present,* and *deponent*). The combination here of the preposition ἐν with the dative article τῷ and the infinitive προσεύχεσθαι gives the present infinitive this temporal force.

Luke 18:5

διά	γε	τὸ	παρέχειν	μοι	κόπον	τὴν	χήραν	ταύτην
διά	γέ	ὁ	παρέχω	ἐγώ	κόπος	ὁ	χήρα	οὗτος
because	yet	—	is causing	for me	trouble	—	widow	this
1223	1065	3588	3930	3427	2873	3588	5503	3778

Finally, the present infinitive also often describes the **cause** of an action. Luke 18:5 records the parable of the persistent widow. The judge grants her request "because this widow is causing trouble" for him. The infinitive παρέχειν (*present* and *active*) is given causal force by the preposition and article (διά . . . τό), a construction that occurs most commonly with present infinitives.

Aorist Infinitive

The **aorist infinitive**, like the aorist tense in the verbal moods explored earlier, portrays aoristic aspect, viewing the action from a distant or zoomed-out perspective. As noted previously, this distant perspective can be expressed in several different ways.

Matt. 20:19

εἰς	τὸ	ἐμπαῖξαι	καὶ	μαστιγῶσαι	καὶ	σταυρῶσαι
εἰς	ὁ	ἐμπαίζω	καί	μαστιγόω	καί	σταυρόω
to	—	mock [him]	and	flog [him]	and	crucify [him]
1519	3588	1702	2532	3146	2532	4717

As is common for aorist verbs, the aorist infinitive often displays a **summary** of the action. Matthew 20:19 offers three *aorist*, *active* infinitives (ἐμπαῖξαι, μαστιγῶσαι, and σταυρῶσαι). These infinitives provide a sequence that presents these actions in a summarized or zoomed-out manner.

Mark 12:12

Καὶ	ἐζήτουν	αὐτὸν	κρατῆσαι
καί	ζητέω	αὐτός	κρατέω
and	they were seeking	him	to arrest
2532	2212	846	2902

Sometimes the aorist portrays an action as a **point in time**. This usually occurs when the action by its nature does not involve any progression or process. In Mark 12:12, the Jewish leaders are seeking "to arrest" or "to apprehend" (κρατῆσαι; *infinitive, aorist,* and *active*) Jesus. The aorist here indicates the punctiliar or point-in-time nature of the action.

Acts 10:41

μετὰ	τὸ	ἀναστῆναι	αὐτὸν	ἐκ	νεκρῶν
μετά	ὁ	ἀνίστημι	αὐτός	ἐκ	νεκρός
after	—	rose	he	from	the dead
3326	3588	450	846	1537	3498

Like the present infinitive, the aorist infinitive can take on temporal significance in certain constructions. While contemporaneous or at-the-same-time temporality is in view with the present, the aorist can describe an action that **occurs prior to** the action of the associated verb. This is typically indicated with the preposition μετά with the article τό preceding the infinitive. In Acts 10:41, we find that God has called the disciples who ate and drank with Jesus "after he rose" (ἀναστῆναι; *infinitive, aorist,* and *active*) from the dead as his witnesses. The aorist infinitive here with μετὰ τό indicates the resurrection occurred prior to the disciples eating and drinking with Jesus.

Matt. 6:8

πρὸ	τοῦ	ὑμᾶς	αἰτῆσαι	αὐτόν
πρό	ὁ	σύ	αἰτέω	αὐτός
before	—	you	ask	him
4253	3588	5209	154	846

Finally, the aorist can also describe an action **occurring after** the action of the associated verb. Typically this is signified by the presence of the preposition πρό and the article τοῦ before the infinitive or the preposition πρίν before the infinitive. Jesus tells his followers in Matthew 6:8 that God already knows their needs before they ask ("before you ask," αἰτῆσαι; *infinitive, aorist,* and *active*) him. The appearance of πρὸ τοῦ here before the infinitive indicates that the infinitive action (their asking) occurs after the action of the verb (God's knowing).

Perfect Infinitive

The **perfect infinitive** occurs far less frequently than the present and aorist infinitives. Like the perfect tense in the indicative mood, the perfect infinitive conveys perfective aspect. You may recall that this means it specifies a state of being or indicates a completed action with an emphasis on the results of the action. We will thus find a number of the nuances of the perfect infinitive similar to those explored in the perfect indicative.

Luke 6:48

διὰ	τὸ	καλῶς	οἰκοδομῆσθαι	αὐτήν
διά	ὁ	καλῶς	οἰκοδομέω	αὐτός
because	—	well	had been built	it
1223	3588	2570	3618	846

Often the perfect infinitive **emphasizes a resultant state** or **effect** from a previous action. In Luke 6:48, Jesus uses the illustration of a well-built house to describe those who follow his teachings. Here he says the house stood firm when the flood came, because "it had been built well" (οἰκοδομῆσθαι; *infinitive, perfect,* and *passive*). The perfect tense here emphasizes the sturdy state of the house as a result of the action of being well built.

John 12:18

ὅτι	ἤκουσαν	τοῦτο	αὐτὸν	πεποιηκέναι	τὸ	σημεῖον
ὅτι	ἀκούω	οὗτος	αὐτός	ποιέω	ὁ	σημεῖον
for	they had heard	this	[that] he	had performed	—	sign
3754	191	5124	846	4160	3588	4592

The perfect also at times **emphasizes the completion of an action.** As the crowd came out to meet Jesus in John 12:18, the reason for their gathering was because of "this sign he had performed" (πεποιηκέναι; *infinitive, perfect,* and *active*) when he raised Lazarus. The perfect here indicates the completion of the action, though providing this as "offline" information, or material supplemental to the main narrative of the text.

1 Cor. 8:2

εἴ	τις	δοκεῖ	ἐγνωκέναι	τι
εἰ	τίς	δοκέω	γινώσκω	τίς
if	anyone	thinks	he knows	anything
1487	5100	1380	1097	5100

Sometimes the perfect tense simply **expresses a state** without necessarily placing emphasis on the completion or ongoing results of an action. The perfect tense in these situations may then be used to give the action prominence in the sentence. This usage is especially common with verbs of knowing or seeing, such as in 1 Corinthians 8:2. Here Paul writes that if anyone thinks they "know" (ἐγνωκέναι; *infinitive, perfect,* and *active*) anything, they do not yet know as they should. The perfect here does not necessarily focus on the completion or results of an action but rather expresses a state that is given a greater degree of prominence with the perfect tense.

Infinitive Functions

We have already explored two common functions of the infinitive (**temporal** and **causal**) by means of their association with the tenses explored above. Other infinitive functions do not necessarily, however, gravitate toward a particular tense. These functions are often quite common. We will explore their basic constructions (how we recognize them) and meanings below.

Matt. 5:17

Μὴ	νομίσητε	ὅτι	ἦλθον	καταλῦσαι	τὸν	νόμον	ἢ	τοὺς	προφήτας
μή	νομίζω	ὅτι	ἔρχομαι	καταλύω	ὁ	νόμος	ἤ	ὁ	προφήτης
[do] not	think	that	I came	to destroy	the	Law	or	the	Prophets
3361	3543	3754	2064	2647	3588	3551	2228	3588	4396

One very common function of the infinitive is to describe the **purpose** or **result** of an action. Jesus states, for example, in Matthew 5:17 that he did not come "to destroy" (καταλῦσαι; *infinitive, aorist*, and *active*) the Law or the Prophets. In other words, he did not come "with the intended purpose of destroying" them. Purpose or result infinitives can be expressed in several different constructions. We may have only the infinitive (as in Matt. 5:17), or it may be preceded by τοῦ, εἰς τό, πρός, or ὥστε τό. The difference between a purpose and a result idea is primarily one of emphasis on intent, where purpose expresses an intended outcome and result expresses an outcome without emphasis on its intent. Here in Matthew 5:17, it seems clear that Jesus is discussing the intent of his ministry, and thus purpose is the better designation.

Rom. 1:13

οὐ	θέλω	δὲ	ὑμᾶς	ἀγνοεῖν
οὐ	θέλω	δέ	σύ	ἀγνοέω
[I do] not	want	now	you	to be ignorant
3756	2309	1161	5209	50

Infinitives often also serve a **complementary** function. In this construction, the infinitive completes the idea of its associated verb. Typically, incomplete verbal ideas fall into this category, which includes verbal notions such as "to be able," "to wish," "to seek," and so on.

In Romans 1:13, Paul offers such an idea with the combination of the indicative verb θέλω and the infinitive ἀγνοεῖν (*present* and *active*). Here the infinitive complements, or completes, the idea of the verb θέλω ("I am not wanting you to be ignorant").

Phil. 1:21

τὸ	ζῆν	Χριστὸς	καὶ	τὸ	ἀποθανεῖν	κέρδος.
ὁ	ζάω	Χριστός	καί	ὁ	ἀποθνῄσκω	κέρδος
—	to live	[is] Christ	and	—	to die	[is] gain
3588	2198	5547	2532	3588	599	2771

Since infinitives are verbal nouns, they often function more like a noun than a verb. They thus sometimes can act like a nominative-case noun and function as a **subject** or a **predicate nominative**. Philippians 1:21 contains two uses of the infinitives (ζῆν, *present* and *active*; ἀποθανεῖν, *aorist* and *active*) as subject. Here both constructions have an implied stative verb (a form of εἰμί; "to be") and an expressed predicate nominative (Χριστός and κέρδος). Thus "to live" functions as the subject of the first clause and "to die" as the subject of the second.

2 Cor. 8:11

νυνὶ	δὲ	καὶ	τὸ	ποιῆσαι	ἐπιτελέσατε
νυνί	δέ	καί	ὁ	ποιέω	ἐπιτελέω
now	so	also	the	doing	complete
3570	1161	2532	3588	4160	2005

Just as the infinitive may function as a subject, it may also function as a **direct object**. In 2 Corinthians 8:11, Paul writes for the Corinthians to complete "the doing" (ποιῆσαι; *infinitive, aorist,* and *active*), meaning to finish the collection that they had begun. The thing being completed here is the infinitive ποιῆσαι ("the doing"), which here functions as the object of the verb ἐπιτελέσατε.

Rom. 8:12

ὀφειλέται	ἐσμὲν	οὐ	τῇ	σαρκὶ	τοῦ	κατὰ	σάρκα	ζῆν
ὀφειλέτης	εἰμί	οὐ	ὁ	σάρξ	ὁ	κατά	σάρξ	ζάω
obligated	we are	not	to the	flesh	—	according to	the flesh	to live
3781	2070	3756	3588	4561	3588	2596	4561	2198

Finally, the infinitive may also **redefine** or **further explain** a previously presented idea. Romans 8:12 illustrates this use. Here the infinitive (ζῆν; *present* and *active*) in the phrase "living according to the flesh" (τοῦ κατὰ σάρκα ζῆν) further explains what it means not to be obligated to the flesh. Often this idea is marked by the presence of τοῦ with the infinitive, which is what we find in this example.

We have examined the aspectual significance of the infinitive tenses as well as the most common functions of the infinitive. It is worth remembering that aspectual significance and function are not mutually exclusive. The aspect of the infinitive portrays the perspective from which the action is viewed, but the infinitive will also have a function (e.g., temporal, result) in the sentence. It is important to attend to both of these issues when interpreting these important words.

Your Turn

I have outlined the most-common functions of the present, aorist, and perfect infinitive. Now it is your turn to apply what you have read. Examine the bolded words in the sentence below. Using an analytical lexicon or parsing tool (see chap. 4), identify the grammatical information for each word. Once you have identified the tense and voice, using the categories described above, determine how each of these words is functioning. After you have made a decision about the form and function, check your answers in the key in appendix 1.

2 Cor. 7:3

εἰς	τὸ	συναποθανεῖν	καὶ	συζῆν
εἰς	ὁ	συναποθνήσκω	καί	συζάω
so that	—	we die together	and	we live together
1519	3588	4880	2532	4800

Words to Memorize

αἰτέω	to ask
γινώσκω	to know
εἰμί	to be
ἔρχομαι	to come, to go
ζητέω	to seek
νεκρός	dead
νόμος	law, Law
πνεῦμα	spirit, Spirit
ποιέω	to do, to make
προσεύχομαι	to pray
σταυρόω	to crucify

13

(Dependent) Greek Participles

We have saved the worst for last! I am, of course (though only partially), kidding. Greek participles are incredibly important for understanding the New Testament. But they are also quite complex. Indeed, they contain the most complex forms and functions of any part of speech in the Greek New Testament. The **participle** is a verbal adjective, meaning that it possesses verbal properties while functioning primarily as an adjective. Participles take *tense, voice,* and their *root* or *stem* from the verb while also taking *gender, case,* and *number* from the adjective. The participle occurs in the present, aorist, and perfect tenses and emphasizes the aspectual significance of each. Participles thus do not contain any independent "time" significance, though temporal ideas can be used in the participle in certain contexts. We will examine each tense in turn before considering the major uses of the participle.

Present Participle

The **present participle** portrays imperfective aspect (an in-process or zoomed-in view of the action). As previously seen, this can take on several different nuances.

Matt. 8:25

καὶ	προσελθόντες	ἤγειραν	αὐτὸν	λέγοντες
καί	προσέρχομαι	ἐγείρω	αὐτός	λέγω
and	[they] came	[and] woke	him	saying
2532	4334	1453	846	3004

Sometimes the present participle focuses on **the beginning of an action** while adopting an up-close or in-process view of the action's progression. In Matthew 8:25, the *present* participle λέγοντες (*active, masculine, nominative,* and *plural*) signals the beginning of the speech that follows, thus introducing it as in progress. This is quite common for verbs of speaking in the New Testament.

Rom. 8:11

διὰ	τοῦ	ἐνοικοῦντος	αὐτοῦ	πνεύματος	ἐν	ὑμῖν
διά	ὁ	ἐνοικέω	αὐτός	πνεῦμα	ἐν	σύ
through	—	who lives	his	Spirit	in	you
1223	3588	1774	846	4151	1722	5213

In adopting an up-close perspective, often the present participle simply points to an action that is **ongoing**. Romans 8:11 illustrates such usage. The *present* participle ἐνοικοῦντος (*active, neuter, genitive,* and *singular*) here emphasizes the current and ongoing role of the Spirit in the life of the Roman believers.

Matt. 9:9

Καὶ	παράγων	ὁ	Ἰησοῦς	ἐκεῖθεν	εἶδεν	ἄνθρωπον
καί	παράγω	ὁ	Ἰησοῦς	ἐκεῖθεν	εἶδον	ἄνθρωπος
and	was going away	—	[as] Jesus	from there	he saw	a man
2532	3855	3588	2424	1564	1492	444

Like the present infinitive, the present participle may describe an action that **occurs at the same time** as the action of its associated verb. In Matthew 9:9, the *present* participle παράγων (*active, masculine, nominative,* and *singular*) takes on the contemporaneous temporal force, indicating that "while Jesus was leaving" he saw Matthew (the ἄνθρωπον mentioned above).

Aorist Participle

The **aorist participle** portrays aoristic aspect (a zoomed-out or summary view of the action). This too can take on several nuances.

Matt. 5:1

Ἰδὼν	δὲ	τοὺς	ὄχλους	ἀνέβη	εἰς	τὸ	ὄρος
εἶδον	δέ	ὁ	ὄχλος	ἀναβαίνω	εἰς	ὁ	ὄρος
[when he] saw	now	the	crowds	he went up	—	the	mountain
1492	1161	3588	3793	305	1519	3588	3735

Often the aorist participle functions temporally where the **participle occurs before the main verb.** An example of this orientation is found in Matthew 5:1. Here the action of the *aorist* participle ἰδὼν ("he saw"; *active, masculine, nominative,* and *singular*) occurs before the verb ἀνέβη ("he went up"). These instances of the aorist participle (referred to as "antecedent" time) are translated with the word "after" or "when." The participle adopts a distant or summarized view of the action.

Matt. 28:19

πορευθέντες	οὖν	μαθητεύσατε	πάντα	τὰ	ἔθνη
πορεύομαι	οὖν	μαθητεύω	πᾶς	ὁ	ἔθνος
go	therefore	[and] make disciples	of all	the	nations
4198	3767	3100	3956	3588	1484

Sometimes the aorist participle indicates the **participle is coordinate with the main verb.** Perhaps the most famous example is found in Matthew 28:19, a text we looked at earlier. Here the *aorist* participle πορευθέντες (*deponent, masculine, nominative,* and *plural*) piggybacks on the action of the aorist imperative μαθητεύσατε, meaning that the primary command is to "make disciples" but the participle also takes on the force of the command. This coordinated use of the participle occurs only when the participle comes before the verb and both the participle and the verb are in the aorist tense (it is referred to as the "attendant circumstance" function of the participle). Again, the participle adopts a distant or summarized view of the action.

Acts 25:13

Ἀγρίππας	ὁ	βασιλεὺς	καὶ	Βερνίκη	κατήντησαν	εἰς
Ἀγρίππας	ὁ	βασιλεύς	καί	Βερνίκη	καταντάω	εἰς
Agrippa	—	King	and	Bernice	arrived	at
67	3588	935	2532	959	2658	1519

Καισάρειαν	ἀσπασάμενοι	τὸν	Φῆστον.
Καισάρεια	ἀσπάζομαι	ὁ	Φῆστος
Caesarea	to welcome	—	Festus
2542	782	3588	5347

In rare cases, the aorist participle will also indicate that the **action of the participle occurs after the action of the main verb.** These "subsequent" temporal uses of the participle usually occur when the participle follows the verb rather than precedes it, as it does in Acts 25:13. Since the *aorist* participle ἀσπασάμενοι (*deponent, masculine, nominative,* and *plural*) follows the verb κατήντησαν, its action likewise occurs after the action of "arriving." Here again, the participle adopts a distant or summarized view of the action.

Perfect Participle

The **perfect participle** portrays perfective aspect (an emphasis on the results of an action or a state). This also takes several different nuances.

Gal. 3:15

κεκυρωμένην	διαθήκην	οὐδεὶς	ἀθετεῖ
κυρόω	διαθήκη	οὐδείς	ἀθετέω
has been ratified	[when] the covenant	no one	declares [it] invalid
2964	1242	3762	114

Sometimes the perfect participle **emphasizes the completion of an action.** In Galatians 3:15, the *perfect* participle κεκυρωμένην (*passive, feminine, accusative,* and *singular*) describes a covenant that "has been ratified," likely focusing on the completion of the covenant being made binding.

Eph. 3:17

ἐν	ἀγάπῃ	ἐρριζωμένοι	καὶ	τεθεμελιωμένοι
ἐν	ἀγάπη	ῥιζόω	καί	θεμελιόω
in	love	[because] you have been firmly rooted	and	established
1722	26	4492	2532	2311

As in the indicative, the perfect participle sometimes **emphasizes the existing results of an action.** In Ephesians 3:17, the *perfect, passive* participles ἐρριζωμένοι and τεθεμελιωμένοι likely focus on the results of these actions, meaning that Paul views his readers as *still* rooted and established in love.

Luke 9:27

εἰσίν	τινες	τῶν	αὐτοῦ	ἑστηκότων
εἰμί	τίς	ὁ	αὐτοῦ	ἵστημι
there are	some	of	here	those standing
1526	5100	3588	847	2476

Finally, the perfect participle may portray simply a **stative** idea with added prominence.[1] In Luke 9:27, the *perfect, active* participle ἑστηκότων (*masculine, genitive,* and *plural*) does not focus as much on the completion of an action or its results as the current state of the activity, which is given added prominence through the perfect tense. There are several markers of prominence in this section that carry important weight for what follows in the transfiguration passage.

Adjectival Participle Functions

We have briefly covered some of the primary ways that the various participial tenses employ their aspectual categories in the Greek New

Testament. We now must examine some of the different constructions used with the Greek participle and their various nuances. We again will focus here not on recognizing the participle (since we are using our tools for that) but rather on understanding its primary functions.

The participial functions can be placed under three broad umbrella categories: adjectival functions (acting like an adjective), adverbial functions (acting like an adverb), and verbal functions (acting like a verb).

We begin with the **adjectival** functions. The **attributive** (also called the adjectival) function of the participle is very similar to the function of the attributive adjective, which we explored above in chapter 8. Here the participle has a noun with which it agrees in gender, number, and case, and the participle usually has an article as well (though not always). In John 4:11, the Samaritan woman asks Jesus about the living water he has just described. The phrase here (τὸ ὕδωρ τὸ ζῶν) contains the noun ὕδωρ with the participle ζῶν, both of which have the article. Since the participle and noun agree (*neuter*, *accusative*, and *singular*), this fits as an attributive participle ("living water").

The **substantival** function of the participle is also very similar to the function of the substantival adjective, which we learned about in chapter 8. Here the participle has no agreeing noun and usually has an article. In this function, the participle acts like a noun, so its case determines the role it plays in the sentence. In John 6:39, Jesus refers to the will of the "one who sent" (τοῦ πέμψαντος) him. The participle πέμψαντος (*masculine*, *genitive*, and *singular*) here has no agreeing noun and has an agreeing article, which clearly identifies it as a substantival participle. Here, in the genitive case, it is connected to the head noun θέλημα, likely as either a possessive or subjective genitive (for a reminder on those terms, see chap. 7).

Adverbial Participle Functions

Adverbial participles act like an adverb, meaning that they tell us something about a verb in the sentence (often a mainline verb). Adverbial participles, unlike adjectival participles, will *never* have an article preceding them. The adverbial functions of the participle are a little more complex than the adjectival functions. There are a number of important nuances to the participle in this category, but the appropriate option is not always immediately clear. We have already explored the temporal adverbial function in our discussion of the tenses above. Below are the other major uses of the adverbial participle.

Acts 5:41

Οἱ	μὲν	οὖν	ἐπορεύοντο	χαίροντες
ὁ	μέν	οὖν	πορεύομαι	χαίρω
they	—	so	went out	rejoicing
3588	3303	3767	4198	5463

Sometimes the participle describes the **attitude** in which an action is carried out. In Acts 5:41, the apostles go out "rejoicing" (χαίροντες; *present, active, masculine, nominative,* and *plural*). The participle here describes the manner, or attitude, that characterizes their departure from the council.

Eph. 1:20

ἐγείρας	αὐτὸν	ἐκ	νεκρῶν	καὶ	καθίσας	ἐν	δεξιᾷ
ἐγείρω	αὐτός	ἐκ	νεκρός	καί	καθίζω	ἐν	δεξιός
raising	him	from	the dead	and	seating [him]	at	right (hand)
1453	846	1537	3498	2532	2523	1722	1188

αὐτοῦ	ἐν	τοῖς	ἐπουρανίοις
αὐτός	ἐν	ὁ	ἐπουράνιος
his	in	the	heavenly [places]
846	1722	3588	2032

Often a participle describes the **means** by which an action is carried out. Ephesians 1:20 contains two participles of means (ἐγείρας and καθίσας). The participles (both *aorist, active, masculine, nominative,* and *singular*) describe the means by which God has displayed his power, which was by raising and exalting Christ.

Matt. 1:19

Ἰωσὴφ	δὲ	ὁ	ἀνὴρ	αὐτῆς,	δίκαιος	ὢν
Ἰωσήφ	δέ	ὁ	ἀνήρ	αὐτός	δίκαιος	εἰμί
Joseph	so	—	husband	her	righteous	being
2501	1161	3588	435	846	1342	5607

Another common adverbial function of the participle is to indicate the **cause** of an action. In Matthew 1:19, the *present* participle ὢν (*active*, *masculine*, *nominative*, and *singular*) likely takes on a causal force in explaining why Joseph does not want to disgrace Mary ("because he was a righteous man").

Heb. 2:3

πῶς	ἡμεῖς	ἐκφευξόμεθα	τηλικαύτης	ἀμελήσαντες	σωτηρίας
πῶς	ἐγώ	ἐκφεύγω	τηλικοῦτος	ἀμελέω	σωτηρία
how	[will] we	escape	so great	[if we] neglect	a salvation
4459	2249	1628	5082	272	4991

Sometimes the participle also implies a **condition** of the fulfillment of an action that the main verb describes. Hebrews 2:3 illustrates this function. Here the author asks, how will we (he and his hearers) escape "if we neglect" (ἀμελήσαντες; *aorist*, *active*, *masculine*, *nominative*, and *plural*) so great a salvation. The conditional function is most likely, from which we infer the "if" used to translate the participle.

Phil. 2:6

ὃς	ἐν	μορφῇ	θεοῦ	ὑπάρχων
ὅς	ἐν	μορφή	θεός	ὑπάρχω
who	in	the form	of God	[although he] existed
3739	1722	3444	2316	5225

Another common adverbial function of the participle occurs when the main verb describes an action that is true **in spite of** the action of the participle. In Philippians 2:6–7, Paul writes that Jesus emptied himself even though he existed (ὑπάρχων; *present*, *active*, *masculine*, *nominative*, and *singular*) in the form of God. In other words, in spite of the fact that Jesus existed in the form of God, he emptied and humbled himself anyway.

Rom. 15:25

Νυνὶ	δὲ	πορεύομαι	εἰς	Ἰερουσαλὴμ	διακονῶν	τοῖς	ἁγίοις.
νυνί	δέ	πορεύομαι	εἰς	Ἰερουσαλήμ	διακονέω	ὁ	ἅγιος
now	but	I am traveling	to	Jerusalem	serving	the	saints
3570	1161	4198	1519	2419	1247	3588	40

Finally, frequently the adverbial participle also describes the **purpose** or **result** of an action. In Romans 15:25, Paul writes that he is going to travel to Jerusalem "for the purpose of serving" (διακονῶν; *present*, *active*, *masculine*, *nominative*, and *singular*) the saints. In other words, it is Paul's intended purpose that he will serve the saints when he arrives in Jerusalem.

Verbal Participle Functions

Though the adjectival and adverbial functions of the participle are most common, the participle can also take on verbal characteristics in various settings. One common verbal function is what is known as the **periphrastic** (pronounced "pair-uh-fras-tic") participle. Like adverbial participles, periphrastics will not have an article. They will also be paired with a stative verb, like a form of εἰμί. The periphrastic combines the tense of the verb with the aspect of the participle and thus forms an indicative verb-tense equivalent (see table 1). The periphrastic construction probably contains added emphasis or significance over an indicative-mood verb, but this must be considered in each context.

Sometimes the participle, like the infinitive, performs a **complementary** function, where it completes an incomplete verbal idea (like wishing, trying, being able, etc.). In Ephesians 1:16, for example, Paul writes, οὐ παύομαι εὐχαριστῶν ὑπὲρ ὑμῶν ("I am not ceasing giving thanks for

Table 1. Periphrastic Participles and Verb-Tense Equivalents

Stative Verb	Participle	Tense Equivalent
Present	Present	Present
Imperfect (Past)	Present	Imperfect
Future	Present	Future
Present	Perfect	Perfect
Imperfect (Past)	Perfect	Pluperfect
Future	Perfect	Future Perfect

you"). The negated verb παύομαι ("I am not ceasing") is completed by the *present* participle εὐχαριστῶν ("giving thanks").

Finally, sometimes, though rarely, the participle may also function as an **imperative** or **indicative** verb. Since participles are usually grammatically dependent, classifying a participle in one of these functions should be avoided unless clear from the context. For example, in 1 Peter 2:18, the participle ὑποτασσόμενοι (*present, passive, masculine, nominative,* and *plural*) takes on the force of an imperative, commanding slaves to be subject to their masters. Since there is no main verb to connect to the participle, the use is fitting in this context.

We have examined the aspectual significance of the participial tenses as well as the most common functions of the participle. It is again worth remembering that aspectual significance and function are not mutually exclusive. The aspect of the participle portrays the perspective from which the action is viewed, but the participle will also have a function (i.e., some adjectival, adverbial, or verbal use) in the sentence. It is important to attend to both of these issues when interpreting these important and frequent words.

Your Turn

I have outlined the most-common functions of the present, aorist, and perfect participle. Now it is your turn. Examine the bolded words in the sentence below. Using an analytical lexicon or parsing tool (see chap. 4), identify the grammatical information for each word. Once you have identified the tense, voice, gender, case, and number, using the categories described above, determine how each of these words is functioning. After you have made a decision about the form and function, check your answers in the key in appendix 1.

1 John 5:1

καὶ	πᾶς	ὁ	ἀγαπῶν	τὸν	γεννήσαντα
καί	πᾶς	ὁ	ἀγαπάω	ὁ	γεννάω
and	everyone	—	who loves	the	[one] who fathers
2532	3956	3588	25	3588	1080

ἀγαπᾷ	καὶ	τὸν	γεγεννημένον	ἐξ	αὐτοῦ.
ἀγαπάω	καί	ὁ	γεννάω	ἐκ	αὐτός
loves	also	the	[one] fathered	by	him
25	2532	3588	1080	1537	846

Words to Memorize

ἀνήρ	man, husband
δίκαιος	righteous
ἔθνος	nation, people
εἶδον	to see
ἵστημι	to stand
οὐδείς	no one
ὄχλος	crowd
πᾶς	all, each, every

14

Back to the Big Picture

We have surveyed the most important parts of speech and grammatical features of the Greek of the New Testament. Our crash course has given us the tools to recognize the various kinds of words we will encounter on the pages of the Greek New Testament as well as the grammatical information that is encoded within them. Moreover, we have explored the most common and most important functions of the various parts of speech of New Testament Greek and have picked up a base of ninety-two vocabulary words along the way, accounting for around 40 percent of the number of word occurrences in the Greek New Testament. This means that based on the small sampling of vocabulary you have learned in this book, you can recognize at least one in every three words in the Greek New Testament (though it may not seem that way yet).

Our goal in this chapter is to step back to the flyover view of the Greek New Testament. In doing so, we want to learn how to pay attention to the overall structure of passages and arguments. We will begin by reviewing what we have established above concerning the independent and dependent nature of various Greek phrases and clauses.

Independent and Dependent Ideas

By speaking of independent and dependent ideas, we again refer to the question of whether a clause can stand on its own, or whether a phrase or clause depends on or modifies another clause. This holds importance for two reasons: (1) because Greek tends to structure sentences around a main clause with a number of dependent or supporting clauses connected to it, and (2) because our English translations, in seeking to make the text more readable in standard English style, often make it difficult to determine the structure of the Greek text. The independent idea in a clause is usually also the main idea, and supporting ideas further expand on it. Identifying and understanding whether an idea is mainline or supporting is important both for how we understand a passage and for how we teach or preach it.

An **independent clause** is a clause that is not subordinate. It normally contains at least a *subject* and *verb* and generally also contains either an *indicative* or *imperative*, or sometimes *subjunctive*, verb. They are typically introduced by a **coordinating conjunction**, like καί, δέ, γάρ, ἀλλά, or οὖν. Sometimes independent clauses are introduced by a prepositional phrase, such as διὰ τοῦτο ("for this reason"), διὰ τί ("why?"), or ἐκ τούτο ("as a result"). Independent clauses contain *main-level* ideas, and generally everything else in a sentence hangs from them.

A **dependent clause** is a clause that is subordinate, either modifying or depending on the independent clause. There are four main kinds of dependent clauses in Greek: *relative*, *infinitival*, *participial*, and *subordinate conjunction*.

- *Relative* clauses are typically introduced by a **relative pronoun** (ὅς, ἥ, ὅ; "who, which") but may also be introduced by a **relative adjective** (like ὅσος; "as many as") or a **relative adverb** (like ὅτε; "when").
- *Infinitival* clauses (containing an **infinitive**) may function substantivally (like a noun, such as when they function as *subject* or *object*), adjectivally (like an adjective, such as when they function

to *redefine* or *further explain* another idea), or adverbially (like an adverb, such as when they function *temporally*). All such functions are dependent.

- *Participial* clauses (containing a **participle**), like infinitives, may function substantivally, adjectivally (*attributive* function), or adverbially (such as the *purpose* or *temporal* functions). (The verbal functions of the participle are usually independent but typically in conjunction with its related verb, such as in the periphrastic.)
- *Subordinate conjunction* clauses are introduced by a **subordinate conjunction**, and their function is determined by the meaning of the conjunction. Our main subordinating conjunctions are ὅτι, ἵνα, εἰ, ἐάν, and ὅτε.

One issue to which we have not yet attended is conditional sentences. A **conditional sentence** is a sentence that has two clauses, one of which conditions, and thus is dependent on, the other. For example, in the sentence "If you keep using this book, then you will more effectively understand the New Testament," the action of better understanding the New Testament is conditioned on continuing to use this book. We refer the condition "if . . ." as the **protasis** (pronounced "prot-uh-sis") and the "then . . ." as the **apodosis** (pronounced "uh-pod-uh-sis"). The protasis ("if . . .") is grammatically dependent, while the apodosis

Table 1. Conditional Sentences

Type	Protasis ("If")	Apodosis ("Then")	General Concept
First Class	εἰ + indicative verb negated with οὐ	any verb	assumed true for the sake of argument
Second Class	εἰ + aorist or imperfect indicative verb negated with μή	aorist or imperfect indicative	assumed contrary to fact for the sake of argument
Third Class	ἐάν + subjunctive verb negated with μή	any verb	used for hypothetical consideration

Note: There is also a fourth-class condition, which is very rare in the New Testament (occurring about 14 times) and uses the optative mood, which is also very rare in the New Testament (occurring 68 times). I have not included it here due to its rarity.

("then . . .") is grammatically independent. In Greek, there are four different ways that conditional sentences can be structured, with each resulting in a different nuance of the condition. Table 1 helps explain the different constructions.

Flow of Thought and Argument

In this section I want to highlight a few important practices that are helpful in analyzing a passage. Some are easier to recognize than others, but all have their value in understanding an author's flow of thought.

Word Order

As we noted earlier and have illustrated throughout, Greek word order has a higher degree of flexibility, though some elements have a certain fixity of order. The style of writing and order of clause elements tend to vary some among the New Testament writers. At times authors will deviate from their normal pattern and move a word or phrase to an atypical location. Recognizing these instances is difficult (it takes having familiarity with the author's general tendencies), but the rearranging of the structure is likely intended to give some prominence to that word or phrase. In general terms, higher degrees of prominence are given to those elements that are moved to the front of the sentence, though when a word is moved back (such as a verb being moved to the end of the sentence), this may also have added prominence. In other words, we need to pay attention both to what an author says and to how they say it.

Flow of Thought

We will talk more in chapter 16 about reading with awareness of the literary context of a work. For now, however, we should appreciate that flow of thought has great importance for our interpretation. We have noticed that the process of translation is a difficult one, not only because of the complexities of Greek, but also because we are working with two languages that are by no means identical. This means that, at times and more often than we might imagine, the grammatical structure of a passage is lost as it is brought into English. The Letter to the Ephesians is perhaps the best example of this. The letter is well known for its long, run-on sentences, the longest of which is Ephesians 1:3–14 (yes, it is one sentence). Our English translations break these long sentences into many shorter ones for the sake of readability. When they do so, however, the structure of the passage can be lost.

Take, for example, Ephesians 5:21–22: many translations not only break these verses apart, but they also create a separate section heading between them (e.g., NASB, ESV, NKJV, HCSB). To do so, however, is to ignore the grammar of the passage. Ephesians 5:21 is connected back to 5:18, where the last main verb is found. All of the other verbal forms, including 5:21, are participles, meaning that they are grammatically dependent on 5:18. Ephesians 5:22 also lacks a verb, so it is likely intended to be read in conjunction with 5:21 ("submitting yourselves to one another in fear of Christ, wives to their own husbands as to the Lord"). When translations break verse 22 off from the preceding flow of thought *and* separate the two with a section heading, they mask the structure of the Greek. Regardless of how one interprets the passage, they should recognize the grammatical situation and base their interpretation on it. This illustrates all the more our need to develop sensitivity to the form and structure of the Greek text and the shape of the text as a whole.

Discourse Analysis

One area of growing emphasis in studying New Testament Greek is what is known as discourse analysis. **Discourse analysis** involves examining how larger units of text fit together. As mentioned in chapter 2, we need to be aware both of the immediate context of a passage and of how this passage fits into the author's flow of thought or argument. To put it another way, using the Sermon on the Mount in Matthew 5–7 as an example, discourse analysis helps to answer questions like, "Where does the sermon begin and end?" "Where does each section begin and end?" "What ties the sermon together?" and "How does the sermon relate to what precedes and follows it?" These are all important questions, indeed, and ones we often overlook in studying Scripture. Some of the significant features that discourse analysis examines are the cues that mark the **boundaries** of a passage (or pericope), the recognition of **prominent features**, and the **elements that hold a discourse together**.

The *boundaries of a passage* are recognized by attending to issues like changes in person or characters, scene or location, time or tense, situation, reference, or action. In addition, the use of certain conjunctions (like δέ) also often marks the boundaries of a unit. In examining these features we are primarily concerned to identify where a particular passage or pericope begins and ends. Recognizing these features can alert us both to the boundaries of an individual section of text and to the way in which an author frames the entirety of the discourse. Often these boundary-marking features occur in recognizable patterns throughout the work.

Prominent features can be recognized when elements indicate emphasis, such as emphatic pronouns, tenses with marked verbal aspect, disruption of the author's normal clause structure, or repetition of particular constructions. With these items we are primarily concerned with what elements in a discourse stand out in some significant way.

The *elements that hold a discourse together* are frequently found in the use of pronouns (Ephesians 1–2 and Galatians 2–4 are interesting test cases), the references to participants in the discourse, the patterns of verb uses, and the way conjunctions are used to connect ideas together. In all of these instances, we are looking at the elements that are used in certain recognizable patterns and create cohesion between the discourses. This means we should pay attention to both grammar and meaning but also to patterns of usage. When a pattern changes (such as first-person to second-person pronouns, or aorist to present verbs, or indicative to imperative verbs), that should signal us to examine more closely the reason for these shifts.

Ultimately, in paying attention to these and other discourse features, we hope to understand (1) how the work is organized, (2) the various discourses as discourses, (3) how they relate to one another, and (4) what conclusion(s) they intend for the reader to draw. A great deal of sensitivity to the Greek language is required to develop these skills. This book will not equip us fully for the task (though note the recommended resources in chap. 18). However, if we lay a foundation of knowledge here that is applied with consistency and expanded over time, the necessary skills can be gained along the way. In other words (as we will discuss more later), we must commit ourselves to a trajectory of discovery, expanding our knowledge as we go and grow. We will not be able to walk through each of these processes in this book, but I hope to chart a course that allows you to better think through texts. We begin by examining the structure of the passage, and we will take a familiar text as our example: John 3:16.

Diagramming Passages

John 3:16 is as familiar as any verse in the New Testament. Most Christians can probably recite it with ease. What often escapes attention, however, is that John 3:16 is a part of a dialogue between Jesus and Nicodemus that begins in John 3:1. Using the principles outlined above, if we attend to the discourse features, we can identify the beginning and end of the passage. John 3:1–2 introduces a new character and setting, prefaced with the use of δέ in 3:1, which often signals the presentation of new information. We have a similar hint in 3:22, where we are told Jesus goes to Judea "after these things" (Μετὰ ταῦτα), indicating that the current scene closes and a new one begins. Thus John 3:1–21 is the context of our passage. We will begin, however, by analyzing John 3:16–18 before examining this larger context.

The method that we will advocate is sometimes called "block diagramming." Here our goal is to *see* the structure of a passage by arranging the passage in such a way that it is visible. The easiest way to do this is to indent the text in a word-processor file, using tabs to delineate the different levels of structure. Our mainline items will be set to the left of the page, and our subordinate items indented, toward the right. We will start with John 3:16.

In order to start our analysis, we need to know how to separate our text. Here we want to identify the beginning and end of phrases and clauses. We will be working with phrases and clauses as a whole as we examine the text. For the sake of space and simplicity, we will use the Greek text alone, so keep your interlinear handy. I explain below how I have separated the units.

> οὕτως γὰρ ἠγάπησεν ὁ θεὸς τὸν κόσμον, (The conjunction γὰρ marks the beginning of the clause. This is a unit with a subject [ὁ θεὸς], verb [ἠγάπησεν], and object [τὸν κόσμον].)
>
> ὥστε τὸν υἱὸν τὸν μονογενῆ ἔδωκεν, (The conjunction ὥστε marks the beginning of the clause. This is a unit with a verb [ἔδωκεν] and object [τὸν υἱὸν τὸν μονογενῆ].)
>
> ἵνα πᾶς ὁ πιστεύων εἰς αὐτὸν μὴ ἀπόληται ἀλλ᾽ ἔχῃ ζωὴν αἰώνιον. (The conjunction ἵνα marks the beginning of the clause. This is a unit with a subject [πᾶς ὁ πιστεύων] and two verbs [ἀπόληται and ἔχῃ].)

With our clauses separated, we will now work on indenting them based on their level of subordination.

> οὕτως γὰρ ἠγάπησεν ὁ θεὸς τὸν κόσμον, (This is a mainline phrase with a coordinating conjunction [γὰρ] and an indicative verb [ἠγάπησεν].)
>
>> ὥστε τὸν υἱὸν τὸν μονογενῆ ἔδωκεν, (This is a dependent clause, introduced by ὥστε, which here indicates result. It is subordinate to the above clause, explaining the result of God's love.)
>>
>>> ἵνα πᾶς ὁ πιστεύων εἰς αὐτὸν μὴ ἀπόληται ἀλλ᾽ ἔχῃ ζωὴν αἰώνιον. (This is a dependent clause, introduced by ἵνα, which here indicates purpose. It is subordinate to the above clause, explaining the purpose of giving the Son.)

Here, then, is the arrangement of our text.

οὕτως γὰρ ἠγάπησεν ὁ θεὸς τὸν κόσμον, (main)
　　ὥστε τὸν υἱὸν τὸν μονογενῆ ἔδωκεν, (subordinate—result)
　　　　ἵνα πᾶς ὁ πιστεύων εἰς αὐτὸν μὴ ἀπόληται
　　　　　　ἀλλ᾽ ἔχῃ ζωὴν αἰώνιον. (subordinate—purpose)

Noting the verse's structure, we can explain it as follows: God's love for the world resulted in the giving of his Son with the intent that all who are trusting in him would have eternal life. Let's take a look also at John 3:17.

οὐ γὰρ ἀπέστειλεν ὁ θεὸς τὸν υἱὸν (main)
　　εἰς τὸν κόσμον (subordinate—preposition [destination])
　　　ἵνα κρίνῃ τὸν κόσμον, (subordinate—purpose)
　　　ἀλλ᾽ ἵνα σωθῇ ὁ κόσμος (subordinate—purpose)
　　　　δι᾽ αὐτοῦ. (subordinate—preposition [means])

The main idea here is that "God did not send his son," which is clarified with two purpose clauses: "in order that he might condemn the world but [contrast] in order that the world might be saved." The ἵνα in both clauses alerts us to their dependency. There are also two prepositional phrases that clarify the destination of the sending (εἰς τὸν κόσμον) and the means by which the world would be saved (δι᾽ αὐτοῦ) and are likewise dependent. Finally, let's look at John 3:18.

ὁ πιστεύων εἰς αὐτὸν οὐ κρίνεται· (main)
ὁ δὲ μὴ πιστεύων ἤδη κέκριται, (main; contrasting, new information)
　　ὅτι μὴ πεπίστευκεν (subordinate—causal)
　　　εἰς τὸ ὄνομα τοῦ μονογενοῦς υἱοῦ τοῦ θεοῦ. (subordinate—
　　　preposition [direction/sphere])

The two main clauses come first, with δέ connecting them and showing their relationship. This is followed by the dependent causal clause introduced by ὅτι, and then the dependent prepositional phrase introduced by εἰς.

In examining the structure of the passage, we can identify which ideas are main ideas and which ideas are explanatory. To summarize our block-diagramming method, we indent the clauses and phrases to show which related groups of words they are modifying. This also allows the main ideas to stand out from the supporting ones. We allow the Greek text to give us pointers about where the divisions of phrases lie, which correspond to the concepts of independent and dependent clauses and phrases we have explored above. We then examine the relationship between these phrases and clauses, identifying mainline and supporting ideas. The information that we have explored earlier concerning how different clauses and phrases relate in terms of their independence or dependence should guide our thinking as we determine the structure of a passage.

If we zoom out a bit from the passage and look at the whole discourse (John 3:1–21), we see that the major actions of the passage are verbs of speaking, alternating between what Jesus says (3:3, 5–8, 10–21) and what Nicodemus says (3:4, 9). There are thus five alternating interactions between the two participants. This passage is a conversation that gives Jesus the opportunity to lay out his mission for Nicodemus (and subsequently for us all). We also notice some thematic connections in the passage by examining how it fits into the first three chapters of John's Gospel. "Spirit" (1:32–33), "water" (1:26, 31, 33; 2:7, 9), "divine birth" (1:13), "signs" (2:11, 18, 23), "kingdom" (1:49), "heaven" (1:32, 51), "world" (1:9–10, 29), "Son" (1:49, 51), "light" (1:4, 5, 7–9), and "darkness" (1:5) are key terms that have been used already in John's Gospel and that will be repeated throughout. If we read this section with that larger context in mind, we will see how John is developing these themes and ideas, building on them through the first two chapters and offering some significant input to them in chapter 3.

We have undertaken a very brief analysis of this section. By examining the structure of the passage, paying attention to which ideas the Greek text indicates are mainline and which ideas are subordinate, we can identify the major assertions of the passage and subsequently identify which phrases and clauses support, clarify, or contrast those assertions. In addition, by paying attention to the boundaries of the passage, we recognize Jesus's words here are a part of a conversation with Nicodemus. Furthermore, by zooming out even further, we see that the Gospel writer builds on previously introduced themes in this section, adding further illumination and clarification to what has preceded. Even in this brief examination, there is much to gain by stepping back and looking at the big picture as we read, interpret, and apply the message of the New Testament.

Your Turn

I have outlined a diagram of a brief section from John's Gospel above. Now it is your turn! Examine the passage below (1 John 1:5), and separate the text into phrases and clauses as illustrated above. Once you have separated the phrases and clauses, determine whether they are coordinate or subordinate, and indent the text accordingly. After you have completed your diagram, check your answers in the key in appendix 1.

Καὶ ἔστιν αὕτη ἡ ἀγγελία ἣν ἀκηκόαμεν ἀπ᾽ αὐτοῦ καὶ ἀναγγέλλομεν ὑμῖν, ὅτι ὁ θεὸς φῶς ἐστιν καὶ σκοτία ἐν αὐτῷ οὐκ ἔστιν οὐδεμία.

15

Comparing English Translations

Students of the Bible often express a desire to use whatever translation of the New Testament is the "most literal." While our translations approach the text through different philosophies, none set out with the goal of misrepresenting the Greek text. Now that we have toured through the various parts of speech and introduced ourselves to some of the complexities of the Greek language, it is no wonder that we find variations between our translations. A number of factors are involved in the process of translation, which we will explore below. After examining how the text of the New Testament is determined from the existing, or extant, manuscripts, we will then discuss the process of translation, the considerations made by translators, the limitations of translations, and some suggestions for how to compare translations in studying a biblical passage.

The Text of the New Testament

It is widely acknowledged among New Testament scholars but often less known among the wider public that we possess no known original

131

manuscripts (or "autographs") of the New Testament. In other words, the original documents attributed, for example, to Paul are not currently in our possession. What we have instead are copies of copies of the original documents. While this sometimes causes consternation for Christians, the New Testament documents are actually the best-preserved texts in all of the ancient world. We will examine some of the evidence for this claim below as well as the process by which experts in the field known as textual criticism analyze and determine the most likely original reading when manuscripts disagree.

The field of **textual criticism** is an ever-growing and ever-changing enterprise. Scholars find and study previously unexamined manuscripts with fair frequency. The Center for the Study of New Testament Manuscripts (http://www.csntm.org), for example, has undertaken the task of better preserving, recording, and studying many previously overlooked or improperly handled documents. Our knowledge of the habits of ancient scribes likewise constantly expands as more insights develop. In spite of this more recent focus on better preservation of New Testament manuscripts, textual criticism has not uncovered any finds in recent history that significantly alter what has been determined as the most likely original text of the New Testament documents.

Most of the nearly six thousand Greek manuscripts in existence date to the second millennium AD. In other words, they are *much* later than the original documents. This does not make them unusable for determining the original text, but experts generally prefer earlier manuscripts to later ones (more on that below). According to New Testament text critic Daniel Wallace, we have almost twenty manuscripts from the second century (and possibly one from the first), representing nearly 43 percent of the words of the New Testament.[1] Furthermore, recent research by George Houston suggests manuscripts could have survived for several hundred years, a number previously estimated at a much lower time frame.[2] While this does not mean that the second- and third-century manuscripts we possess are direct copies of the originals, it certainly at least lies within the realm of historical possibility. Furthermore, when compared with the number of copies of secular ancient works, the New Testament documents are far more widely attested and far earlier attested, often by several hundred years.

In addition to these earliest manuscripts, Wallace informs us that sixty-four manuscripts from the third century and forty-eight from the fourth century exist and are recognized as such today. In comparing this with other ancient texts, Wallace states,

> If we are comparing the same time period—300 years after composition—the average classical author has no literary remains. Zip, nada, nothing. But if we compare all of the manuscripts of a particular classical author, regardless of when they were written, the total would still average less than twenty, and probably less than a dozen—and they would all be coming much more than three centuries later. In terms of the extant manuscripts, the New Testament textual critic is confronted with an embarrassment of riches. If we have doubts about what the original New Testament said, those doubts would have to be multiplied a hundred-fold for the average classical writer. . . . The New Testament is far and away the best-attested work of Greek or Latin literature from the ancient world.[3]

Why does this matter? The fact that we lack the original manuscripts does not mean we have no idea what the original wording of the New Testament writings would have been. We actually have a great degree of certainty, greater than we have for any other documents from the ancient world. This does not mean, of course, that there are not questions or places where the original reading is debated. The majority of the New Testament text, however, has a solid textual basis that is widely accepted by New Testament scholars.

Understanding the examination of the text of the New Testament is a complex endeavor. We will seek to summarize here the major contours of the field of textual criticism while recognizing that we are merely scratching the surface. There is a mountain of evidence that contributes to our knowledge of the New Testament text. In addition to the actual Greek **manuscripts**, we also have **ancient translations** of the Greek text (such as in Latin, Coptic, and Syriac), **citations from the early church fathers,** and **ancient lectionaries** (books containing collections of Scripture readings). While the Greek manuscripts are generally the heaviest-weighted witnesses, an early patristic citation, for example, may be more valuable than a late Greek manuscript. Greek manuscripts also come in several different forms. We have copies written on papyri, parchment, and (later) paper, as well as texts written in "capital" lettering (known as **uncials** or **majuscules,** which are our earliest witnesses) and "lowercase" script (known as **minuscules,** which are much later witnesses). Experts can discern the date of a manuscript by the type of material used as well as the type of script used.

In addition to these material considerations, text critics acknowledge the existence of three major families of manuscripts, or **text types:** the Alexandrian, the Western, and the Byzantine. These families are organized based on the general copying tendencies used by the scribes who reproduced the text. In the earliest transmission of the New Testament, it appears that literate, but likely often untrained, copyists did the copying work, which then gave rise to variants.[4] As the copies multipled, so did the variants. Eventually trained scribes took over the process, but this was not the case in the early period of transmission.

The textual families provide a mechanism for grouping the general tendencies of the copyists.[5] Manuscripts of the **Alexandrian** text type, associated with Alexandria, Egypt, well known for its prowess as an educational center, display a high degree of care and accuracy in copying, are evidenced as early as the second century, and are generally preferred over the Western and Byzantine text families. The **Western** text type is also attested as early as the second century but tends more toward paraphrasing, harmonization, and the inclusion of explanatory material not original to the text. The **Byzantine** text type is attested as early as the fourth century and evidences completeness while also tending to expand on the text and smooth out difficult wordings. The Byzantine text family became the dominant text type by the eighth century and is sometimes referred to as the Majority Text, since about 80 percent of existing manuscripts come from this later text family. For this reason, text critics do not simply count manuscripts to determine the best reading, since that would nearly always favor the later, less reliable reading of the Byzantine text type. It is also worth noting that a single manuscript may evidence traditions from more than one text type, especially in the larger codexes (basically books that contain multiple documents bound together).

The field of textual criticism is necessary because, as noted above, the various manuscripts do not agree in every detail of the text. The differences between the manuscripts are known as **variants**, and the process of textual criticism analyzes the textual data in order to determine which of the variant readings are most likely original. The variants are often as minor as a single letter of difference but may include as much as a word, phrase, or, in rarer instances, entire verses or paragraphs. The most famous of the major variants in the New Testament manuscripts are the longer endings of Mark (16:9–20), John 7:53–8:11 (the woman caught in adultery), and the longer form of 1 John 5:8. Based on the manuscript evidence, most New Testament scholars hold that these variants likely were not a part of the original text. Interpreters should work hard to familiarize themselves with the tools available to digest the text-critical data and to implement these tools in the critical and exegetical study of a passage. We will give a brief overview of the available tools, but first, we should examine how text critics make judgments about variant readings.

A number of criteria feed into the decision as to which reading among the evidenced possibilities is to be preferred.[6] We have already mentioned that the **text type** and **date** of a reading are a part of the equation. The Alexandrian text, being less prone to explanation and embellishment, is thus generally favored and is also among the earliest of the manuscript traditions. When a reading also has **broad geographical attestation**, meaning that it is evidenced by various text types or kinds of textual data (patristic quotations, lectionaries, etc.) from different regions of origin, this adds further support to the reading. In addition to this *external* evidence, text critics also consider the *internal* evidence in making a decision about variant readings.

One factor that comes into the discussion is the possibility of **scribal error**. Here the range of possibilities includes a copyist misspelling a word, unintentionally skipping a word or even several lines of text, or adding a word or phrase. Adding material may at times be unintentional, but it may also be an attempt by the scribe to clarify a **difficult reading**. Thus text critics tend to favor more-difficult readings to smoother ones, assuming it to be less likely for a copyist to make the text harder to read or understand. Text critics also tend to favor the **shorter reading** of a text, again assuming it to be more likely for a scribe to add material than to consciously omit it. For the Gospels or texts where there may be parallel material (like quotations of the Old Testament), text critics also generally prefer the **less harmonious** reading, since copyists were more likely to harmonize two parallel texts than to make them different. Finally, text critics also consider the tendencies of an individual author in their assessment of the data. Here the author's **style** and **vocabulary** and the **context** in which the variants occur all come into play. All of these criteria contribute to the analysis of a textual problem. A balanced approach to textual criticism considers all of these factors, when applicable, to evaluating the evidence.

I fully recognize that nonspecialists will not likely become immersed in the field (though for those who may, by all means do!). So how does the average reader access this information provided by the work of text critics and factor it into their exegetical processes? In critical editions of the Greek New Testament, such as the UBS[5] (United Bible Society, 5th edition) or the NA[28] (Nestle-Aland, 28th edition), readers can access the most pertinent text-critical information by means of the **textual apparatus**.[7] Taking the UBS[5] as an example, the excerpt in figure 1 shows the textual evidence for two variants in Matthew 1:18.

The superscript number at the beginning of each entry correlates to a footnote in the text that identifies the location of the textual issue. For our first example, the text has four possible renderings, with each rendering separated by //. The first rendering is Ἰησοῦ Χριστοῦ, the second is Χριστοῦ Ἰησοῦ, the third is Ἰησοῦ, and the fourth is Χριστοῦ. Each textual issue reported in the apparatus is preceded by a capital

Fig. 15.1

---

⁵ **18** {B} Ἰησοῦ Χριστοῦ 𝔓¹ ℵ C L Z Δ Θ *f*¹ *f*¹³ 28 33 157 180 205 565 579 597 700 892, 1006 1010 1071 1241 1243 1292 1424 1505 *Byz* [E P Σ] *Lect* syr^{p, h, pal} cop^{sa, meg, bo} arm (eth) geo slav Diatessaron^{arm} Irenaeus^{gr} Origen Eusebius Didymus^{dub} Epiphanius Chrysostom Theodotus-Ancyra Nestorius // Χριστοῦ Ἰησοῦ B Origen^{lat}; Jerome // Ἰησοῦ W Ps-Athanasius // Χριστοῦ it ^{a, aur, b, c, d, f, ff1,} ^{g1, k, q} vg syr^{c, s} Irenaeus^{lat}; Chromatius Jerome Augustine

⁶ **18** {B} γένεσις 𝔓¹ ℵ B C P W Z Δ Θ Σ *f*¹ 579 arm Eusebius Ps-Athanasius // γέννησις L *f*¹³ 28 33 157 180 205 565 597 700 892 1006 1010 1071 1241 1243 1292 1424 1505 *Byz* [E] *Lect* it^{a, aur, b, c, d, f, ff1, g1, k, q} vg slav Irenaeus^{gr} Origen Didymus^{dub} Epiphanius Chrysostom Theodotus-Ancyra Nestorius; Chromatius Jerome Augustine

---

letter in braces (between A and D), which indicates the editorial committee's certainty with the selected rendering (A being high certainty and D being low certainty), followed by the evidence that supports each reading, with papyri (e.g., 𝔓¹) and codexes (e.g., ℵ) indicated first, followed by other witnesses, such as other manuscripts, lectionaries, translations, and patristic quotations. At first glance, it is noticeable that the majority of witnesses favor the first reading (Ἰησοῦ Χριστοῦ) and that the variant readings are primarily supported by quotations from the church fathers. Since the weight of the evidence favors the first reading, the committee gave a B rating to the first textual issue, indicating they were more confident than not that the first reading is original.

In addition to the textual apparatus, Bruce Metzger's *Textual Commentary on the Greek New Testament* gives an immensely valuable summary paragraph of the committee's decision on each variant presented in the UBS apparatus, reviewing the evidence that factored into their judgment. For this particular issue in Matthew 1:18, the summary reads:

> It is difficult to decide which is the original reading. On the one hand, the prevailing tendency of scribes was to expand either Ἰησοῦς or Χριστός by the addition of the other word. The Western reading Χριστοῦ in Old Latin and Old Syriac witnesses seems to have a certain appropriateness, but it may be an assimilation to ἕως τοῦ Χριστοῦ of the preceding sentence. It can also be argued that in the narrative of his birth one would

expect to find the personal name "Jesus," yet Ἰησοῦ in W may have been conformed to the following command by the angel (v. 21).

On the other hand, though the external evidence in support of Ἰησοῦ Χριστοῦ appears to be overwhelming, the reading is intrinsically improbable, for in the New Testament the definite article is very rarely prefixed to the expression Ἰησοῦς Χριστός (only in inferior manuscripts in Acts 8:37; 1 John 4:3; and Rev. 12:17).

In the face of such conflicting considerations, the Committee judged that the least unsatisfactory course was to adopt the reading that was current in many parts of the early church.[8]

It should be obvious that this resource is indispensable for the nonspecialist in that it provides a summary of the evaluation of the material presented in the apparatus. Since this companion volume corresponds to the UBS text, those who use the Nestle-Aland (NA) will find that the larger number of textual variants provided in the NA apparatus will not always correspond to Metzger's commentary. Regardless, however, whether using the UBS text, which gives fewer variants but more-detailed evidence for them, or the NA, which provides more variants but less-detailed evidence, Metzger's commentary is a very valuable resource.

As you will notice from the example above, not every text-critical issue affects the interpretation of a passage. Minor variants often provide little impact on our understanding of a passage. This does not mean text-critical issues never influence the interpretation of a passage, for they certainly at times do. In those instances, greater care should be given in order to evaluate the evidence for the variant readings before delving too deeply into the interpretation of the text. The textual commentary, exegetical commentaries, and even scholarly essays and monographs can be consulted when necessary to examine significant textual issues. Once care has been given to studying the text-critical data, an interpretation can be rendered based on what has been determined as the most likely reading of the passage. It should go without saying that determining what the text actually says is absolutely vital in the process of interpretation.

The Science of Translation

We have already seen one good reason why our translations differ in various places. Depending on what text type undergirds the translation, there may be significant textual issues at work behind the scenes that are then brought to the fore in the translation. Probably the best example of this is the KJV translation, which relies on the Byzantine manuscript tradition. When compared with other translations, such as the NIV or NASB, which use an eclectic text (i.e., one established by evaluating the text-critical data on a case-by-case basis), the differences are obvious. As we noted above, the Byzantine text type is much later and tends to expand on the earliest manuscripts. Thus, we would expect to find some significant differences between these translations.

Most modern translations, however, are based on an eclectic or critical text, and thus we find fewer glaring differences where phrases or verses are inserted in one version but not in another. This does not mean, however, that we find no differences between them. Many factors influence how translations render passages. For starters, there are some genuine disagreements about issues of **grammar** and **syntax** in the text concerning how certain phrases are to be understood (we have mentioned a number of these in earlier chapters). Different translators may interpret the data differently since there are situations when these constructions are polysemantic (i.e., conducive to more than one meaning). **Lexical** considerations also factor into translation since words, like phrases, have more than one possible meaning. Interpreters may agree on the grammar of a particular passage but disagree on which meaning in a word's range of meaning was intended by the author (more on this in chap. 17). As always, context should be the determining factor as to which rendering is best, but even here valid disagreements exist.

Furthermore, there is the problem of the **compatibility of the receptor language**. When moving, as we have been doing, from Greek to English, we must recognize that the two languages have striking differences. We have already seen how inflection and sentence structure differ greatly between the two. Furthermore, the semantic range of words in English and Greek is not identical. This means that as translators translate, they make decisions about what they think is the best way to render the intended meaning in Greek into English. In doing so, there is inevitable loss of some meaning, which is why the original languages are so important. Things like rhyme, rhythm, and wordplay are simply lost in translation. This is no fault of the translators but is rather simply one limitation involved in producing a translation.

The Art of Translation

As we have seen in our tour through Greek grammar, developing a "literal" translation of the Greek New Testament is difficult. The most literal of our translations are interlinears, which reproduce the order of the Greek text. These often produce, however, nonsense readings in English since the word order of the two languages differs significantly. Thus, when people ask for a "literal" translation of the Greek New Testament, they often don't really know what they are asking for! Such a translation often sounds more like Yoda than like good English. Take Luke 3:16, for instance, which we examined earlier, which "literally" would read: "I with water am baptizing you, but coming is one more powerful than I" (wise you are, young padawan). While we get the gist of what is being said, the translation is certainly lacking. Imagine trying to read an entire chapter or book of the Bible that way!

Translators frequently acknowledge that all translators are "traitors." While these seem like harsh words, they are true ones. There is simply no way to exactly replicate the original grammar, syntax, and meaning of the text in English. Since our grammatical forms, syntactical constructions, methods of emphasis and structuring, and lexical nuances vary greatly between English and Greek, no translation can perfectly reflect the original text (though a translation can, and many do, quite adequately reflect it). The question becomes what trade-offs to make and what points of emphasis to draw out, even if they result in poor English. For example, we have seen that Greek sentences can be highly complicated, containing a number of dependent ideas hanging from a single independent idea. English translations often will break these larger sentences into multiple sentences. In doing so, the text is made more readable for English readers, but the structure of the original text, with its flow and emphases, is largely lost. Furthermore, the nuances of a Greek word may have no exact equivalent in English. Scholars debate how to understand and translate the meanings of words such as πίστις ("faith") and δικαιοσύνη ("righteousness"), for example, whose ranges of meanings do not have exact equivalents in English.

Translating is thus largely a balancing act. For example, when dealing with an **idiom** (a figurative expression with a nonliteral meaning, like "kick the bucket") in the Greek text, reproducing the idiom often results in a loss of meaning for a modern English audience, so we must translate the sense of the passage rather than the individual parts. In other words, no translation can be totally literal all the time. There are some that opt for what is frequently called **formal equivalence**, meaning that they try to reproduce the text in its original grammatical structure as much as possible. Even here, though, most of these translations will break up a passage such as Ephesians 1:3–14, which is one continuous sentence in Greek, or make other necessary adjustments to convey the meaning better in English. Other translations operate using a **functional equivalence** approach, meaning that they try to reproduce the intended idea of the passage with less concern for how it is structured grammatically. On the far end of the spectrum we also have **paraphrase** translations, which are concerned with rendering the text in more modern or "culturally appropriate" forms of English vernacular (and so, in addition to the Message and the Voice, we also have the Cotton Patch Version, *Da Jesus Book* [Pidgin English version], and Word on the Street [along with the more absurd Klingon Language Version and LOL Cat Bible]).

If we put some of the most commonly used modern English translations (LOL Cat Bible excluded) on a spectrum from formal to functional equivalence,[9] we would find the breakdown shown in figure 2.

Fig. 15.2

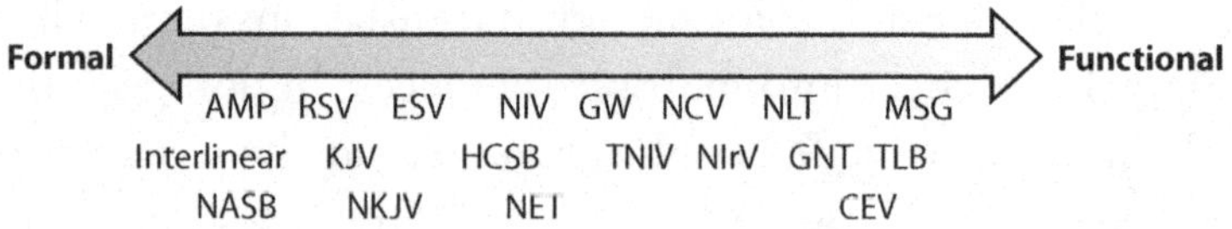

The more formal-equivalent translations tend toward more rigid and complex grammatical structures and often reproduce theological jargon in a long-standing tradition of English translation. The more functional end of the spectrum will opt for shorter sentences, better English readability, and less jargon-heavy terminology. There is not necessarily an inherently "good" or "bad" way to approach translation, though not all translations are equally successful in communicating the original message of the Greek text.

Often what determines where a translation falls on the spectrum is the intended **audience**. The more formal translations tend to be written for more serious use in Bible study and for those with more refined reading skills, while the more functional translations are aiming at a wider audience. While the NASB, for instance, operates at a high school reading level, the NIV operates at a middle school reading level and the Message at an upper elementary–middle school level. This does not mean any of these translations dumb down the Bible, but rather they translate for a wider audience. In fact, some studies estimate the average American reading level at around the seventh grade,[10] so the NIV is appealing to the majority of English readers rather than the upper tier as the most formal-equivalent translations do.

Translations also vary in their degree of **interpretation** when translating. First, we should recognize that all translation involves interpretation, and there is no bias-free translation available (again underscoring the importance of the languages). All translators see things through a grid that influences how they render certain passages. A good example here occurs in 1 Corinthians 6:9. Here two debated terms, μαλακοί and ἀρσενοκοῖται, are found in the text. To show the variations, the NASB translates them as "effeminate" and "homosexuals," the NIV as "men who have sex with men," the RSV as "sexual perverts," the NLT as "male prostitutes" and those who "practice homosexuality," and the NKJV as "homosexuals" and "sodomites." According to BDAG and Louw-Nida, standard lexicons for New Testament interpretation, μαλακός means one who is "passive in a same-sex relationship" and ἀρσενοκοίτης means "a male who engages in sexual activity with a person of his own sex." The range of translations given show the variations between how translators interpret these terms in the context of 1 Corinthians 6. The NIV gives a solid and simplified translation of the two terms, while the NASB and RSV are lacking in their accuracy ("effeminate" does not necessarily reflect well the meaning of μαλακοί in this context, and "sexual perverts" is far too broad a term).

Sometimes, as we have seen in our grammar review, the Greek text is **vague** and **imprecise**. Here translators must decide whether or not they will clarify, and thus give added interpretation to, a verse. A good example of this is found in Galatians 3:10. Here the Greek "literally" reads: "For as many as are from works of law are under a curse." Our translations frequently add a verb into the translation, which weakens the function of the preposition that Paul has been using with great consistency since earlier in chapter 2. The NIV, ESV, and RSV read: "all who rely on (the) works of the law"; the NLT reads: "those who depend on the law to make them right"; and the NIrV has: "all who depend on obeying the law." The drawback with these translations, regardless of how one judges their meaning, is that they add an interpretive layer to the verse that is absent in the Greek. The NASB and NKJV leave the verb as a stative one and thus present the text without an interpretive addition. At times such clarifications are necessary where things implicit in Greek must be made explicit in English. At other times, however, clarifications may actually detract from the intended meaning of the passage.

Often our translations also clean up the language of the New Testament that might be viewed as **crass** or **too explicit**. For example, when Paul writes about the "uncircumcised" in his letters, the term he uses (ἀκροβυστία) literally means "foreskin," though modern English translations do not usually render it as such. In addition, when Paul refers to all things as "rubbish" in Philippians 3:8, the word σκύβαλον sometimes refers to excrement or feces rather than garbage. Thus some have suggested Paul intends the term to essentially mean "crap" here (or some have suggested even a more crass English equivalent), while others take it to mean "garbage" or "trash." It has also been suggested that 1 Thessalonians 4:4, where Paul, in condemning sexual immorality, commands the Thessalonians to know how to control "their own vessel," is a reference to sexual organs. Needless to say, most translations, for various reasons, will not opt for some of the more dramatic translation possibilities in these examples (and probably with some wisdom). When translations do this, however, if the original authors intended some shock value to their words in these cases, the shock is removed in their English renderings.

Every translation also has some degree of **theological bias** and deals differently with **theological language**. For example, the title Χριστός means "Anointed One," but most translations render it as "Christ" (a transliteration), thus not indicating the significance of the term. The same goes for the cognates of βαπτίζω, which means "to wash" or "to immerse in water" yet is rendered rather consistently as "baptize" in most translations, allowing for a range of denominational preferences to be included. The same goes for a loaded term like ἱλαστήριον in Romans 3:25, which some translations render as "propitiation," though others suggest the concept of "expiation" or "place of mercy" or some other notion is in view. There are obvious theological considerations that go into the selection of the term in this example. None of this should be taken to mean that translators or translation committees necessarily set out with a preconceived theological grid to foist on the text (though some fringe translations have done so). Rather, these biases may sometimes be unrealized or a matter of one's tradition or theological heritage or the result of some committed study on a particular word or issue. Those translations that best avoid capitulating to a single theological perspective tend to be made up of a group of diverse translators from various theological backgrounds and persuasions (such as the group involved with the NIV translation), thus minimizing the influence of the presence of theological bias.

Translators must also wrestle with the question of when and where to use **inclusive language**. This issue has created a firestorm on several occasions, most notably with the 2011 NIV translation. At times translators will take a term like "sons" (υἱοί) or "brothers" (ἀδελφοί) and render it with a gender-inclusive word like "children" or "siblings." Often this is seen as an attack on the traditional view of male/female identity and is interpreted as acquiescing to broader cultural norms. While there may be some truth to that claim in certain contexts, we must also necessarily recognize that masculine (and neuter) plural nouns were frequently used in Greek to be gender-inclusive terms. The question is not whether a gender-inclusive interpretation is appropriate in some instances, for it certainly is (when Paul frequently addresses the ἀδελφοί in his letters, he does not usually refer only to male believers).[11] The question is *when* such a rendering is appropriate, and here Greek usage and context should be determinative. We do have translations that seek to be completely gender neutral, which is a serious mistake, but translating with gender-inclusive language when an inclusive idea is intended by the author's own choice of words is not. In these cases we have to remind ourselves again that Greek is not English. This is where the grammar and function of the original language must compel us to ask which linguistic equivalent in our own language is most appropriate. That is, after all, the goal of translation: to bring the meaning of a text into another language system.

Comparing Translations

A number of very good Bible translations exist today.[12] We have briefly examined a few of them above. No translation perfectly represents all the originally intended meaning of the original-language text. Such an accomplishment is simply impossible. Most of our modern translations do represent well the intended meaning, but in light of these shortcomings and controversies, interacting with the original languages becomes all the more important. This does not mean, however, that we should discard our modern translations. Much good, thorough, and difficult work has gone into producing them. Rather, this means we should use them carefully, and use many of them. Too often readers of the Bible hunker down into a single, favorite translation. While reasons for doing so may be admirable, studying the Bible well necessarily entails that we do not allow ourselves to rely on a single source. The Bible (and most importantly, the Triune God who inspired it) should be our source for truth. No single translation, commentary, theologian, or preacher has an unmediated and infallible claim on God's truth. As the saying goes, the only theologian I ever always agree with is myself, and even then we have arguments! Every human has epistemic limitations, so our study should first be humble, recognizing our limitations and seeking after wisdom and discernment. Using multiple translations gives us a wider window into understanding the biblical text, as does reading various authors, listening to various preachers, and understanding various theologians.

With all of the translations available, how do we decide which translations to incorporate into our study? When we interpret a text, we certainly cannot review them all. I'd like to first set out that there is not a one-size-fits-all, completely comprehensive, objective, results-assured method to studying the Bible that gives any individual absolute, certain, indisputable knowledge of the entirety of the biblical text. We have lots of good methods available (more on that in the next chapters), as well as many not-so-good ones (the worst of which is probably having no intentional method at all). What I outline below, then, are what I consider some valuable suggestions for gaining a clearer picture of the biblical text.

First, using several different translations that span the spectrum of translation approaches gives us a very good first step.[13] I suggest incorporating three or four translations as a part of your in-depth study: one formal (e.g., NASB, RSV, ESV), one formal/functional (NIV, HCSB, NET, etc.), one functional (NCV, NLT, CEV, etc.), and one paraphrase (MSG, TLB, etc.). Though figure 2, which we looked at above, does not give us hard delineations, it illustrates how these translations may be thought of along the spectrum of approaches. In examining different translations, and in particular at least one in each of these areas of the spectrum, we can see how different translation philosophies result in different attempts to render the text of the New Testament. Furthermore, when there is significant disagreement or a wide variety of translation options found when comparing translations, particularly where the meaning becomes either unclear, confusing, or even contradictory between different translations, this provides a good signal for us to slow down and examine the text in more detail.

Second, our review of the translations should be compatible with our examination of the features of the Greek text (through our inter-linear interactions explored earlier). Translations provide a helpful go-between for those still developing Greek-reading skills or lacking enough proficiency to work exclusively from the Greek text. This does not mean, however, that comparing translations should be the end of the road in thinking about the passage.

Taking our advice above, let's look at a familiar text, Philippians 2:6–8, and see how different translations from the spectrum of approaches measure up. In what appears below, I have bolded some of the major areas of difference between these translations.

NASB: ⁶who, although **He existed in the form of God,** did not regard equality with God **a thing to be grasped,** ⁷but **emptied Himself,** taking the form of a bond-servant, *and* being **made in the likeness of men.** ⁸Being found in appearance as a man, He humbled Himself by becoming obedient to the point of death, **even death** on a cross.

NIV: ⁶Who, **being in very nature God,** did not consider equality with God **something to be used to his own advantage;** ⁷rather, he **made himself nothing** by taking the very nature of a servant, **being made in human likeness.** ⁸And being found in appearance as a man, he humbled himself by becoming obedient to death—**even death** on a cross!

NLT: ⁶Though he **was God,** he did not think of equality with God **as something to cling to.** ⁷Instead, he **gave up his divine privileges;** he took the **humble position** of a slave and was **born as a human being**. When he appeared in human form, [8]he humbled himself in obedience to God and **died a criminal's death** on a cross.

MSG: He had **equal status with God** but didn't think so much of himself that he had **to cling to the advantages of that status no matter what.** Not at all. When the time came, he set aside the privileges of deity and took on the status of a slave, became *human*! Having **become human, he stayed human. It was an incredibly humbling process. He didn't claim special privileges. Instead, he lived a selfless, obedient life and then died a selfless, obedient death—and the worst kind of death at that—a crucifixion.**

As you can see, there is not a tremendous amount of variation among our formal, formal-function, and functional translations. A few key phrases, however, are rendered quite differently and raise some obvious questions. Did Paul write that Jesus "existed in the form of God," was "in very nature God," or "was God"? Was equality not "a thing to be grasped," "something to be used to his own advantage," or "something to cling to"? Did Jesus "empty himself," "make himself nothing," or "give up his divine privileges"? As we move through the translations we see layers of interpretation added on to the text. That does not nescessarily mean these interpretations are bad or wrong, but they are added interpretations nonetheless. As we look at the Message, there is very little materially identical with the other three translations. Those who teach Bible study methods will often say that paraphrase translations should not be heavily used in serious Bible study, except perhaps to give a different angle on the text, and this is why. We lose the poetic nature of the text in that translation as well as the careful vocabulary and structure employed. Though it may capture some essence of the passage, it leaves out quite a bit. It is also considerably longer than our other translations. These translations can provide helpful insights, but ultimately as we drive toward the Greek text, we will depart farther from most paraphrase translations. The phrases bolded above should alert us to areas of the Greek text that we would need to explore further in order to examine carefully the language used. We will say more about that process in the next few chapters.

Ultimately, comparing translations, as I have tried to illustrate above, should serve as a sort of triage process whereby we are alerted to potential interpretive issues or theological questions that must be handled with more attention in the exegetical process. We must avoid the temptation to simply go with our favorite translation when these difficulties arise or, even worse, to pick the one that sounds the best (and yes, this is an all too common practice even among preachers and teachers of the Bible). Our investigation should lead us into giving more attention to the questions that comparing English versions uncovers. These questions ultimately must be answered by addressing the context(s) of the passage.

16

Bridging Contexts

The field of textual criticism is vital for exegeting, or "drawing out," the meaning of a passage. Textual criticism undergirds the process by establishing the base text of the New Testament. Most people, however, will not make a career out of textual criticism, so we are dependent on trusting the experts and their analysis. Likewise, most will not endeavor to develop their own translations or be a part of a translation committee. Being aware of these disciplines and processes is important in interpretation and especially in understanding how the New Testament was composed and transmitted. These issues undergird interpretation, which is something we all, knowingly or not, undertake when we read Scripture. The question of interpretation, like that of theology, is not *whether* we interpret (or whether we "do" theology) but rather whether we do it well. The fact of the matter is that each of us brings baggage to the Bible when we read it. Whether they come from our upbringing, our theological traditions, our families, or our cultural situation, we have preconceived ideas about God, Jesus, truth, and religion. When we open the Bible, those ideas do not disappear. Rather, they inform, for good or for ill, how we read the biblical text.

Some have suggested in light of this that no hope remains for accessing any sense of the originally intended meaning of a text. Rather, they suggest, we should embrace our situation and presuppositions and read them freely into all texts. There are many problems with this view, which we will not unpack here.[1] Suffice it to say, there is a middle ground here where we can gain an understanding of the intended meaning even if we cannot exhaust it. We must find a balance between uncritical, free interpretations (i.e., whatever it means to me is what it means) and overcertain, narrow readings of a text (i.e., my interpretation is the only one worth hearing or considering). Seeking to understand a text means that we must *stand under* it rather than *stand over* it. We must as much allow the text to read us, to reshape our presuppositions and to reform our mind, as we read it.

Approaching the Bible with this kind of epistemic humility means we allow it to critique our previously conceived beliefs and interpretations rather than find ways for it to reinforce them (something known as confirmation bias). We must approach the Bible with an open attitude, meaning that even if the results of our study run against the grain of our presuppositions or previously held beliefs, we embrace the biblical teaching anyway. So how can we avoid being handcuffed by the influence of our presuppositions? The first step is being aware that they exist and that we do not have a God's-eye view of the world that guarantees our objectivity (though again, not succumbing to a defeatist mentality that therefore no significant sense of meaning can be found). The second is to immerse ourselves in the thought world of the Bible itself, and this means examining its contexts.

You will notice that I said "contexts" here rather than "context." We will explore that concept as we progress through this chapter. We should not necessarily think of the context of a passage as a singular idea. Rather, the biblical text can be illumined through considering several kinds and layers of context. There is, of course, the **historical context** of the passage, in which we examine the passage in a specific temporal and geographical situation. We also have the **social context** of a passage, in which we read the text with sensitivity to the social situation *of the work* (and so not reading our own social situation and concerns into it), such as the political, economic, gender, and ethnic dynamics surrounding it. The **cultural context** contains those elements of ancient life, such as religion, commerce, family, and government, that enveloped the events and ideas of the ancient world.[2] The **literary context**, perhaps the one both most and least (in terms of its ancient aspects) familiar to modern readers, focuses on these texts as texts. The **intertextual context** reads the work with sensitivity to its connection to other texts, most prominently its Old Testament connections, though including also connections to Greco-Roman and extrabiblical Jewish writings as well as other New Testament works. Finally, the **canonical context** considers the passage in light of the whole thrust and theological framework of the entire biblical canon. Though we could possibly include others, these six areas of context each bring unique kinds of insight to our reading of the New Testament and act as hermeneutical safeguards for modern readers. The more we can immerse ourselves in the events, beliefs, and dynamics of the first-century world, the better we will understand these texts that emerged from it. My goal in what follows is both to set out some of the primary issues that arise from these contexts and then to briefly consider some examples in the New Testament that fruitfully connect to these larger contextual elements. We will begin by looking at the historical context of the New Testament.

Historical Context

We often underappreciate the fact that the New Testament comes to us, particularly as Westerners, from a world that is very different from our own, both in space and time, but also in its cultural setting. Too often Western readers insert the "I" into the text where it does not belong and read the New Testament documents as if we were their original recipients. This is simply not the case. This does not mean, of course, that the basic message of the gospel or the New Testament is not understandable to us, but neither does it mean that we should be satisfied to apprehend only its basic message without appreciating its depth. In order to do that, we must insert ourselves into a world far removed from our own.

We cannot in the space allotted here approach anything like an adequate history of the ancient Mediterranean world leading up to the time of the New Testament. We will seek to outline some of the larger historical points. More important, however, we hope to establish the necessity of thinking about the New Testament as a historically situated collection of documents. This does not mean we should abandon the idea that it holds some relevance for us (we will cross that bridge in chap. 18). Rather, it means that we should not think about its relevance for us before we have adequately considered its original contexts and purposes.

The ancient world, much like our own, was complex. Though some aspects of ancient life were obviously simpler than our lives today, others were equally, if not at times more, complex. In historical terms, a great deal of important insights come to us from the time between the Testaments, which is sometimes referred to as the "intertestamental period," but more commonly now as "Second Temple Judaism," "early Judaism," or, more broadly, the period of the "early Roman Empire." Even here, we notice how the different terminology used is influenced by the concerns we have in investigating the period (Christians may be more apt to think of the "intertestamental period," those focused on Judaism of "Second Temple" or "early Judaism," and classicists of the "early Roman Empire"). Since Jewish concerns are our primary interest here, I will default to that terminology.[3]

The Old Testament ends with a bit of a cliffhanger. The northern and southern kingdoms have been exiled, events described as God's punishment for Israel's waywardness and inclination toward idolatry and syncretistic activities. As the Old Testament time line ends, a restoration of the Jewish people to the land of Israel has begun, though only a partial one. The rebuilding of Jerusalem is under way, but the picture given in the prophetic books of the restoration of Israel and the abundance of blessings that await the faithful remnant has not yet come to fruition. Israel is still under the rule of a foreign power. The nations are not gathering to Jerusalem to worship YHWH.

Unfortunately for the Jewish people, the end of the exile did not bring the end of the turmoil they would face. Alexander the Great would eventually conquer the region and establish yet another foreign reign over the Jewish people, ushering in the Hellenistic period. Alexander died shortly after expanding his kingdom. His kingdom was eventually split under the rule of four of his generals, with the Ptolemaic dynasty ruling Egypt (to the south of Judea) and the Seleucid dynasty ruling Syria (to the north of Judea). The two regions jostled for control of Judea, with the Seleucids finally winning out. Antiochus III was the Seleucid ruler who took control of Judea, and the historical record indicates that he apparently treated the Jewish people with respect.

Such was not the case with his successor, Antiochus IV. The events of his reign greatly impacted aspects of Jewish self-identity for the remainder of the period. The motive of Antiochus's antagonism toward the Jewish people is debated, but it was likely a combination of several factors. Part of the problem likely arose from some conflict among the Jewish people that involved the buying of the high priesthood by unfit bidders. Further, some apparent attempts to bring Hellenistic practices to Jerusalem that conflicted with traditional Jewish practices also occurred. This led to some discord among the Jews of Jerusalem, of which Antiochus possibly caught word. Whatever the events that prompted Antiochus's response, he invaded Jerusalem, desecrated and looted the temple, and eventually forbade the Jewish people from practicing their customs (e.g., circumcision, Sabbath, food laws). He destroyed their sacred texts, established idol worship in Jerusalem, and threatened all defectors with death.

Needless to say, the devout in the Jewish community were not so pleased with this situation. According to 1 and 2 Maccabees, Mattathias and his sons remained faithful and initiated a revolt in Jerusalem that also extended to surrounding areas. Using guerrilla warfare tactics, the Maccabean revolters, led chiefly by Mattathias's son Judas, held off the

Seleucid forces and reclaimed Jerusalem. The temple was purified and rededicated, and the Jewish people enjoyed a brief period of self-rule by the successors of the Maccabees, the Hasmoneans.

The Hasmonean dynasty, however, was not without its own controversies. Due to the Hasmoneans combining the roles of king and high priest, many Jewish traditionalists viewed the Jerusalem temple as corrupted under their reign. The Hasmoneans also enjoyed varying degrees of peace among the people since they were not always popular rulers. We also see the rise of the Pharisees and Sadducees during this time, who held influence among the people, though their influence often depended on whether or not they were "in" with the Hasmonean rulers.

The brief period of Jewish self-rule came to an end in 63 BC. The Romans had been expanding their territory around the ancient world, and eventually Jerusalem was brought under their jurisdiction. The Hasmonean dynasty ended, and the Herodian family eventually took over leadership of Judea. It is these governors whom we find overseeing Judea during many of the events described in the New Testament.

This (very) brief survey gives us an idea of the historical contours that preceded the ministry of Jesus and the growth of the earliest church. With the exception of a brief period of time under the Hasmoneans, the Jewish people lived under the authority of foreign rulers for the majority of the Second Temple period. We find them in this same state, under Roman rule, in the pages of the New Testament. This backstory no doubt informs their understanding of their religious history and identity as well as shapes their religious practices. Understanding this backstory and its relevance for the Jewish people during this period opens up important avenues for understanding the message of the New Testament itself.

One such place where this backstory is evident in the New Testament is in John 10. In 10:22–24, we find the Jews (or "Jewish leaders"; there is some debate over how John uses Ἰουδαῖοι in his Gospel) asking Jesus to tell them plainly if he is the Messiah. John notes that this conversation happened in Jerusalem during "the Feast of Dedication." This festival, also known as Hanukkah, celebrated the rededication of the temple after the Maccabean revolt. Given that the Maccabean revolt represented what many Jews thought the Messiah would be and do (a leader to bring freedom from political oppressors), the setting and the question together give additional force to the situation. At this time, when the nation's deliverance from its Seleucid oppressors was remembered, the question to Jesus about his messianic identity is all the more intriguing. Jesus's messianic identity did not meet the politically charged expectations of many of the Jewish people, which may explain his hesitation to use the term outright. Recognizing the setting of Hanukkah, and the historical background of the Maccabean revolt, thus gives us an added dimension of understanding to this passage that we would otherwise lack.

As we apply the lens of historical study to passages in the New Testament, we must communicate that information in ways that make it relevant. As we teach, preach, discuss, or think through a passage, we should ask what historical information may have relevant bearing on it. In other words, I would not recommend recapping the history (as I have done above) for the sake of recapping it in, say, a sermon, teaching lesson, small group discussion, or exegetical paper. We should grow in our awareness of these historical elements, but ultimately we should bring them to bear on explaining a passage only when we add value to our hearers or readers by doing so. A good rule of thumb is to ask the question, "Does presenting this information give any additional or essential insight into the meaning of the passage?" If the answer is no, we would do best to leave it out, though that does not mean we should ignore it in our process of study.

Social Context

The social world of the ancient Mediterranean peoples was vastly different from our own. Social taboos, structures, expectations, and values in the ancient world, though overlapping in places with our own, often operated on completely different systems than Westerners in particular experience. Many aspects of the ancient Mediterranean world diverge from our own. We will mention a few below as a means of illustrating the importance of being aware of the social setting of the New Testament.[4]

The person in the ancient world operated within a basic sense of group identity rather than an individual one. This does not mean they did not possess a sense of individual identity, but it means that identity was formed primarily through how it related to its group connections (ethnicity, family line, place of origin, social class, etc.). These group connections formed the essence of an individual's identity and largely determined what social spheres they would move within. Far different from the Western notion of making a name for yourself, in the ancient Mediterranean world, your name was basically made for you (whether you liked it or not). This aspect of the New Testament's social world in and of itself has major implications for how we read and understand the New Testament. When Paul describes believers as sharing in a common identity centered around Jesus, and when Jesus himself calls his followers to place allegiance to him above even allegiance to their families, we see here the collective framework of the ancient world being present while also being radically reoriented. Awareness of this aspect of ancient life has major implications for our understanding (and application) of the New Testament.

One of the social dimensions alluded to above was that of the family. Family identity largely established the identity for an individual. It usually determined their social status, their occupation, and their geographical location, among other things. Since the ancient world operated largely as an honor-and-shame culture, the honor of the family was of utmost importance, and bringing shame to one's family was loathsome. In general, the father's reputation influenced the reputation of the family, and blood relations were considered as of primary significance. The father was, of course, the head of the household, meaning that he ruled its affairs and held authority over its operations. Women and children in the home were to submit to his authority and live modestly. Slaves also inhabited the household in the Greco-Roman world, supporting the work of the family, though not sharing in its success or honor. Scholars sometimes speak of Jesus establishing a fictive kinship or a surrogate family, meaning one based on something other than blood relations, which were so important in the ancient world.[5] For Paul to refer to his fellow believers as "siblings" (ἀδελφοί) illustrates the radical way in which the New Testament church saw itself as a unified family.

The ethnic tensions that undergirded the social relationships between Jews and gentiles in the ancient world also provide important insights for understanding the New Testament. The Jewish people tended to view the gentile world as fundamentally at odds with God and dangerous to associate with, since it might tempt them toward idolatry or intermarriage or defile their purity. Likewise, the gentiles often viewed the Jews with contempt, for example, seeing them as lazy for not working on the Sabbath, viewing their monotheistic beliefs and practices of dietary regulations and circumcision as peculiar, and taking offense at their tendency to isolate themselves from gentiles. Paul's most extensive discussions of "justification" (δικαι- words) occur in two letters loaded with the Jew-gentile tension (Romans and Galatians). The emphasis on understanding the social setting of the New Testament in recent years has led to many rereadings of those letters since many interpreters believe traditional lines of interpretation neglect the centrality of the social dynamic portrayed within them. In other words, we should ask why Paul's most pointed discussions of justification occur primarily in a context of dealing with Jew-gentile distinctions, recognizing that social makeup influences how we understand those texts. Here again we find an important and fruitful point of study that arises from this larger contextual setting.

We have mentioned here but a few of the layers of social context in the world of the New Testament. Ethnic, familial, lingual, spiritual, group, class, gender, and geographic nuances give us important windows of understanding into the meaning and message of the New Testament. As with the historical context, cultivating an awareness of these elements takes time, effort, and mental energy. We learn here to ask questions of relevance for the original situation, such as "Why is table fellowship so often an issue in the New Testament?" "What is the significance of identifying figures like tax collectors and 'sinners' in the Gospels?" or "What did those terms signify in the ancient world?" We receive great rewards by our effort to examine these social layers of the text, since we thus may escape reading our social situation into the New Testament and gain a deeper insight into the situation evidenced in the New Testament and subsequently into the way that message and its setting can transform us today.

Cultural Context

As with the social context, the cultural context of the New Testament provides us with some important insights into its message. The Greco-Roman world and its religious, political, and cultural dynamics operated quite differently from our Western context today. The known world was largely united under the expansive Roman Empire, and thus its values, economy, beliefs, and religion(s) were influenced by that empire and its Greek cultural heritage. As we saw above, these belief systems created tensions with Jewish monotheists, who generally observed a more restricted lifestyle.

One particular aspect of cultural significance was the Roman emperors themselves. The "cult of the emperor," as it has become known, developed during this period, in which deceased Roman emperors, and eventually living ones, were deemed deities. Eventually this resulted in worship practices dedicated to the emperors, in which good citizens of the empire were expected to participate. Neglecting the imperial cult was viewed as treason against the empire and was punishable by death. The Jewish people, as a recognized religion, were exempt. Nonetheless, the centrality of honor for the emperors created a significant tension with early Christians referring to Jesus as κύριος ("Lord") and σωτήρ ("Savior"), titles attributed at times to the emperors. Understanding this background context can shed some important light on aspects of the New Testament's message.[6]

The ancient world was also heavily polytheistic. A plethora of gods existed in the Greek and Roman pantheons, and regional deities also played an important role in everyday life. While the major deities of the pantheon were known across the empire, different regions tended to favor a deity or group of deities, usually related to their major agricultural or economic trades. We find some evidence of the diversity of religious expression in the empire in the writings of Paul. Paul's Letters, written to former pagans whom he wished to set securely in their following of the Father, Son, and Spirit, address different issues for different locations. Paul writes and instructs the Colossians, with their own set of religious and cultural difficulties, differently from the Corinthians. An awareness of these regional religious tendencies helps inform our understanding of the issues that Paul addresses in his writings.

The ancient Greco-Roman world also operated on a very different economic system. Much of the ancient world relied on agricultural production for economic sustenance. Only a small percentage of the population (the wealthy and elite) owned land. The majority of the population (upward of 90 percent) were laborers, tending to fields or working on some other labor-based trade (such as carpentry, fishing, herding, pottery, etc.). Many of the analogies used by Jesus in his teachings draw precisely from these forms of livelihood that dominated the economic landscape. Slavery was also common in the Greco-Roman world. Slaves typically lived within the household of their owner rather than in separate quarters. People were often enslaved as a result of war, slave trading, kidnapping, orphaning, criminal punishment, or being born to slaves. It is estimated that between 15 and 30 percent of the population of the Roman Empire were slaves.[7]

The value system of the ancient world also varied considerably from our own (though comparabilities existed as well). True power and influence were rare commodities in the Roman world, reserved for the elite class, and an individual's worth was largely determined by factors outside their control. Birthplace, family lineage, social class, occupation, ethnic background, literacy, and gender were among the factors that determined a person's place in society. Though there were instances of social mobility, it was generally uncommon for a person to move up in the world, an ideal embraced so often in the West. The honor-and-shame values system played a major role in social standing in the ancient world. Courage, virtue, wisdom, and justice were prized values, and often ethical instruction centered on how to act properly within given household and societal roles. The household was viewed as a microcosm of the empire, in which the emperor himself held the position of *paterfamilias*.

All of this holds a great deal of importance for how we understand the New Testament. Taking the New Testament household codes as an example (Eph. 5:22–6:5; Col. 3:18–4:1; 1 Pet. 3:1–9), we face the danger, when not examining the cultural context when interpreting these texts, of reading *our* cultural setting and values back into these texts and interpreting them in the wrong context. When we invest ourselves in the Greco-Roman and Jewish cultural contexts, we can better understand the significance of those passages and avoid anachronistic interpretations.

As another example, the issue of whether or not to eat meat that was sacrificed to idols comes across as quite strange in our cultural perspective (1 Cor. 8–10). Paul devotes significant attention to this matter in 1 Corinthians, showing us that this was an issue of importance to him for that congregation. If we lack appropriate perspective concerning the cultural dynamics at play in Corinth, and in the larger Greco-Roman world, we may end up with a confused interpretation of this passage and misapply its teachings. Recognizing, however, the social and religious background strengthens our interpretation and our application of this and many other texts.

Literary Context

The Bible in general, and the New Testament in particular, is a *collection* of various writings. It is not a seamless document written from start to finish in chapter-by-chapter sequence. This is apparent as readers transition from Matthew to Mark. Mark does not pick up where Matthew left off; it tells the good news of Jesus again, with slightly different emphases and order, but the same story nonetheless. When we recognize that the New Testament is a collection of writings from various authors who were eyewitnesses of Jesus and the early Jesus-movement, we should be prompted to ask, "What kind of writings are these?"

This raises the question of literary **genre**. The New Testament contains twenty-seven different writings that were composed in at least four major genres: *gospels, theological narrative* (Acts), *epistles*, and *apocalypse*. These are the major categories, and each category has its own unique features that are vital to understand in order to comprehend the message of writings in that category.

The **Gospels** (Matthew, Mark, Luke, and John) present portraits of the life, death, and resurrection of Jesus.[8] Each Gospel contains some unique material (John being the most unique in comparison to the three Synoptic Gospels), while they also follow the basic plot line of Jesus's ministry, conflict with the Jewish religious leaders, betrayal, and crucifixion. Sometimes the question arises as to why we have four Gospels. Each Gospel emphasizes certain aspects of Jesus's life and ministry and likely also shapes the story to better influence its intended audience. The Gospels, though containing historical material that we should recognize as reliable, do not ultimately seek to give a purely historical description. They seek to present the story of Jesus in order to reach some effectual end for the readers. As we will suggest with the Epistles, we must work to understand the intended audience of each Gospel (which is not explicitly stated but nevertheless existed) and its intended outcomes.[9] The Gospel of Matthew, for example, seems focused on a primarily Jewish audience with its frequent connections to the Old Testament and the way in which it frames Jesus's story as recapitulating elements from Israel's history. The Gospel of John, however, in that it frequently explains Jewish elements to the audience, was probably intended for those unfamiliar with Jewish customs.

We should also recognize that the Gospel writers frame their stories, sometimes the same story, differently in order to accomplish different purposes. The ordering of the Gospel accounts, for example, differs from one to another, and in particular the order of the Synoptics differs from that of John. Does this mean that one of the Gospels got the history of Jesus "right" and the others "wrong"? Asking such a question reveals our orientation to history. We think of history as a strict, factual retelling of an event or sequence of events. Ancient history did not quite work that way. It was expected that the historian would shape the material to retell the story as well as to accomplish certain goals in doing so. The fact that Mark and John may order certain events differently does not mean they present us with historical contradictions. Rather, they intend to frame the story differently in order to accomplish their differing literary purposes. For example, Jesus's temptation is recorded in the three Synoptic Gospels (Matt. 4:1–11; Mark 1:12–13; Luke 4:1–13). While Mark's account records only that Jesus endured forty days of temptation from Satan and was with wild animals and was served by the angels, Matthew and Luke both offer fuller accounts. Although they record similar accounts, they include different information (such as Matthew's fuller quotation of Deut. 8:3 in 4:4). Matthew presents the order of events as wilderness, temple, mountain, while Luke presents them as wilderness, mountain, temple. Does this mean Matthew contradicts Luke? Not likely. Depending on one's view of the synoptic problem (that is, the order in which the Synoptics were written and the extent to which each had access to the others' material), the two accounts could be independent, Matthew could have revised Luke's order, or Luke could have revised Matthew's.[10]

This has led some to suggest that the Gospel writers, in light of this, were simply inventors of certain aspects, or even the entirety, of Jesus's life.[11] This too is a hasty conclusion. A historical contradiction would be one Gospel telling us Jesus was crucified and another that he was stoned to death. We do not find those kinds of contradictory stories in the Gospels. We do find, however, that the Gospel writers shape different elements of the stories differently. What matters most as we study the Gospels is that we pay close attention to the frameworks that the Gospel writers themselves offer us (which we will say more about shortly). Different stories or teachings could be placed in different contexts by the Gospel writers to serve different purposes.[12] But the pliability of these stories and teachings also reveals to us their depth in that they could be used to achieve several different purposes. Thus in studying the overlapping elements of the Gospels, we should attend as much as possible both to the individual context of a teaching or event in each Gospel and to the diverse contexts found in their parallels.

The **theological narrative** found in the New Testament is the book of Acts. Acts shares many similarities to the Gospels with the exception that it is not a *bios*, or an ancient biography. Rather, it traces the spread of the early church through its key early leaders, and in particular through Peter and Paul. Acts, like the Gospels, is not a purely historical document. It too is selective, meaning that it chooses some material and omits other data. The selectivity is, likewise, for a purpose, to construct a historical account, but also to paint a theological picture of the growth of the early church and to paint that picture in a captivating manner. It too has goals that it wished to accomplish with its original recipients. Thus many of the issues we mentioned for the Gospels, about attending both to their details and to the framework, apply to Acts.

Acts also contains a number of speeches and sermons. According to what we know of ancient narratives, authors would often summarize or paraphrase the content of the sermon rather than give verbatim accounts. We would expect that the short sermons in the book of Acts, which can be read in just a few minutes, were likely longer when originally delivered. Luke thus probably provided us with the "Cliffs Notes" version of these sermons. Again here we recognize that Luke shaped this material and selected that which he thought would best accomplish his literary purpose. This all the more reinforces the importance of reading these sermons in the larger narrative context in which they occur. Doing so helps us to see why Luke includes the material he does and helps us to gain a better picture of the overall goals he sought to accomplish.

Narratives are also not necessarily *prescriptive* but are at bottom *descriptive*. The biblical "heroes" were not necessarily intended to be emulated. It is more important that we should understand the progress of the story, and God's role in it as the True Hero, than to find moral principles or establish patterns of action from the human characters. This does not mean that no qualities worth emulation may be present at all, but rather they are not the primary concern of biblical narratives. Since narratives are descriptive, we should also be careful about normalizing certain events or activities we find in them, which applies both to the Gospels and the book of Acts. When we find a pattern of activity, that may indeed alert us to something that the author intends to be prescriptive (a pattern to be followed), but ultimately we must carefully reflect on the context of these occurrences and consider how that pattern may be relevant for us as well as how the pattern compares with other biblical material. When we jump too quickly to assuming that the narrative gives us an action to emulate, we may miss the original intent of the author in including certain events in the first place.

The New Testament **Epistles** constitute a significant portion of the New Testament. These are usually divided into the Pauline Epistles (Romans, 1 and 2 Corinthians, Galatians, Ephesians, Philippians, Colossians, 1 and 2 Thessalonians, 1 and 2 Timothy, Titus, and Philemon)[13] and the General Epistles (Hebrews; James; 1 and 2 Peter; 1, 2, and 3 John; and Jude). Perhaps the most important thing to recognize about the New Testament Epistles is that they are occasional documents: each letter was written for a specific purpose (or purposes) to a specific recipient group (or groups). They are not contextless theological treatises. This does not mean they are not theological, for they are *deeply* theological. But that theology must be understood in the context of the occasion that prompted it. Even the Letter to the Romans, which many a commentator has said is a theological treatise or Paul offering a systematic soteriology, is occasioned. Among other things, the letter focuses on the relationship between Jewish and gentile Christians, a sociocultural issue with theological implications. To remove that element from the letter is to run the risk of serious misinterpretation. In some cases a specific issue or group of issues is not readily determined (such as Ephesians). This does not mean the letter is any less historically situated but rather that we lack the details to more fully construct its situation.

When the historical details are not apparent, either from internal or external evidence, New Testament scholars often deploy some form of mirror reading, meaning that they read with an eye to the issues that the letter addresses in order to attempt to reconstruct (even if tentatively) its historical situation. In a letter like Galatians or 1 Corinthians, sufficient internal evidence is present for us to understand the situation being addressed. In a letter like Colossians or 1 John, where the author does not specify historical details, mirror reading can help us better understand how to situate the content of the letter. Each letter or group of letters (such as the Corinthian correspondence) has its own historical, cultural, and social situation that should be understood in relation to its occasional nature. Such understanding will shed valuable light on the letters of the New Testament.

The **apocalypse** of the New Testament is the book of Revelation. Apocalyptic materials were not necessarily rare in the ancient Jewish world. We find apocalyptic elements in the books of *1 Enoch*, the *Assumption of Moses*, and *4 Ezra*, among others. Apocalyptic writings generally have a narrative style but contain otherworldly images and figures, often include some cataclysmic event or judgment, and have the chief purpose of revealing some yet unknown aspect of the future with the goal of changing the behavior of readers in the present.[14] The book of Revelation, as with the other New Testament writings, had an originally intended audience and purpose. This does not mean, of course, that the events of the book were solely intended for its audience, but rather that the way the book lays out the eschatological future was intended to accomplish a specific purpose (or purposes) with that original audience. The imagery in the book has been its biggest obstacle throughout the history of interpretation. Too often interpreters jump to some allegorization of the images ("the horsemen are *really* . . ."), failing to appreciate them in their original context. These images have a historical context that is drawn from the period itself and the theological pool of Jewish ideas. The images serve to reach into the imagination of the hearers and are not intended as some obscure and impossible puzzle to be solved. As the images unfold, we must also realize that they may not necessarily be presented in a precise chronological sequence, a phenomenon we see in other extrabiblical apocalypses as well. The more we immerse ourselves in the context and purpose of the work, the better we will understand the message of Revelation and its relevance for us today. We should also recognize that the imagery of Revelation, strange as it may be to us, finds precedent both in the Old Testament (primarily Daniel and Ezekiel, though other texts as well) and in Jewish literature of the period. Again here, recognizing the elements that make up this reservoir from which Revelation draws deepens our understanding of the book and its message.

No New Testament writing is, however, pure in its genre. Each writing has a primary genre (which we examined briefly above), but we find numerous literary **subgenres** throughout. The Gospels, for example, in addition to providing narrative details about Jesus, also contain subgenres, such as genealogies, parables, prayers, wisdom sayings, prophecies/apocalypses, and discourses.[15] We also find creedal material in the book of Acts, along with sermons, discourses, and other material. The New Testament Epistles also include subgenres, such as prayers, hymns, creeds, apocalyptic material, and historical summaries. The book of Revelation, in addition to its apocalyptic features, also contains epistolary material and prophetic content. As we interpret the New Testament, we must read with a sensitivity to the main literary function of each work, while also recognizing when we find these subgenres in each of the New Testament writings.

We should also recognize that the New Testament documents were written for a primarily **oral function**. While local congregations in the early church may have had copies of many, or even perhaps most, of the writings that would become the New Testament, each copy would have served a collective function. There were likely very few personal copies of the New Testament. So when the local assemblies shared in the reading of these writings, it was orally, with one member reading and/or explaining the text. Therefore, the documents were intended to be *heard*, as is indicated by so many phrases in the New Testament that emphasize the *hearing* of the material ("if anyone has ears to hear, let them hear," not "if anyone has eyes to read, let them read"). The documents were also intended not just to communicate information but to prompt action, to change a person's beliefs and practices. And the means by which that activity of persuasion occurred could take various shapes and forms. Different devices and forms of argumentation, such as diatribe, narrative, proverb/parable, refutation, and comparison, were implemented, depending on the context and which one the persuader thought would be most effective. We see Jesus, for example, relying heavily on parables but also using refutation and other forms of persuasion. Paul in Romans uses a form of diatribe, conversing with an "interlocutor" who raises questions against his teachings. In Ephesians we find a form of epideictic rhetoric, full of language of praise and reinforcement, used to communicate to that audience.[16]

When we think about the literary context, we must also consider the **immediate context** of the passage. We have discussed this already previously, but a brief reminder will not hurt. Since the New Testament writings are forms of contextualized theology, and since individualized verses occur in a flow of thought, we must consider what comes before and after the verse. This works differently for different books of the Bible. In the Gospels and Acts (and partly in Revelation as well), we must consider where the passage occurs in the story of that work. The individual pericopes, or units (such as a particular parable or scene), are not isolated materials, stitched together haphazardly with no cohesion. They collectively form the larger literary unit of the work itself. We thus must take our cues concerning the meaning of individual words, sentences, and units from where and how they fit into the larger flow of thought. Likewise, for Epistles, a particular section must be considered in light of what has preceded it and what follows it. When we isolate a passage without consideration for its larger context, we run the risk of reading foreign ideas into it. What we will find as we pay attention to the larger context is that the New Testament authors connect elements together, building on what has preceded or foreshadowing what is to come. Many of Paul's Letters, for example, follow an indicative-to-imperative pattern, where Paul develops his (contextualized) theological argument in the beginning of the letter and then draws forth applications from that material, making obvious connections to what has gone before. To ignore either of these elements is to miss the intent of Paul's Letters, which is to ground real-life behavior in theological truth.

We have suggested earlier that *diagramming* passages can help us to understand the flow of thought in a particular unit and reveal the structure of primary ideas and supporting ideas. As we look across an entire literary work, we may find larger **structural elements** that tie it together, but we should also attend to *repeated vocabulary* (words, phrases, or clauses, such as Matthew's "kingdom of heaven" language); *repeated grammatical structures* (such as Paul's rhetorical questions in Romans); *changes in characters, locations, or events* (such as the transition from Peter to Paul in Acts); *changes in verbal patterns* (such as the aforementioned indicative-to-imperative, but also changes in tense, etc.); *conjunctions signaling transition* (such as δέ); or *changes in theme or issue being addressed* (such as we find repeatedly in 1 Corinthians). Noticing these elements and transitions helps us to identify these larger units and also to see how the work as a whole fits together. As we think about literary context, we should thus think about the genre, the immediate context around the passage, and the larger context of the work as a whole.

Intertextual Context

Another significant area of attention in New Testament scholarship in recent years is the area of intertextuality. **Intertextuality** very simply refers to the relationships between texts. We may find intertextual connections between the New Testament writings themselves (such as between the Gospels, or between Acts and the Pauline Epistles). But there is another layer of intertextuality that I wish to examine in this section, and that is the relationship between the New Testament and non–New Testament texts, primarily the Septuagint (LXX), the Hebrew Bible, and extrabiblical Jewish literature.

The **Septuagint** itself possesses a very interesting history. According to several ancient sources, the Septuagint was commissioned by Ptolemy II, who assembled seventy or seventy-two translators (hence the abbreviation LXX) to translate the five books of Moses. The *Letter of Aristeas* states that the translators completed the work in seventy-two days. The story of the translation of the rest of the Old Testament does not survive in such an account. It seems likely enough, though, that the translated works in the Septuagint came from several different translators, as there is a good bit of unevenness in their translation approaches. Some fairly woodenly follow the Hebrew text, while others, especially in the poetic and prophetic texts, translate more loosely and sometimes hardly reflect the Hebrew text (at least as we have it) at all. Often this is the result of a difficult Hebrew reading that the translator smooths over, an alternate text from which the Septuagint was translated, or a different translation approach. The Septuagint is invaluable for biblical studies for a number of reasons, but most important, it provides important text-critical information for the text of the Old Testament (it is among the oldest witnesses to the Old Testament we possess), it gives us another window into Second Temple Judaism, and it is used heavily by the authors of the New Testament. The majority of the quotations of the Old Testament found in the New appear to be taken from the Septuagint (roughly 80 percent of the time). When examining quotations of the Old Testament in the New Testament, students of the text must thus consult both the Hebrew critical text and the Septuagint.[17]

The issue of the base text represents one of the many difficulties that face interpreters when examining the **use of the Old Testament in the New Testament**.[18] Related to that problem is the way in which the New Testament authors integrate the Old Testament into their writings. We sometimes find straightforward quotations, other times partial quotations, and at other times allusions and echoes, which call on some theme or passage but do not give verbatim detail. At times the New Testament authors also adapt certain texts to better fit their purposes, either by reapplying to a new (usually christological) context, or by adjusting the wording of the passage, making interpretation for us in the twenty-first century all the more complicated.[19] For example, in Ephesians 4:8, Paul quotes from Psalm 68:18, but the Hebrew and Septuagint texts record that God received gifts rather than gave them. This raises the question as to whether Paul adjusted the quotation to fit the context or he was working with a different text. Likewise, in Ephesians 5:14, Paul tells us that "it says" without clarifying the "it." Some suggest that Paul is possibly alluding to several different texts from Isaiah (Isa. 26:19; 51:17; 52:1; 60:1), while others think Paul may be quoting an early Christian creed or hymn here. Both of these examples represent instances where identifying the source of the quoted material poses some difficulty.

Furthermore, we also have situations where the referent of the quoted passage is altered. Matthew 2:15 offers a famous example of this. Here the quoted text from Hosea 11:1 references Israel. The Septuagint reads that God called "his [Israel's] children" (τὰ τέκνα αὐτοῦ) out of Egypt, while the Hebrew reads that God called "my [God's] son." Both references in the context, however, refer to the exodus event and the children of Israel. Matthew reapplies this quotation as a reference to Jesus, so while the meaning of the text is retained, the referent is changed. Matthew's Gospel frequently presents Jesus as the "new" representative of some Old Testament person or theme (Moses, Israel, exodus, etc.). This use of Hosea is thus in keeping with Matthew's view that Jesus recapitulates and fulfills the Old Testament expectations. Another issue surfaces in the Gospel of Mark's introduction. Here Mark introduces his Old Testament quotations by stating, "As it is written in Isaiah the prophet," but he quotes from both Malachi and Isaiah in what follows in 1:2–3. These issues all alert us to the fact that we must carefully attend to the way the New Testament authors use the Old Testament, examining both the original source (when possible) and its original context.

We also must recognize the importance of studying **noncanonical Jewish and Greco-Roman materials** in order to shed further light on the New Testament. The Apocrypha, Old Testament Pseudepigrapha, Dead Sea Scrolls, and Greco-Roman writings contain invaluable insights for understanding Jewish theology and Greco-Roman thought and practices during the period surrounding the New Testament. While most often we find implicit connecting points between these texts, what is less commonly realized is that we also find actual quotations from and allusions to this noncanonical literature in the New Testament. For example, we find a quotation from *1 Enoch* in Jude 14, and some have suggested Paul demonstrates familiarity with the Wisdom of Solomon in Romans 1–2. Beyond these few clear connections, however, understanding Jewish thought is crucial for understanding the New Testament. The New Testament is almost exclusively a Jewish document (depending on the ethnicity of Luke), written by individuals steeped in the Old Testament and Jewish thought patterns, proclaiming the arrival of the Jewish Messiah for the world. Furthermore, many of these Second Temple Jewish writings were primarily preserved by Christians in the centuries after the inception of the church, indicating that they found value in retaining these writings. Thus, we should recognize that the more we understand Judaism on its own terms, the better we will understand the writings of the New Testament.[20]

One area of fresh insight that has taken hold in New Testament scholarship as a result of deeper engagement with Second Temple Jewish writings is a revision of the common understanding of Judaism among scholars. Much of late Christian interpretation, going back to the Reformation and beyond, has viewed Judaism, in particular through the lens of Paul's critique, as a works-righteousness religion, meaning that Jews understood salvation to be merited (i.e., earned) through good works. This is often the framework used when interpreting Romans, Galatians, and Philippians in particular, though other New Testament writings could be included in that list. In the last forty years or so, a growing consensus has emerged, through interaction with the Second Temple texts (much of which was reinvigorated by the discovery of the Dead Sea Scrolls), that questions that framework. The so-called new perspective understands Judaism not as a works-righteousness religion but rather as a covenantal one.[21] This covenantal foundation is understood or expressed in various ways, but many New Testament scholars now agree that we should not describe Second Temple Judaism as a works-based faith. This has subsequently, then, led to various proposals on how we should read Paul's critique of the "works of the law." In this, and many other, areas, paying close attention to the texts of the ancient world that surround the New Testament period leads to new and helpful insights on the message of the New Testament itself.

These complicating factors should not cause us, however, to shy away from investigating this important area of context. Indeed, these intertextual connections often provide very important clues for how to interpret the passage. We may be left asking how exactly we should approach this difficult area of interpretation. I suggest several important steps: (1) identify the source of the quotation or allusion; (2) examine the original context of the source material; (3) examine the usage of the text in the New Testament context, and compare to the original usage; (4) consider the extrabiblical background or interpretive traditions; (5) consider the theological implications to draw from steps 1 through 4. In examining intertextual connections, we must also recognize that the New Testament authors do not necessarily all employ the same methods when interacting with these texts. Matthew's use and Paul's use, for example, are comparable but not identical. We should thus consider broadly the patterns by which individual authors make intertextual connections. Different passages will present their own unique challenges, but keeping these steps and frameworks in mind will no doubt bear much interpretive fruit.

Canonical Context

While most of the contextual areas examined above need not necessarily be examined in a particular sequence, I strongly suggest that the **canonical context** should be. As we examine the New Testament texts, our method should be to understand individual passages in light of their larger literary context within the particular work as well as within its historical, social, cultural, and intertextual contexts. So when studying Philippians, the focus of our examination should remain within this letter as much as possible before extending beyond it. In other words, we must examine individual arguments and portrayals in individual works before seeing how those works fit together into the Bible as a whole. This is not to say we should hesitate to place an individual work in the larger canonical context, but rather that we should do so only after we have gained some appreciation for the meaning and emphases of the work as a whole.

The Bible as a whole informs the life and practice of the church, and so a canonical reading of Scripture is ultimately necessary for those committed to Christ and his church. And such a reading is all the more legitimized by the fact that the Bible itself is intertextually connected. The Old Testament books as well as the New contain links, both explicit and implicit, to other canonical writings, and so in order to appreciate individual books, we must also appreciate the web of connection that occurs throughout the canon. So we should examine how an individual passage or book fits within the whole of the canon. But we must also recognize the diversity in the canon along with the unity. Different books contain different emphases, and sometimes these emphases create tensions with other passages in the Bible (such as the famous tension between God's sovereignty and human freedom). We must learn to appreciate and glean from the whole canon, but our examination should begin with the contextualized study laid out above. In other words, we must appreciate the individual witnesses while also examining the collective voice. Like different voices in a choir, they all sing in tune.

As an illustration, one of the questions that arises in New Testament interpretation is the relationship between the writings of Paul (in particular Romans and Galatians) and the Epistle of James. Here the limitations of employing only word studies, which we will examine in the next chapter, become apparent. Paul states, and quite adamantly, in numerous places in Romans and Galatians that a person is "justified" or "declared right" only ἐκ πίστεως ("from/by faith[fulness]"). James, on the other hand, in 2:24, tells us a person is "justified" or "declared right" ἐξ ἔργων . . . καὶ οὐκ ἐκ πίστεως μόνον ("from/by works and not from/by faith[fulness] alone"). Paul and James appear to be in direct conflict here. What many interpreters do to relieve this tension is immediately put the Pauline grid on James and assert that whatever James means, he cannot mean that people are saved by works. The error in this approach is that it fails to appreciate the contexts of both statements. In other words, it rushes to the canonical context without first adequately examining the contexts of the passages themselves. We find by examining these larger contexts that Paul addresses the issue of gentile inclusion in the people of God and James addresses the lack of charity among (probably Jewish) affluent believers. Likewise, Paul is not opposed to works, since he speaks of the "obedience of faith" in Romans 1:5, but rather he is dealing more narrowly with the role of the law in gentile justification. If we rush to judgment to resolve the apparent conflict, we can easily miss the point of both Paul's and James's arguments, which address different issues in different contexts.

Bridging Contexts

We have explored above some key contexts in which we must situate the text of the New Testament to understand it well. Our aim should be to come to the text asking what *the authors' and audiences'* questions were rather than bringing *our* questions and foisting them on the text. This requires a careful and conscientious effort to immerse ourselves in their world. We must consider *their* historical setting. We must ponder *their* social constructions. We must examine *their* cultural structures. We must ask how these texts functioned in *their* world and in the earliest churches. We must consider the way in which *they* reinterpreted the Old Testament in light of the revelation of Jesus. By gaining this bigger picture of the world around the New Testament, we can more accurately interpret the New Testament itself. And through that more accurate interpretation, we can approach the story of the whole canon of Scripture through clearer lenses.

None of this happens overnight, and neither is our work in aiming at a deeper understanding ever complete. We are introducing the journey here, but this is certainly only a beginning point (see the suggested resources in chap. 18 for further avenues of study). Grant Osborne has described the process of interpretation as a "hermeneutical spiral," by which Osborne means a movement between the text, context, and application: "I [the interpreter] am spiraling nearer and nearer to the text's intended meaning as I refine my hypotheses and allow the text to continue to challenge and correct those alternative interpretations, then to guide my delineation of its significance for my situation today."[22] The analogy captures well the necessary approach for reading the Bible. Our journey is not linear, mastering a text and then moving to the next and eventually reaching a final destination. Rather, we continue to refine our understanding of texts that we have previously perused as well, enlarging our understanding of context, text, and application as we continue to progress.

As we bring these various contexts to bear on the meaning of a text, our process should be to think through the historical, social, and cultural situation of the text, to situate the passage in the flow of thought of the work as a whole, and then to inquire about the meaning of the details of the passage. In doing so, we formulate a hypothesis of what we think the passage might mean, but we must maintain a willingness to continue to learn and to grow, recognizing that our view of a passage may change as we get more information. Interpretation is a process, and one that requires repetition and humility to pursue successfully. We have attended here to the larger questions of reading and interpreting a text. We now zoom in further to the word level to consider how we think about the meaning of individual terms.

17

Word Studies

Most people, it seems, receive their introduction to Greek through doing word studies. I have intentionally saved this part of the process for last. More exegetical errors are probably made through haphazard word study than in any of the other steps in the process. As we suggested and reiterated earlier, words alone do not have meanings. Individual words usually have a bundle of meanings, but we must understand the meaning of a given word based on its use in a particular context. Too often word studies commit a number of missteps, or fallacies, which often result in an incorrect interpretation. In this chapter, we will first examine some of these common fallacies before suggesting some steps and principles to help guide us into the correct implementation of word studies in the exegetical process.

What Not to Do with Word Studies

Because word studies allow those with minimal knowledge of the biblical languages to engage in some primary-language usage, they may at times be approached without appropriate care. We should note, however, that it is not only those with minimal knowledge who may make these missteps but also those with considerable experience with the biblical languages. Thus we must all proceed with some caution as we analyze the words of the New Testament in order to do so with care and thoughtfulness.

One misstep we must avoid when examining biblical words is to assume we can adequately define them with **English resources**. English resources are a good place to start, but unfortunately *Webster's Dictionary* was never intended to give us much of an adequate understanding of New Testament terminology. This is especially true of theological vocabulary. Examining the English meaning for "propitiation" or "justification" will not provide us with any significant understanding of how these terms were used in the first century. Rather, we will understand only what they mean now, and thus we will be prone to misunderstand the New Testament words by failing to begin at the proper starting point. If a runner starts running the Boston Marathon in Los Angeles, they are set up to fail from the start!

Another related misstep is the issue of **anachronism**, where a modern meaning of a word is read back into the Greek. This occurs most often with words that have some etymological relationship in English. In popular preaching, for example, it is sometimes said that δύναμις ("power") should be thought of as "dynamite" power, the explosive and impressive power of God. The problem with this analogy is that it does not represent what δύναμις actually means. While the word may be used to refer to great strength or ability, it can carry simply a functional sense ("capable" or "able"). Understanding the word as "dynamite power" would create a very odd reading in places like Hebrews 11:11, where Abraham and Sarah receive the *ability* (δύναμιν) to procreate even though Sarah is barren.

We must also avoid the **etymological** or **root fallacy**. This misstep results from assuming that the origin of the word sufficiently determines its meaning. In English, for example, while the word "skateboard" gives us a sufficient idea of the concept, "football" doesn't necessarily, since in football (at least the American version), the ball only rarely touches the players' feet. An illustration in Greek would be a word like ἀναγινώσκω, which is a compound of the words ἀνά ("up") and γινώσκω ("to know"). The word does not, however, mean "to know up" but rather "to read," so relying on etymology can lead us into some serious misunderstandings. Likewise, the Greek word used for "repentance" in the New Testament (μετανοέω), though a compound of μετά ("after") and νοέω ("to think"), should not be thought of as only a "change of thinking" or "change of mind." Rather, repentance involves the reorientation of one's life toward God (cf. Acts 26:20), not just in thought but also in behavior. Paul makes this idea explicit, for instance, in 2 Corinthians 12:21, where he fears that when he returns to Corinth he will find those who "have not repented of the corruption and sexual immorality and self-abandonment that they practiced." The context of the term, not its etymology, must determine how we understand its meaning.

Related to this, we must also be careful not to read ontological statements (statements about reality) from the **structure of the language**. For example, as we explored earlier, Greek has grammatical gender, but grammatical gender does not usually imply biological gender, though the two are sometimes correlated. So we should not assume, for example, that the Spirit is an impersonal force simply because the word πνεῦμα is in the neuter gender. Likewise, we should not assume God is male because he is normally referred to with masculine pronouns.

This also raises the issue of how we think of **word meanings and time**. Linguists often refer to two different ways to approach word meaning: diachronic and synchronic. *Diachronic* approaches examine a meaning of a word "through time." Since meanings develop over time and since meanings aren't always (or perhaps even usually) restricted to the original form of the word, such an approach gives us an idea of how the meaning of a word changes. For example, the English word "husband" originally referred to a male who owned property rather than specifically to a male in a marital relationship. That original meaning gives us a historical perspective of the term, but it is largely irrelevant for understanding the predominant use of the term today. *Synchronic* approaches look at the meaning of a word "within time," or at a specific point in time. Since the meaning of a word changes over time, a synchronic study will be most valuable for those interested in exegesis. The use of a particular term by Plato likely has less immediate relevance for understanding Paul than a use by Josephus, who is more of a contemporary with the apostle. This does not mean we should not explore meanings diachronically, but we should prioritize those meanings that are attested most closely to the period of time associated with the text under consideration.

We must also work to avoid **word-concept confusion** when performing word studies. In this misstep, the exegete errs when they assume they have sufficiently addressed a concept in Scripture by studying the associated terminology. For example, if we examined the words in the New Testament for "love" and assumed that, having completed our study, we exhausted what the New Testament says about the matter, we would fall into the trap of word-concept confusion. Concepts are much bigger ideas than words. Concepts are expressed, no doubt, through words, but a single word or group of words does not adequately capture an entire concept. We would need to examine other associated words as well as ideas (like "covenant" and "mercy") to explore the broader connections of the concept in the New Testament.

Sometimes exegetes, eager to appreciate the fact that words have a range of meanings, might try to force the whole bundle of meanings into a single use of the word. This misstep is sometimes referred to as **meaning overload** or **illegitimate totality transfer**. We would not, for example, see a use of the word "ball" in English and assume at once that it refers to a spherical object ("soccer ball"), baseball terminology ("ball two"), and a formal dance ("masquerade ball"). Rather we would recognize that there is likely a single meaning intended that we would derive from the context surrounding the word. Likewise, when we come across a word like ἀρχή in Greek, which could mean "beginning," "corner," "ruler," or "rule," we should not assume that a single use can carry all these meanings at once. Rather, the context will illuminate which meaning is most likely intended.

Finally, we must also beware of determining the contextual meaning of a word by **word count**. This approach assumes the most common use of a word should be inserted in the context at hand. This is logically illegitimate since this means that we would, in practice at least, restrict words to a single meaning based on which meaning is most frequent. While we might assume that common meanings will be frequent (groundbreaking, I know!), we should not restrict possible meanings based on frequency. Rather, whatever meaning is most appropriate in the context, given the word relationships ordered there, is the meaning we should set forward as the intended meaning in the passage.

What to Do with Word Studies

To put it in an overly simple fashion, **a word is a symbol** that refers to a concept or entity. Thus there is nothing about the word "chair" that is inherently connected to its associated object. Rather, it is a linguistic symbol or sign that signifies its referent. Likewise, as we have explored previously, words carry not a single sense but **multiple senses.** Some words carry more senses than others, but all words have a degree of flexibility in their meaning. We must be aware of this fluidity as we study individual words since, again, words derive their meaning primarily from the context in which they are used. The question that we pursue when examining the meaning of a word in a given context is "What sense is present here?" or "What concept is the word intending to invoke here?" Take even the word "God" (θεός). While Christians would most commonly perceive that this word represents the Supreme Being that they worship, the word can take a range of referents, all of which share in common that some divine or supernatural entity is in mind. So even though the New Testament most commonly uses θεός to refer to "God the Father," we find the word as a reference to a negative spiritual power in 2 Corinthians 4:4 ("the god of this age"; ὁ θεὸς τοῦ αἰῶνος τούτου). We would thus be incorrect if we suggested the word θεός is a special term for the God worshiped by early Christians. Rather, the context in which the word is used must guide how we understand the term. We recognize, then, that a combination of lexical data and contextual analysis is necessary to properly understand the intended meaning of individual words.

In addition to words having multiple meanings, we must also think carefully about the phenomenon of **synonyms**. Often multiple words carry similar senses, and so we must consider what significance (if any) is present when a certain term is used over another. Take, for example, the verbs for "knowing" in the Greek New Testament (γινώσκω, οἶδα, ἐπίσταμαι, σοφίζομαι, etc.). While these words at times carry special nuances, in other places they may be roughly synonymous. So how might one tell the difference or know when a particular nuance is present? We must first consider whether words act synonymously in similar contexts, and we must also consider an author's general tendencies with the word usage. In other words, we must use due diligence before making a claim that, for example, γινώσκω and οἶδα always carry certain, special nuances that distinguish them from one another. We should also remember that the word that we will focus on is the Greek word rather than its English equivalent. Since we examined how to use interlinears and lexicons in previous chapters, we will not repeat those steps here, but they are assumed in what is outlined below.

In terms of process, we can think of word studies taking place across **three basic steps**. First, we need to know what words we should study. Not every word will necessarily contain the same amount of theological weight (though all of them are important and to some extent necessary), so we should first consider examining those words that convey some amount of *theological significance*. We should also consider carefully examining *repeated words* in a given passage or context, such as Paul's δικαι- terminology in the Letter to the Romans. In addition, *uncommon words* (such as hapax legomena, which are words that occur only once in a work or corpus) should also prompt our attention during the exegetical process. We might further consider examining words that are *translated differently* by the translations examined or that simply convey an *unclear meaning* to the reader. Our word studies will not necessarily be limited only to these options, but these provide some helpful parameters in deciding which words to investigate.

Second, the lexical data for the word should be examined. Ideally, this would mean looking at critical lexicons, and particularly at *A Greek-English Lexicon of the New Testament and Early Christian Literature* (BDAG), the *Greek-English Lexicon of the New Testament: Based on Semantic Domains* (Louw-Nida), and theological dictionaries, such as the *New International Dictionary of New Testament Theology and Exegesis* (*NIDNTTE*) or the *Lexham Theological Wordbook* (*LTW*).[1] We should be aware, however, that with theological dictionaries we have moved closer toward interpretation in these resources, and so their insights should be incorporated carefully.[2] The goal in this step is to gain an understanding of the possible range of meanings for the word as well as to consider the other terms that share similar meanings. We should remind ourselves here that in order to examine the range of meaning, we will need to find the lemma or lexical form of the word, most likely by identifying it in our interlinear (unless we have memorized it). Once we locate the lexical entry, these resources will provide the range of meaning for the word, usually with accompanying explanations, suggested translations, and examples of the use from the New Testament or other ancient literature.

We must also be aware here of the issue of **diachronic** versus **synchronic** linguistics. In a diachronic approach, the use of the word through a period of time is examined (e.g., most theological dictionaries look at Greco-Roman, LXX, and New Testament usage). In this "through time" approach, any and all relevant data is incorporated. Thus we may examine the Liddell-Scott *Greek-English Lexicon* to consider the Greco-Roman meanings, look at Lust's *Greek-English Lexicon of the Septuagint* to consider the possible range in the Septuagint, and then move on to our New Testament lexicons.[3] While diachronic study can be helpful, we should not privilege it over synchronic study (or "within time"). In a synchronic examination, those uses of the word that are closest to the period of the writing being considered are prioritized.

Taking our example of the etymology of "husband" that we used earlier, just because the word could mean a property owner at some point in its history does not mean we would expect that meaning to pop up in most uses of the term today. So while we must not ignore or neglect to incorporate the broader findings of a diachronic approach, we should prioritize the information that is most relevant to the word and context at hand.

To help find other uses of a particular word or lemma, we can search either through the electronic resources mentioned in chapter 4 or through the use of a concordance. Concordances allow us to locate all the various uses of a word. Most concordances will order the search based on the lemma, or root of the word, meaning that you can find all occurrences of that term regardless of the forms in which it may occur. As we employ concordances, though, we must be sensitive to the diachronic/synchronic distinction made above as well as to the contexts in which the terms occur.

It may be helpful to think of these different pieces of data as a series of **concentric circles**, as we did when we looked at words, groups of words, sentences, and paragraphs earlier (chap. 2). Our most immediate concern is with the immediate context and how the word is used there. But we have larger, outer rings that inform that context. The use of the word within the same book, for example, would be our first outer circle. This would be followed by use of the word by the same author, the usage in the same Testament, the usage across the canon, and the usage outside the canon. In all of these layers or rings, we would be particularly interested in those uses of a word that occur in the same or a similar context. And the closer we are to the innermost circle (the immediate context), the more we prioritize the information found there over other uses further removed.

All of this lexical and linguistic analysis can seem overwhelming. We are fortunate to have many good resources available from which to draw in our study of the New Testament. We have mentioned a few good resources above that are necessities for those interested in serious and thorough study of the New Testament. But this area, as with the others we have examined, is not mastered overnight. It takes time, dedication, and mental effort to persist through the process. But the persistence ultimately pays great dividends!

Finally, the third step in the process is where the rubber meets the road. Here we consider all of the data culled from our resources and make a judgment about which of the possible meanings of the word is most appropriate in the context at hand. There are dangers here. We should not, for example, privilege the usage that sounds best, or that bests fits our theological tradition, or that best fits the way we want to interpret the passage. We must look carefully at the immediate context and the data from the innermost circles of our lexical study to determine which meaning *the author intended*. Thus we should compare any other uses of the word by the author, and especially those in proximity to this use or in a similar context. We must also consider not only the word but the words with which it is associated either by modifying them or being modified. Thus a noun, for example, must be examined in relation to the verbal idea with which it is connected, along with any accompanying modifiers.

As we finalize our assessment about how to understand the word in its context, we must allow all of the **contexts** previously explored to speak into the matter. In particular, the historical, social, cultural, literary, and intertextual contexts must have a voice in the discussion at this point. Whatever meaning we determine fits best into the immediate context of the passage must also make sense given what we know of the historical situation, the social dynamics, the cultural matrix, the literary dimensions, and the intertextual quotations and allusions. As we test the possible meanings, we must allow these areas of study to inform our results.

A Test Case

One of the most heavily debated issues in New Testament studies of late is the meaning of Paul's δικαι- terminology, which is often associated with the theological concept of "justification." Though we will not rehash the debate here, we will note that the traditional Reformed Protestant understanding of justification as a forensic activity by God, through faith, wherein God graciously imputes righteousness to the believer, as is found articulated in the Reformed confessions (e.g., Augsburg, Heidelberg, Westminster), has been much scrutinized, and various counterproposals have been offered.[4] The question here certainly concerns more than the δικαι- word group, as issues such as the historical and literary context of Paul's Letters, theological implications, and concerns with denominational traditions all factor into the debate. Questions persist in the debate as to the biblical basis for holding to imputation, whether justification is a declaration or something more (or something else entirely), whether justification should be thought of as forensic in nature, the place of justification in the order of salvation, whether justification also makes one righteous, and whether justification should be understood as the main act of God in salvation.

So, where does this leave us in analyzing the δικαι- terminology? As suggested above, our theological formulations should not drive our exegesis, but rather our understanding of the contexts of a work along with our careful attention to individual words should serve as a foundation *before* we venture on to theological explanation. It may help for us here to examine a few examples of Paul's δικαι- language to illustrate what we have outlined above. This should not be assumed to be an exhaustive attempt at constructing Paul's thought in this area but rather is merely a brief application of the steps outlined above.

Word Selection

We could go to a number of places to look at Paul's δικαι- terminology, but the Letter to the Romans is probably the most well known. Paul's use of this word group occurs throughout the letter.[5] A few of his uses are more controversial than others, but I will seek to highlight three as a means of illustrating the process I have suggested above. For our purposes, I will focus on the verbal form δικαιόω in Romans 2:13; 3:20; and 6:7. The reason for our selection of these passages is that they are highly debated and give us three different flavors of Paul's justification language. As we will see, there are good reasons for all the debate. In terms of our criteria for word selection, the terminology we have chosen represents a recurring word group, a theologically loaded word group, a word group whose meaning is not immediately clear, and a word group that is handled differently by our translations. In terms of our criteria for what words to study, we obviously have succeeded.

Lexical Analysis

Our next step is to examine the possible range of meaning for the term. We will look here primarily at lexical data, though in a fuller study we would want to look at theological dictionaries and other articles as well. To limit our study, we will primarily look at four lexicons: one to examine the Greco-Roman uses (Liddell-Scott), one to examine the LXX uses (Lust), and two to examine the New Testament data (BDAG and Louw-Nida). Liddell-Scott gives us three different glosses for δικαιόω: (1) "set right," (2) "deem as right," and (3) "do right" or "do justice." We might say, then, that we have two action-oriented senses ("to make something right" and "to do what is right") and one more cognitive or declarative sense ("to recognize something as right"). Along similar lines, Lust's lexicon recognizes two primary senses for δικαιόω: (1) "to pronounce as righteous," or "to vindicate" or "acquit"; and (2) "to be shown to be righteous."[6] Since both of these definitions contain "righteous" in their explanation, we might look further to get a better idea of the senses that the word contains in the LXX. The *NIDNTTE* entry notes that δικαιόω is often connected to the covenant stipulations and thus conveys the idea of "declaring someone in the right" or "doing what is right."[7] Moving on to our New Testament lexicons, we find that BDAG provides four different possible senses for δικαιόω: (1) to take up a legal cause ("show justice," "do justice," "take up a cause"), (2) to render a favorable verdict ("vindicate"), (3) to cause someone to be released from personal or institutional claims that are no longer to be considered pertinent or valid ("make free/pure"), and

(4) to demonstrate to be morally right ("prove to be right").[8] Finally, Louw-Nida provides the following glosses for our verb: (1) "put right with," (2) "show to be right," (3) "acquit," (4) "set free," and (5) "obey righteous commands."[9] From our survey, we find some considerable overlap between the Greco-Roman, LXX, and New Testament senses, noting, however, that the LXX typically contextualizes the term in a covenantal framework. Now that we have developed the range of meaning for our verb (though only very briefly), we can examine the three uses of the verb that we have selected for our study.[10]

Contextual Analysis

We begin first with Romans 2:13. In the preceding context (Rom. 2:1–11), Paul has asserted that God's judgment will come against humanity based on their deeds. Judgment comes to those who do evil, but eternal life comes to those who persevere in good works. The judgment will come without any prejudice, both to Jews and gentiles, on those who practice evil. Likewise, blessings will come without prejudice, both to Jews and gentiles, for those who do good. For those who know Paul as the defender of justification by faith, apart from any works, this sure does sound a lot like salvation by works. This necessitates all the more our reading of a text in its entirety rather than examining only isolated passages. This all brings us to the immediate context of Romans 2:13. In 2:12, Paul states that those who sin without the law perish without the law, and those who sin under the law will be judged by the law. Paul appears here to continue the Jew/gentile distinction made in 2:1–11. He affirms that judgment will come on those without the law (gentiles) and those under the law (Jews). We then find our selected word in 2:13, where Paul states that the doers of the law, not the hearers, δικαιωθήσονται ("will be set right"). This verb is a future, passive, indicative, which suggests this is a future event. Since we have framed the context (if only briefly), we now should consider which of our possible meanings best fits the context. It seems that the best possibilities here are "to acquit" or "to set right," since "doing right" and "setting free" don't seem to work well in the context. The future-oriented context seems to indicate that Paul has in mind here a final justification, or an eschatological verdict.[11] This raises questions, obviously, on how this passage fits with what Paul will argue in Romans 3–8, and again confirms the need to appreciate the whole argument of a letter when doing exegesis.[12]

In Romans 3, Paul continues his argument that all people, Jews and gentiles, have committed sin against God. Paul recognizes that the Jews have the advantage of possessing the oracles of God, yet some "refused to believe," presumably, as Paul will later clarify, in Jesus. In spite of this advantage, the Jews, along with gentiles, still live under the curse of sin. Paul then states, in 3:20, that "from the works of the law, no one δικαιωθήσεται." We have here the same form of the verb (future, active, indicative) as in 2:13, though here it is singular instead of plural. Paul then explains (γάρ) his statement by stating that knowledge of sin comes through the law. We obviously here would again ask which sense of δικαιόω is intended, and it seems again that the sense of "doing right" is not intended. It is possible that the "set free" sense could be intended, though the "set right" or "acquit" senses also fit in the immediate context. In Romans 3:24, however, the sense of "set free" seems to fit better, since Paul there speaks of "justification" occurring through the "redemption" or "release" (ἀπολυτρώσεως) that is in Christ Jesus.[13] What is less clear here is whether or not Paul has the final judgment in mind. So we have two possible senses that could fit into the context here that should be examined in light of the larger argument to determine which is most likely.

Finally, Romans 6:7 seems to point in yet another direction for δικαιόω. In the preceding section (Rom. 5:12–21), Paul has explored the Adam/Christ contrast, recognizing that the results of Adam's disobedience (sin and death) have been undone in the obedience of Jesus, so that God's gracious gift might reign instead of sin in death. Paul then affirms in Romans 6:1–6 that this gracious gift results not in the continued following of sin but rather in the severing of sin's sway through the believer's participation in the death and resurrection of

Jesus. This was done "for us to no longer be enslaved by sin" (Rom. 6:6). Paul then asserts in 6:7 that "the one who has died δεδικαίωται from sin." Here it seems unlikely that the notions of "doing right" or "recognizing as right" or "acquitting" fit since the verbal action is done "from sin." Rather, it seems Paul clearly has in mind the "set free" dimension of the verb that we suggested was a possible reading for Romans 3:20 and 24.

In all three of these examples we identified the word to isolate, developed the semantic domain, and then examined which sense or senses best fit in the immediate context of the passage. So how do we adequately assess and construct our understanding of these passages and how they might relate to one another? First, we obviously cannot do that in the space allotted here.[14] It is no wonder we have a vast array of commentaries available and an ever-expanding mass of specialized literature on Paul, justification, and Romans. The issues involved in apprehending the details of Paul's message are legion. To grasp the intricacies of this letter, we must wrestle with the relationship between Paul's writings and Second Temple Judaism, the Jew/gentile context that occurs throughout, the meaning of the phrase "works of the law" and its significance in Paul's argument, the overall purpose of the Letter to the Romans, the role of works at the final judgment, and the background of the δικαι- language in the Old Testament, along with many other important issues.

Word studies alone do not bring us sufficient clarity on the meaning of a passage. If all we do in the exegetical process is to examine theological vocabulary, we will not find much success in constructing a thoughtful interpretation of these texts. We indeed must plunge into grammatical and syntactical relationships and historical, social, cultural, literary, and intertextual contexts, and ultimately we must keep the whole argument of the letter in mind. All this again brings further awareness of our need to read Paul's Letters, and the New Testament writings in general, contextually in the fullest possible sense. Examining a verse or series of verses apart from the larger argument and contexts is simply insufficient for understanding the depth of the intended message. Can the basic message be ascertained without those steps? Yes, absolutely. Should we settle for understanding only the basic message? Of course not, at least not if we are committed to loving God with our minds. And so, we must view word studies as a part of the journey, a part of the hermeneutical spiral, committing ourselves to the entirety of the process in order to submit ourselves properly to the message of the New Testament. We do not easily recover two thousand years of distance. It takes time and effort. But it is time and effort well spent and well rewarded.

18

The Grammar of Theology
(Putting It All Together)

We have covered a great deal of ground and uncovered the importance of a number of different elements that must converge as we study the biblical text. This may leave some wondering, "Is there any hope for actually understanding the biblical message in light of the enormity of the task?" I would say there is great hope indeed! What becomes immediately apparent, and reinforces a good theological commitment, is that interpretation cannot take place on the island of the self. We rely on a great host of others who have gone before us to examine the Bible and its world. We rely on them not uncritically but rather reflectively, in dialogue with the text, ourselves, and others. Interpretation in isolation will no doubt lead to error. Interpretation that draws on the best elements of scholarship and the best of our Christian heritage will be rich indeed. But I would suggest there is a process that must be carefully undertaken in bringing these interpretive elements together; if we do not follow it, we could potentially short-circuit our efforts.

The Hermeneutical Spiral

As previously noted, Grant Osborne has referred to the interpretive process as a "hermeneutical spiral."[1] This means we do not move in a linear trajectory. Interpretation is an ongoing conversation, one in which, as we learn new information and expand our horizons, we continue to dialogue with our interpretive theses and refine them. We discount the journey when we view interpretation only as a destination. We do have a destination in mind, but we run on precarious ground when we assume we have arrived. The biblical text is true and reliable, but this does not guarantee that our interpretations are so. Therefore, commitment to the process of interpretation is vital.

At the risk of short-circuiting this spiraling process, I would suggest a method of approach that can be applied to a passage to help us think through its meaning well. The suggested process below is not a formula for objective interpretation. Rather, I offer it as a possible process that seeks to incorporate the elements discussed above in our examination of the passage. This should not be seen as a "seven steps and I've arrived" journey, but rather a repeated spiral that is consistently applied and reapplied as we dive into the deep waters of the New Testament.

Explore the background of the text. As mentioned above, this step is not necessarily a linear one. It takes hard work and requires the building up of knowledge over time. The best place to begin is in reading the primary sources from the period, which would include, at least, the Apocrypha, Old Testament Pseudepigrapha, Dead Sea Scrolls, and Josephus. We would do well also to examine the Greco-Roman background. Good, and generally accessible, translations of these materials are available. When, however, primary-source reading is not a possibility, there are some very good introductions to historical, social, and cultural contexts that should be consulted to expand our knowledge of the world around the New Testament. In general, exegetical commentaries are a helpful starting point since they often include the background information pertinent to the letter or book being examined. We will mention more of these resources below.

Read the text as a whole (and aloud), if possible, but if not, at least read the surrounding context. This step is vital in properly placing a text within the overall argument or story of a book. As we read, we should make mental or physical notes of recurring words, themes, and ideas. We should pay attention to the movement of the story or argument, and the natural section breaks that occur. As much as possible, we should try to read the book or letter in Greek, using an interlinear, so we can note lexical connections as we go and point out potential areas of significance or needed study. If we are right that the earliest Christians would have received these texts orally and in one sitting, we should aim to receive them that way ourselves whenever possible. In doing so, we will gain a greater appreciation for the parts in light of this whole.

Compare translations of the passage. As we dig into the exegetical details of the passage at hand, we should, again, consult the Greek text primarily. This does not mean, however, that our English translations lose their value. Rather we should compare different translations via the process suggested in chapter 15. Doing so will reveal points of tension in these translations that will also highlight exegetical issues to which we will need to attend.

Examine significant lexical and grammatical/syntactical issues. Here, again, the Greek text or an interlinear is indispensable. At this point we have already noted areas of needed focus. We now need to explore the relationships between words (something outlined in some detail in chaps. 2–14) to understand how these ideas fit together. This is where examining grammar and syntax functions and developing a structural outline of the passage are vital. In doing so, we can recognize which ideas are primary and which are secondary as well as determine which phrases and clauses are intended to modify which corresponding ideas. The result of this process should be a clear picture of the flow of thought of the passage and the relationship between its constituent parts, and especially those parts that we identified previously as needing special attention. At this point we would also pursue the various word studies that we have identified a need for through our reading and examination of the passage.

Develop a tentative description of the passage's meaning. We have by now developed some understanding of the background of the passage, read through the passage carefully, compared translations and noted points of disagreement, and examined some details of the Greek text. We at this point can formulate a tentative description of the passage's meaning. I say "tentative" for several reasons. First, we should always be willing to test and retest our interpretive hypotheses. Epistemic humility (recognizing that we are not omniscient) is vital in interpretation. Second, as we examine secondary literature, we may find new avenues of interpretation to explore that we did not uncover in our initial study. This does not mean our interpretive hypothesis will necessarily be completely reconstructed, but it can and should be refined. Third, our hypotheses are something we should revisit and refine over time as we continue to expand our understanding of the message of the New Testament.

Examine commentaries, books, and articles on the passage. At this point we have interacted with a number of sources but have not focused primarily on examining what others say about our text. We intentionally have saved this step for after our analysis is completed. If we go to the commentaries and secondary literature first, not only do we shortcircuit our learning process, but we may adopt a conclusion about the passage that our independent study of it would not have produced. As we examine commentaries, books, and articles on the passage, we should make note of and compare the various interpretations we come across. Good exegetical commentaries will often outline these for us. If we find in our reading that we are not coming across divergent interpretations, we are not reading broadly enough. And as we read, we must test the hypotheses of the secondary literature against our own analysis. We may find points that further support our ideas and points that correct some deficient aspect of our own interpretation. Again, I will suggest some starting places for secondary literature below.

Refine the description of the passage's meaning. Having done our own firsthand analysis and then invested some time in examining the analyses of others, we are now ready to refine our description of the passage. We should, again, be willing to hold aspects of our interpretation loosely. Though we are convinced now that we have produced an accurate description of the meaning of the text, new information or further study down the road may alter it. We must also remember that we are not now at the end of the process, as if we have exhausted the meaning of the text, but rather we have completed one loop of an ongoing spiral.

Attitudes

I have introduced at some length some important methods for examining the Greek text of the New Testament and immersing ourselves in the context of the New Testament. It would be negligent, however, not to recognize that we are dealing here not simply with a collection of literature (though it is that) but with sacred writ. As a result, we do not come to the text merely to analyze it and fill our minds with new, good information. Rather, we come to it to be transformed by the Triune God to whom it gives witness. This means that not only do we need a correct approach to the text, but we need to approach it correctly. We thus must think about the **attitude** with which we study the Holy Scriptures.

First, we must recognize that our commitment to a disciplined, contextual reading of Scripture does not nullify our need to be **dependent on the Holy Spirit**. Sometimes eager students or pastors will comment that all of this study is unnecessary since the Spirit will lead us to truth. Usually John 14:26 is in mind here, but understanding the context helps us to see that the conclusion sometimes drawn from this text isn't what Jesus intended. Jesus is speaking here to his disciples and tells them that the Spirit will bring to their remembrance his teachings. This presupposes that they have received and understood these teachings. Yes, the Spirit will aid us in proclaiming Jesus to others, but, as Ben Witherington has stated so well, it would be a shame not to give the Spirit more to work with.[2] Further, from a logical perspective, if the Spirit is leading both of us and we come to contradictory interpretations, this means either we assume the Spirit is really leading only one of us (me, of course!) and the others are wrong, or the Spirit is contradicting himself. Either way, we are left with quite the logical conundrum. The Spirit brings illumination and remembrance, but this does not mean the need for serious study is eliminated. I hope I have demonstrated throughout this volume the great value of reading carefully, contextually, and in the original languages.

Second, we must also be **open to correction**. I suggested earlier that we all come with presuppositions and biases to certain theological ideas and traditions. We bring that baggage with us when we read the Bible. In order to avoid simply reading our theological preferences into the text, we must delve deep into the contexts of Scripture. Ultimately this means we must be willing to hear what the New Testament says, in its original context, to its original hearers, and accept that message as divinely inspired truth. When our contextual interpretation rubs against our theological tradition, we must be open to correct our beliefs rather than maintaining them against the grain of Scripture. To put it another way (again), we must be committed to *under*-standing the text rather than *over*-standing the text. When we stand over the text, we impose our views on it. When we stand under the text, we humbly accept its message.

Third, this means, in part, we must be **committed to a trajectory of discovery**. As we have seen, the interpretive process does not progress along a linear path. As we gain new information, we enhance our understanding of the text and our ability to communicate it. If we read Scripture to confirm our existing beliefs, we risk not hearing what it, and ultimately God through it, has to say to us. If, however, we posture ourselves in a position of openness and discovery, we will be all the more ready to absorb and apply its teachings.

Fourth, we must avoid the temptation to make the interpretive process an isolated one. Study and application of Scripture must come in a **communal context**. When we divorce ourselves from the community of faith, we put ourselves in opposition to the pattern outlined in the New Testament. I suggested earlier that there are good reasons to believe these texts were used in collective settings in the earliest churches. When these letters were read, they were read to a corporate community and received for corporate practice. When we look, for example, at the commands of the New Testament, very few of them can be carried out in an individual setting. Take the fruit of the Spirit, for example. What good do love, joy, peace, patience, kindness, goodness, and self-control have apart from a community in which to exercise them? The same is true of reading Scripture. Our interpretations will be best served by discussing them in a community context, learning from one another, and growing in community. Just as we must rely on the work of others in our grammatical, lexical, and contextual study, so we must interpret and apply the text in community.

Finally, I must reiterate that we do not study Scripture merely to gain new or more information. Rather, we study Scripture to **experience transformation**. The New Testament should not be set off as some ancient relic to study for only historical purposes. We should study the New Testament as a historical document. But as Scripture, it must be allowed to inform our life, thoughts, attitudes, and relationships. To rightly take hold of the New Testament means to allow its message to take hold of us. As we grow in deeper understanding and appreciation of the message of the Lord and the teachings of his earliest followers, we must receive that message as having an authoritative voice in our life, both individually and collectively as the church.

This phenomenon stands out in many of Paul's Letters. As mentioned previously, Paul often structures his letters in an indicative-imperative construct. This means he begins first with theological realities (primarily about the Triune God and his activity) and then draws from those realities implications for living as God's people. Ephesians provides a helpful example of this. The first three chapters of the letter, though also including prayers, primarily, through a heightened form of rhetoric, remind the recipients about the reality of the divine work that they have experienced. The final three chapters focus on imperatives, or commands, for working out that reality in their everyday life as God's people. To ignore the transformative intent of the New Testament is to miss its central purpose. As speech-act theory has reminded us, texts do not just have something to say, but they have something to do. They expect to elicit reactions and behaviors, perlocutionary effects, from their readers. We must keep this intent in mind as we interpret the New Testament and respond to those intended effects accordingly.

Aids

In addition to the proper attitude, we also need the right kind of **aids** to help guide us deeper into the New Testament and its world. We spoke at some length in chapter 16 about what areas of context we should attend to as we examine the text. In this section I will recommend some specific aids to help with that enterprise. What I hope to do here is offer some starting points for examining the various layers of the context of a passage.

Historical, Cultural, and Social Context Resources

As we mentioned earlier, reading the primary sources is ideal, but when these are not accessible, other resources give helpful insights to the ancient Mediterranean world. The resources that address historical, cultural, and social issues often overlap in their focus, so I have combined them here under one heading. Two excellent and rather comprehensive dictionaries provide a very helpful reference tool for examining these background items. The *Dictionary of New Testament Background* (part of a whole-Bible dictionary series that includes several other New Testament and post–New Testament volumes) and *The Eerdmans Dictionary of Early Judaism* give readers a thorough introduction to the major literature, cultural and social dynamics, and historical events and persons of the Greco-Roman and Jewish worlds. Both are written by a collection of experts in the issues and topics covered. In addition, the *Anchor Bible Dictionary*, *Eerdmans Dictionary of the Bible*, and *Lexham Bible Dictionary* include helpful articles on background items and biblical interpretation issues as well.[3]

While most exegetical commentaries will also give an account of the historical situation of particular books of the New Testament, the *IVP Bible Background Commentary: New Testament* supplies important historical and cultural contextual information in a verse-by-verse format, making it an excellent resource for exegetical purposes. There are also works, such as C. K. Barrett's *New Testament Background* and Craig Evans's *Ancient Texts for New Testament Studies*, that are helpful introductions to the literature of the period. *The World of the New Testament* (ed. Green and McDonald) also provides readers with insightful articles by top-notch scholars on historical, cultural, and social background issues in the Jewish, Hellenistic, and Greco-Roman contexts. Everett Ferguson's *Backgrounds of Early Christianity* also constructs a helpful framework of the world of the New Testament and beyond, covering historical, political, cultural, social, and religious background issues. Likewise, Bruce Malina's *New Testament World* gives important insights into the social setting of the New Testament, dealing with cultural values, social structures and relationships, and religious identity. Many other sources could be recommended, but these will offer readers a thorough orientation to the world of the New Testament.[4]

Literary, Intertextual, and Canonical Context Resources

As with the previous section, the resources that address literary, intertextual, and canonical connections often overlap. First, a number of more in-depth exegetical texts are available that take readers deeper into the process than what we have been able to outline here. One of the go-to volumes for some time now has been Klein, Blomberg, and Hubbard's *Introduction to Biblical Interpretation*, which covers with some thoroughness the history of interpretive methods, canonicity, the role of the interpreter, literary considerations, and the implications of interpretation. Bock and Fanning's *Interpreting the New Testament Text* also offers a helpful introduction to the process while providing a number of exegetical examples from leading New Testament scholars. Bauer and Traina's *Inductive Bible Study* explains a very helpful and thorough method for thinking through texts, developing hypotheses, and evaluating and refining them. Two shorter, but very helpful, volumes are Blomberg's *Handbook of New Testament Exegesis* and Erickson's *Beginner's Guide to New Testament Exegesis*, which are accessible introductions to the exegetical process that are full of examples applying the principles outlined and practical advice for readers.[5]

Beyond exegetical introductions, several other types of resources can give helpful insights in these areas. Moisés Silva's *Biblical Words and Their Meaning* is a helpful introduction to understanding the structure of language as it relates to word meaning. Ben Witherington's *New Testament Rhetoric* presents an introduction to ancient rhetorical strategies and their application in the New Testament. Likewise, Joel Green's *Hearing the New Testament* introduces and offers illustrations of various methods of interpretation, providing readers with a diverse swath of methodologies and showing the value of their application to the New Testament. While many helpful works are available for examining the use of the Old Testament in the New Testament, probably the two most important for the interpretation process are the *Commentary on the New Testament Use of the Old Testament* and *Old Testament Quotations in the New Testament*.[6]

Finally, we must also mention a few of the very helpful commentary series available. For less-technical commentaries, these are some recommended series:

NIV Application Commentary (Zondervan)

Baker Exegetical Commentary on the New Testament (Baker Academic)

Pillar New Testament Commentary (Eerdmans)

Tyndale New Testament Commentaries (Eerdmans)

Expositor's Bible Commentary (Zondervan)

Socio-Rhetorical Commentary Series (Eerdmans)

New American Commentary (B&H)

Interpretation (Westminster John Knox)

Abingdon New Testament Commentaries (Abingdon)

Story of God Bible Commentary (Zondervan)

On the more technical side, some helpful series are the following:

Word Biblical Commentary (Thomas Nelson)

New International Commentary on the New Testament (Eerdmans)

New International Greek Testament Commentary (Eerdmans)

Zondervan Exegetical Commentary on the New Testament (Zondervan)

International Critical Commentary (T&T Clark)

Anchor Yale Bible Commentaries (Yale)

New Testament Library (Westminster John Knox)

Baylor Handbook on the Greek New Testament (Baylor University Press)

Exegetical Guide to the Greek New Testament (B&H)

Since our goal is to more deeply examine the text of the New Testament in its original context and language, the more-technical commentaries will offer more-detailed interactions with the Greek text. This is not to say that the less-technical commentaries do not base their interpretation on the Greek text or yield insights from time to time. Rather they provide less-focused and less-consistent insights on the Greek text, whereas the New International Greek Testament Commentary, for example, gives more-consistent critical examination. The downside is that the more-technical commentaries are more difficult to work through for those who are new to the biblical languages. That being said, some combination of the two lists will afford a helpful balance in working through the interpretive insights of others. Many more series could be included in these lists, so this should not be thought to be exhaustive. Rather, they are provided to give some starting points for exegetical resources.

Application

We have emphasized in the preceding material the historical, cultural, and social situatedness of the New Testament writings. We might wonder at this point, "If the New Testament writings were intended for such specific audiences and purposes, how are they relevant for us today?" First, we can assume that they are because the message that they proclaim still endures. The lordship of Jesus does not come with temporal restrictions. Second, they were written to inform the life of local churches in the ancient world. Thus, though they come temporally situated, we do well to hear and heed the instructions they convey. Third, they have informed the life of the church for two thousand years, giving guidance to believers everywhere in varying geographical and temporal contexts.

This does not mean that application comes easy, however. If we approach these documents with common sense and consistency, we should readily admit that the text of the New Testament *cannot mean for us what it did not mean in its original context*. In other words, as we think about application, our application must take into account— indeed, must depend on—how the text was intended to function for its original recipients. When we consider how to apply the text in our own situation, we must examine how comparable our context is to theirs. If we are honest with ourselves, we all have misapplied Scripture through various means, whether by "claiming" a verse that contextually has nothing to do with how we use it, or by hoping to find divine direction through flipping pages and pointing to a random passage for direction. Can God use our silly and feeble attempts to reveal his will? Absolutely! Should that, however, be our default mode of operation? Likely not. While we do not have a one-size-fits-all formula for guaranteeing appropriate application of a passage when we move from the ancient context to our contemporary setting, there are some helpful guidelines we can follow to aim at accomplishing application with contextual sensitivity.

What Did It Mean?

The first step necessary to approaching a contextually sensitive application is to understand the meaning of the passage in its original context. I have said much about this previously, particularly in chapter 16, so I will not rehash that conversation here. If we intend to understand what the passage meant, we must gain appreciation for the historical, social, cultural, literary, intertextual, and canonical factors at work. In doing so, we will develop a more robust understanding of what the author intended to communicate to the original audience.

What Was the Intended Response?

As discussed earlier, the books of the New Testament intended not just to transmit new information but to bring personal and communal transformation. The various genres all expect behavioral responses from their readers. As we saw with Paul, sometimes this pattern moves from theology (indicative) to application (imperative), in a two-step process. When a direct command emerges, we can give thought to its motivating purpose (Is there a specific issue, or is it a general charge?) as we consider the role the command plays in the larger literary context. Other times the expected behavioral responses emerge less overtly, through parable, symbol, narrative, or some other form. Before we move to thinking about how a text should inform our thoughts and actions, we must first consider its intended effects for its original hearers. We must consider the perlocutionary intent for the first audience before reflecting on its intent for us.

What Is the Level of Contextual Comparability?

Having sufficiently considered the contextual meaning and originally intended effects, we are now ready to begin translating the text to our world. There are commands in the Bible that are time and culture bound and no longer apply to us today. The purity laws in the Old Testament book of Leviticus, for example, do not maintain legal force today for several reasons. First, they were intended for a theocratic situation that no longer exists. Second, the New Testament indicates that gentile Christ-followers should not feel obligation to keep various aspects of the Old Testament law. This does not mean that we can learn nothing or gain nothing in terms of personal devotion and behavior from studying them. Rather, it means we cannot read them as if they had direct bearing on our situation.

Not every command in the New Testament, however, is restricted or bound to a particular context or situation. When Paul, for example, proclaims in Acts 17:30 that God expects that "all people everywhere should repent," we should readily recognize a universal thrust to how we receive that message. Or when Paul says in 1 Timothy 2:8 that he desires for "men everywhere to pray," we can assume that a fairly universal application emerges. We find no contextual indications that there were explicit cultural motivations for this action that would restrict our own application of it. What about, however, when we keep reading in 1 Timothy and find that women should not have "elaborate hairstyles or gold or pearls or expensive clothes" (1 Tim. 2:9 NIV)? Would we say this command is culture bound or universal? And what about when Paul writes, "A woman should learn in quietness and full submission. I do not permit a woman to teach or to assume authority over a man; she must be quiet" (1 Tim. 2:11–12 NIV)? The application (and interpretation) of this passage is debated. When Paul brings up Adam and Eve in the passage, is he pointing toward a universal expectation rooted in creation? Or does the connection with the fall indicate this might be reversed "in Christ"? And what implication does Paul's issue with false teachers in chapter 1 of the letter have for what he says here? And what should we make of Paul stating this is something "he" does not permit? Does that mean it is apostolic preference or a divine command? These and other interpretive questions on this passage have obvious implications for the meaning of the text. But they also have major implications for application. If we determine the passage has some cultural or situational conditioning, this would obviously lift the restriction many denominations have against women preaching to or teaching the congregation. If we determine it has universal intent, then those denominations have instead properly appropriated the passage into their context.

These are the kinds of questions we ask at this point in the application process, and this step is vital to correctly applying the passage at hand. If we overlook cultural particulars, we run the risk of taking a situational command and universalizing it. Likewise, if we restrict a passage that had intended universal application, we move again in the wrong direction. Some questions here can help guide us through the process:[7]

Does the text present a broad principle or a specific command? We would expect that the more specific a command, the greater the possibility it has some cultural restrictions, while the more general a command, the greater the possibility it has broader application. As we saw with our example above, this is part of the core of the issue in how various interpreters approach 1 Timothy 2. When we find Paul speaking about head coverings in 1 Corinthians 11, we must inquire *why* this command was given, what cultural particulars are connected to it, and subsequently what relevance it has for us today.

Does the larger context of the book limit its application? We find an issue similar to that in 1 Timothy 2 in 1 Corinthians 14, where Paul writes, "Women should remain silent in the churches" (1 Cor. 14:34 NIV). We might take this injunction to be corroborative evidence for how to interpret 1 Timothy 2. Returning to 1 Corinthians 11, however, we find there that Paul states women are to pray and prophesy with their head covered (1 Cor. 11:5). If they are praying or prophesying in the setting of corporate worship, it is difficult for them to be silent! We must thus consider the whole of the argument in our interpretation unless we take Paul to be contradicting himself in a span of just a few chapters.

Is the command limited by a later teaching, or does it occur on a canonical trajectory? The concept of progressive revelation instructs us to interpret Scripture with Scripture by examining earlier writings in light of later ones. Returning to the question of the law and the gentile Christian, when we find Paul adamant in Romans and Galatians that gentile Christians need not be circumcised, we understand that new revelation has refined the previous understanding of divine expectations.

A clear example of this phenomenon is found in Matthew 5:38–42. Here Jesus, referencing Exodus 21:24; Leviticus 24:20; and Deuteronomy 19:21, states that instead of an "eye for an eye and a tooth for a tooth," retribution should not be sought against an evil person. Rather, he instructs his hearers to "turn the other cheek," to give their tunic and outer garment, and to go two miles. Jesus redirects and restrains the original commandment given through Moses. Likewise, in Matthew 19, Jesus restricts the Mosaic allowance for divorce (cf. Deut. 24:1) to applying only in situations of sexual immorality. That earlier teaching has been clarified by Jesus.

So, we must consider the canonical witness as we think about application. When we come to an issue like slavery, which is allowed in Old Testament Israel, yet we find Paul stating there is "neither slave nor free" (Gal. 3:28) and apparently urging Philemon to release Onesimus (Philem. 15–22), we seem to see a trajectory of development in the scriptural witness. Our application of texts must recognize such trajectories if and when they are present.

Is a clear cultural restriction present that limits the application of the passage? We earlier raised the question of the head coverings of 1 Corinthians 11. Many interpreters would say that the passage is restricted in application because it offers the command specifically to address cultural expectations. For men to have short hair or women to have long hair is not a universal truth or good. Rather, in an honor-and-shame culture like Paul's (notice how much honor-shame language is present in the passage), to overstep these expectations would have sent mixed messages to the Greco-Roman and Jewish world. Paul's commands seem to have, at least in part, an apologetic orientation rather than a universal standard of hair length in mind. (Fortunately, it seems God is not quite so concerned about our preferred hairdo. He is concerned, however, with the impressions the behavior of his people might give to outsiders, especially ones that are potentially linked with unwholesome or corrupt practices.) Or again, when we read 1 Corinthians 10:14–22, we recognize that we do not share the same cultural particulars as the Corinthians since eating meat sacrificed to idols is not a common phenomenon in the Western world.

How does the command or teaching compare to other ancient cultural teachings? As we have already noted, being aware of the cultural and social situation of the ancient world greatly enhances our understanding of the New Testament. When we understand the prevailing roles and expectations in the ancient world, we can see with greater clarity how the teachings and commands of the New Testament push against those entities. Ephesians 5:21–25 provides a helpful example. In Paul's instructions, several elements stand out as fairly radical. Instructing the Ephesian believers to submit to one another was certainly a countercultural idea and bypassed the way in which social life was structured in the Greco-Roman world. Likewise, though wives were expected to submit to their husbands in the Roman household, Paul qualifies this with "as to the Lord," grounding his teaching in a spiritual reality rather than in a social framework. Further, Paul's teaching for husbands to love their wives in a self-sacrificial manner is likely the most radical of all, since such a command seems to find no precedent in the Greco-Roman or Jewish worlds. Thus, understanding the social expectations for ancient households can greatly inform how we understand Paul's admonitions in this passage.

Does the command or teaching present conditions or limitations on what is stated? Another question to consider as we examine the application of the passage is what limitations a passage presents for its application. This is probably one of the more common areas where passages are misapplied. Philippians 4:13 provides a notoriously misused example. Here Paul writes, "I am able to do all things through the one who is strengthening me." This verse has become a slogan for Christian success, adopted as a motto and taken to mean that we can achieve our dreams and goals through the power given to us by Jesus. In the context of the passage, however, Paul addresses living during both times of abundance and times of need. His statement in 4:13 must be understood in light of what precedes it, where Paul says, "I have learned to be content in whatever *circumstances* I am" (Phil. 4:11 LEB).

Likewise, the words of Jesus in Matthew 7:7 (NASB)—"Ask, and it will be given to you; seek, and you will find; knock, and it will be opened to you"—are sometimes taken to mean that God will give us whatever we want. In the context, Jesus has in mind specifically the "good things" that God delights to give to his people (cf. Matt. 7:11). And in the larger context of the Sermon on the Mount (since chapter 7 is a part of a larger discourse), we find Jesus instructing that the prayer of his followers should be kingdom oriented and for God's will to be done (cf. 6:10) and also that his followers should accumulate not wealth on earth but treasure in heaven (cf. 6:19). Likewise in Matthew 6:33, where Jesus admonishes his hearers to "seek first his kingdom and righteousness, and all these *things* will be added to you" (LEB), "all these things" refers back to God providing (specifically food, drink, and clothing here) for his creatures (cf. 6:25–32). So we should not take these instructions in Matthew 6:33 and 7:7 to mean that God will give us whatever we ask (e.g., that Ferrari you've always wanted), but rather they mean that he will supply us with what we need as it accords with his will and as we seek his kingdom above all else.

If Contexts Are Not Comparable, What Is the Underlying Principle?

If there is a high degree of comparability between the ancient context and our own, it is likely that the application will be quite similar. If, however, there is not, we should consider the underlying principle at work in that original situation. We will likely find a principle that can be applied to our situation even if the original application cannot.

Sometimes this principle might be made explicit in the text itself, while other times we must, through carefully considering the passage and its contexts, derive the principle ourselves.

When we come to a passage like 1 Corinthians 16:1–4, we obviously do not share identically in the circumstances. Paul here writes to the Corinthians, asking for their participation in the "collection for the saints," which likely refers to his desire to bring some financial relief to the poor, struggling Jewish believers in Jerusalem (cf. Rom. 15:26; 2 Cor. 8:13; 9:12; Gal. 2:10). We cannot participate in that collection (barring the invention of some time-travel capability). Our situation is not identical. Our situation is, however, comparable. Just as Paul expected each believer to give as they were able to help these impoverished believers, so too we can and should give from our means to help those in need, and particularly those of the household of faith (cf. Gal. 6:10). The principle here is that each believer should be involved in helping those in need as they are able, and the principle is readily extended into our own situation.

A little more difficult, perhaps, is a passage like 1 Corinthians 10:14–33, which we have briefly mentioned already. Since the worshiping of idols and the question of whether or not to purchase and eat meat sacrificed to them generally is not relevant for us today, we do not share the particulars of the original situation, and we cannot directly apply the text. Paul, however, clarifies the underlying motivation of his instructions. In 1 Corinthians 10:28–29, Paul states that these instructions are given as a matter of respecting conscience. Though Paul recognizes one may eat in good conscience, he forbids knowingly partaking of food sacrificed to idols for the sake of the conscience of others (cf. 1 Cor. 10:29–33). Paul seeks to create unity and to prevent offense among fellow believers. Though some may not object to the practice, others will and will take offense at it, and thus believers should avoid it. The principle that emerges here is clear even if the situation is not comparable: *In matters of conscience, avoid living in a way that would cause offense to fellow believers*. There are numerous specific situations in which this principle can (and should) apply for believers today even if we do not share in the particulars of the original situation.

What Are Specific Ways the Principle Can Be Applied Today?

As we move from ancient context and text to modern context and application, avoiding the temptation to produce generic applications will produce more fruitful results. Too often applications end at developing principles. But principles and applications are not one and the same. In a teaching setting in particular, finding specific means of application will produce helpful benefits. This does not mean that the principle should be restricted to a particular form of application but rather means that context-appropriate suggestions for how to actually apply the text should be offered. As an example, I suggested above that the principle derived from Paul's discussion of meat sacrificed to idols can be summarized as follows: *In matters of conscience, avoid living in a way that would cause offense to fellow believers*. So what does this look like? What matters of conscience would apply here? Things like alcohol consumption, what kind of media we consume (TV, music, movies, etc.), and gambling come to mind. In other words, what morally questionable activities relate to the principle of avoiding offense to fellow believers? Those are the kinds of issues that could be specifically addressed via the principle suggested. We are not talking here about things specifically forbidden in Scripture, such as sexual immorality, stealing, or lying. Rather, we have in mind specifically potential gray areas of moral action. Providing specific examples fitting to the context of the contemporary community in view can foster a stronger link between principle and application.

The task of bringing a two-thousand-year-old text to bear on our lives today is not always simple or straightforward. Not all of the teachings and commands of the New Testament elude our understanding due to deep cultural embedding. Some are more straightforward than others. This does not mean we should assume that we can properly navigate them, however, without first understanding their larger background and, second, examining the context in which they occur. We find some significant challenges when the situation is not comparable, and this is where we must examine the original situation and ours carefully to determine how the text speaks to us today.

A word of caution is necessary here. We should not get lost in the trees of application and miss the forest of the biblical story. The Bible reveals to us the character and plan of the Triune God. We must avoid the narcissistic tendencies of Western culture in making the Bible a book about us. Quite simply, it is not. The Bible has meaning and implications for us, but it is not about us. The Bible is about God: Father, Son, and Spirit. And it is about God's plan to rescue and restore his world and his creatures. We are not the hero of the Bible, and neither are its many characters, honorable though many of them may be. We are the captives set free by the Hero. As we read Scripture, we *should* ask how it intends to transform us. But we err if we make the Bible merely a storehouse of information to help us live better. The Bible has transformative value, but only because it comes from a loving and powerful Father who brings transformation in his Son and through his Spirit.

Nonetheless, as we embrace the biblical story, the God it reveals, and the world in which it was formed, we do so recognizing, as a part of the church, that it does have intended outcomes for our life. We must not neglect, then, as we consider the relevance of various passages for our life today, to approach these questions with the proper attitude and disposition. Our journey to live rightly in an upside-down world must find a central role for prayer. Reflective prayer. Petitioning prayer. Praising prayer. Prayer in the Spirit. We dare not come to the text and ignore the spiritual dimension. We also must recognize the role of community, as we have already mentioned, in how we live out the text. We cannot follow the patterns outlined in the New Testament apart from the community of faith. And that means our prayer, interpretation, application, and fellowship should all take place individually *and* corporately. There we will find the fullest possible sense of spiritual learning and growth.

Where Do We Go from Here?

I have already suggested some aids for helping to develop contextual sensitivity in the exegetical process. We should not neglect, however, to remind ourselves that we must also aim to integrate Greek into our study of the New Testament at the grammatical and syntactical levels. What I introduced in chapters 2–13 sought to provide a basic framework for doing just that. We looked at grammatical and syntactical basics by parts of speech and attempted, by making the most of our English tools, to gain a functional understanding of Koine Greek. I must present here both a word of caution and an exhortation.

This functional understanding of Greek will open new doors for studying the New Testament. Resources and ways of thought that were far off have been brought near. We must remind ourselves, however, that this does not give us any level of expertise. We have the ability to understand some grammatical frameworks and interact with good exegetical commentaries and essays. We even have some ability to evaluate those resources. We have not, however, developed proficiency with the language. As a student and teacher of the language, I find it my duty to caution here against overestimating what we have gained from this study.

I also find it necessary to encourage you to move forward in exploring grammar and syntax. It is not within our scope to do that here. There are, however, many excellent resources available that will take you beyond our introductory and functional approach to developing a more comprehensive understanding of the language. If I have whetted your appetite here (and I hope I have), by all means, please continue!

First, many excellent **grammars** are available that take their readers through all the forms of Koine Greek. In our functional approach here, we have interacted minimally with morphology (how words are formed), though I have provided key paradigms in an appendix. To develop reading proficiency, we need deeper familiarity with grammar and morphology. The first, and probably most widely used, grammar is William Mounce's *Basics of Biblical Greek*. Mounce's text gives an excellent introduction to Greek grammar and provides very helpful resources to aid students in the transition. I would also recommend Rodney Decker's *Reading Koine Greek*, which offers a bit more of an in-depth approach and also seeks to develop exegetical skills along with the grammatical exploration. Finally, Stanley Porter's *Fundamentals of New Testament Greek* also gives an in-depth and slightly more technical and likewise comprehensive introduction to Greek grammar.[8]

Beyond the grammatical introductions, several important **syntactical resources** are also available. The standard remains Daniel Wallace's *Greek Grammar beyond the Basics*. Wallace provides an exhaustive introduction to syntactical issues and also gives the reader a very valuable reference tool. Wallace also now offers a less-extensive companion, entitled *The Basics of New Testament Syntax*. A less-exhaustive (or exhausting, depending on your perspective!) but equally helpful treatment is Stanley Porter's *Idioms of the Greek New Testament*, which supplies insightful analysis and treatment of intermediate grammar and syntax issues. Also to be recommended is Steven Runge's *Discourse Grammar of the Greek New Testament*, which takes a more function-oriented approach to how the Greek language operates. For Logos users, Runge's *Discourse Greek New Testament Bundle* offers a useful integration of Runge's analysis with the biblical text. David Alan Black's *Linguistics for Students of New Testament Greek* also is a very useful introduction to the field of linguistics for the intermediate student of Greek. Finally, several more-specialized works that deal with specific aspects of the language should be consulted. Constantine Campbell's *Basics of Verbal Aspect in Biblical Greek* provides a very helpful introduction and practical framework for understanding and integrating verbal aspect into exegesis. Finally, Murray Harris's *Prepositions and Theology in the Greek New Testament* is a useful tool for examining those small but very important words.[9]

A Final Word

I have approached this text intent on accomplishing two things: (1) laying a foundation for those who lack formal training in the biblical language to gain insights from the original language of the New Testament, and (2) providing an exegetical framework to help guide the way in which those insights are developed. If those two things have been accomplished, then I am grateful indeed.

I have tried to reiterate throughout that one voice, or one book, or one author, or one interpreter is entirely insufficient for the task of rightly interpreting the New Testament. We must commit ourselves as much to the process of interpretation as to its principles. Learning and growth are processes, and to prioritize the goal over the process means that neither will be accomplished. In other words, if we focus solely on the end in mind (i.e., the information itself), we miss out on how learning actually occurs. My prayer is that this book spurs its readers on to undertake a trajectory of going further and deeper in studying the New Testament, both in the original languages and in exegetical method.

I have provided a brief and condensed language foundation. Those who wish to build some reading fluency and a more refined understanding of Greek grammar should continue with the sources mentioned earlier in this chapter. There is far more to the language of the New Testament and the skills necessary to explore it with some exactness than what is offered in this book. Further grammatical and syntactical study is necessary to gain some mastery. What I hope to have achieved in this book is to offer an introduction to allow the basic contours to be navigated with some awareness of the intricacies, dangers, and rewards of the process. We must remind ourselves again that this entails neither mastery of the intricacies of nor expertise in even all of the grammatical basics.

I also hope to have conveyed the importance of not confusing our interpretations with inspired revelation. While we work to make our interpretations correspond to the intended meaning of the text, we do well to recognize the difference between what philosophers refer to as "ontology" and "epistemology." "Ontology" refers to what is, or reality, and "epistemology" to knowledge, or what is known. The "ontological meaning" of the text refers to its original, intended sense as penned by the author and received by its audience. The "epistemological meaning" refers to what we know of the text, or our interpretation of it. The goal of exegesis is to bring the two into conformity. The epistemic humility I advocated earlier is vital in committing ourselves to the process. Possessing this mentality means we are both open to correction and continuing to pursue a deeper understanding. As Paul reminds us in 1 Corinthians 13:12, "For now we see in a mirror dimly, but then face to face; now I know in part, but then I will know fully just as I also have been fully known" (NASB). So now we press on to fuller knowledge, awaiting the day when we will know face to face instead of through these reflections alone.

"Your Turn" Answers

Chapter 6 (1 John 1:9)

- ἁμαρτίας: feminine, accusative, plural; direct object
- πιστός: masculine, nominative, singular; predicate nominative (the implied subject of the verb, "he," is the subject)
- δίκαιος: masculine, nominative, singular; predicate nominative (the implied subject of the verb, "he," is the subject; also when two words of the same case are connected by καί as in this example, they usually share the same function)

Chapter 7 (Colossians 1:3)

- θεῷ: masculine, dative, singular; indirect object
- πατρί: masculine, dative, singular; simple apposition (modifying θεῷ)
- κυρίου: masculine, genitive, singular; relationship
- ἡμῶν: 1st person, genitive, plural; relationship, possession, or subordination

- Ἰησοῦ: masculine, genitive, singular; simple apposition (modifying κυρίου)
- Χριστοῦ: masculine, genitive, singular; simple apposition (modifying κυρίου)

Chapter 8 (Matthew 26:18)

- εἰς: preposition; specifies direction (*"into* the city")
- τήν: article; feminine, accusative, singular; particularizes πόλιν
- πρός: preposition; specifies direction (*"to* a certain man")
- τόν: article; masculine, accusative, singular; substantiver (with δεῖνα)
- δεῖνα: adjective; masculine, accusative, singular; substantival adjective
- αὐτῷ: personal pronoun; masculine, dative, singular; replaces noun; functions as indirect object

Chapter 9 (1 John 1:2)

- ἐφανερώθη: aorist, passive, indicative, 3rd person, singular; summary
- ἑωράκαμεν: perfect, active, indicative, 1st person, plural; emphasizes completion
- μαρτυροῦμεν: present, active, indicative, 1st person, plural; in progress or repetition

Chapter 10 (Revelation 3:19)

- ζήλευε: present, active, imperative, 2nd person, singular; in the context, this is probably a command to begin and continue an action

- μετανόησον: aorist, active, imperative, 2nd person, singular; summary or beginning of action

Chapter 11 (Revelation 19:7)

- χαίρωμεν: present, active, subjunctive, 1st person, plural; hortatory
- ἀγαλλιῶμεν: present, active, subjunctive, 1st person, plural; hortatory
- δώσωμεν: aorist, active, subjunctive, 1st person, plural; hortatory

Chapter 12 (2 Corinthians 7:3)

- συναποθανεῖν: aorist, active, infinitive; purpose/result
- συζῆν: present, active, infinitive; purpose/result (remember, when two words of the same form are connected by καί, as in this example, they usually share the same function)

Chapter 13 (1 John 5:1)

- ἀγαπῶν: present, active, participle, masculine, nominative, singular; substantival
- γεννήσαντα: aorist, active, participle, masculine, accusative, singular; substantival
- γεγεννημένον: perfect, passive, participle, masculine, accusative, singular; substantival

Chapter 14 (1 John 1:5)

Καὶ ἔστιν αὕτη ἡ ἀγγελία (main)
　　ἣν ἀκηκόαμεν (subordinate—relative-pronoun clause)
　　　ἀπ᾽ αὐτοῦ (subordinate—prepositional phrase)

καὶ ἀναγγέλλομεν ὑμῖν, (subordinate—relative-pronoun clause, continued)

ὅτι ὁ θεὸς φῶς ἐστιν (subordinate—content clause, introduced by ὅτι)

καὶ σκοτία . . . οὐκ ἔστιν οὐδεμία (subordinate—content clause, continued)

   ἐν αὐτῷ (subordinate—prepositional phrase)

APPENDIX 2

Greek Paradigms

The following pages contain paradigms for the various Greek parts of speech. These are not comprehensive but are intended to serve both as a reference point for those who may not have quick access to parsing tools and as a study aid for those who want to further develop their reading skills by memorizing these common paradigms.

Nouns

Table 1. First-Declension Nouns

Case, Number	First Declension (fem.; ε, ι, ρ stems)	First Declension (fem.; σ, ξ, ψ stems)	First Declension (fem.; other stems)	First Declension (masc.)
nom., sg.	ἡμέρα	δόξα	φωνή	προφήτης
gen., sg.	ἡμέρας	δόξης	φωνῆς	προφήτου
dat., sg.	ἡμέρᾳ	δόξῃ	φωνῇ	προφήτῃ
acc., sg.	ἡμέραν	δόξαν	φωνήν	προφήτην
nom., pl.	ἡμέραι	δόξαι	φωναί	προφῆται
gen., pl.	ἡμερῶν	δοξῶν	φωνῶν	προφητῶν
dat., pl.	ἡμέραις	δόξαις	φωναῖς	προφήταις
acc., pl.	ἡμέρας	δόξας	φωνάς	προφήτας

Table 2. Second-Declension Nouns

Case, Number	Second Declension (masc.)	Second Declension (neut.)	Second Declension (fem.)
nom., sg.	ἄνθρωπος	δῶρον	ὁδός
gen., sg.	ἀνθρώπου	δώρου	ὁδοῦ
dat., sg.	ἀνθρώπῳ	δώρῳ	ὁδῷ
acc., sg.	ἄνθρωπον	δῶρον	ὁδόν
nom., pl.	ἄνθρωποι	δῶρα	ὁδοί
gen., pl.	ἀνθρώπων	δώρων	ὁδῶν
dat., pl.	ἀνθρώποις	δώροις	ὁδοῖς
acc., pl.	ἀνθρώπους	δῶρα	ὁδούς

Table 3. Third-Declension Nouns

Case, Number	Third Declension (masc.)	Third Declension (masc.)	Third Declension (fem.)	Third Declension (neut.)
nom., sg.	ἄρχων	τίς	χάρις	ὄνομα
gen., sg.	ἄρχοντος	τίνος	χάριτος	ὀνόματος
dat., sg.	ἄρχοντι	τίνι	χάριτι	ὀνόματι
acc., sg.	ἄρχοντα	τίνα	χάριν	ὄνομα
nom., pl.	ἄρχοντες	τίνες	χάριτες	ὀνόματα
gen., pl.	ἀρχόντων	τίνων	χαρίτων	ὀνομάτων
dat., pl.	ἄρχουσι(ν)	τίσι(ν)	χάρισι(ν)	ὀνόμασι(ν)
acc., pl.	ἄρχοντας	τίνας	χάριτας	ὀνόματα

Personal Pronouns

Table 4. First-Person and Second-Person Personal Pronouns

Case, Number	First Person	Second Person
nom., sg.	ἐγώ	σύ
gen., sg.	(ἐ)μοῦ	σοῦ

Case, Number	First Person	Second Person
dat., sg.	(ἐ)μοί	σοί
acc., sg.	(ἐ)μέ	σέ
nom., pl.	ἡμεῖς	ὑμεῖς
gen., pl.	ἡμῶν	ὑμῶν
dat., pl.	ἡμῖν	ὑμῖν
acc., pl.	ἡμᾶς	ὑμᾶς

Table 5. Third-Person Personal Pronouns

Case, Number	Third Person (masc.)	Third Person (fem.)	Third Person (neut.)
nom., sg.	αὐτός	αὐτή	αὐτό
gen., sg.	αὐτοῦ	αὐτῆς	αὐτοῦ
dat., sg.	αὐτῷ	αὐτῇ	αὐτῷ
acc., sg.	αὐτόν	αὐτήν	αὐτό
nom., pl.	αὐτοί	αὐταί	αὐτά
gen., pl.	αὐτῶν	αὐτῶν	αὐτῶν
dat., pl.	αὐτοῖς	αὐταῖς	αὐτοῖς
acc., pl.	αὐτούς	αὐτάς	αὐτά

Indicative Verb Endings

Table 6. Present Indicative

Person, Number	Present, Active	Present, Middle/Passive
1st, sg.	λύω	λύομαι
2nd, sg.	λύεις	λύῃ
3rd, sg.	λύει	λύεται
1st, pl.	λύομεν	λυόμεθα
2nd, pl.	λύετε	λύεσθε
3rd, pl.	λύουσι(ν)	λύονται

Table 7. Future Indicative

Person, Number	Future, Active	Future, Middle	Future, Passive
1st, sg.	λύσω	λύσομαι	λυθήσομαι
2nd, sg.	λύσεις	λύσῃ	λυθήσῃ
3rd, sg.	λύσει	λύσεται	λυθήσεται
1st, pl.	λύσομεν	λυσόμεθα	λυθησόμεθα
2nd, pl.	λύσετε	λύσεσθε	λυθήσεσθε
3rd, pl.	λύσουσι(ν)	λύσονται	λυθήσονται

Table 8. Imperfect Indicative

Person, Number	Imperfect, Active	Imperfect, Middle/Passive
1st, sg.	ἔλυον	ἐλυόμην
2nd, sg.	ἔλυες	ἐλύου
3rd, sg.	ἔλυε(ν)	ἐλύετο
1st, pl.	ἐλύομεν	ἐλυόμεθα
2nd, pl.	ἐλύετε	ἐλύεσθε
3rd, pl.	ἔλυον	ἐλύοντο

Table 9. First Aorist Indicative

Person, Number	First Aorist, Active	First Aorist, Middle	First Aorist, Passive
1st, sg.	ἔλυσα	ἐλυσάμην	ἐλύθην
2nd, sg.	ἔλυσας	ἐλύσω	ἐλύθης
3rd, sg.	ἔλυσε(ν)	ἐλύσατο	ἐλύθη
1st, pl.	ἐλύσαμεν	ἐλυσάμεθα	ἐλύθημεν
2nd, pl.	ἐλύσατε	ἐλύσασθε	ἐλύθητε
3rd, pl.	ἔλυσαν	ἐλύσαντο	ἐλύθησαν

Table 10. Second Aorist Indicative

Person, Number	Second Aorist, Active	Second Aorist, Middle	Second Aorist, Passive
1st, sg.	ἔλιπον	ἐλιπόμην	ἐγράφην
2nd, sg.	ἔλιπες	ἐλίπου	ἐγράφης
3rd, sg.	ἔλιπε(ν)	ἐλίπετο	ἐγράφη
1st, pl.	ἐλίπομεν	ἐλιπόμεθα	ἐγράφημεν
2nd, pl.	ἐλίπετε	ἐλίπεσθε	ἐγράφητε
3rd, pl.	ἔλιπον	ἐλίποντο	ἐγράφησαν

Table 11. Perfect Indicative

Person, Number	Perfect, Active	Perfect, Middle/Passive
1st, sg.	λέλυκα	λέλυμαι
2nd, sg.	λέλυκας	λέλυσαι
3rd, sg.	λέλυκε(ν)	λέλυται
1st, pl.	λελύκαμεν	λελύμεθα
2nd, pl.	λελύκατε	λέλυσθε
3rd, pl.	λελύκασι(ν)	λέλυνται

Table 12. Pluperfect Indicative

Person, Number	Pluperfect, Active	Pluperfect, Middle/Passive
1st, sg.	ἐλελύκειν	ἐλελύμην
2nd, sg.	ἐλελύκεις	ἐλέλυσο
3rd, sg.	ἐλελύκει	ἐλέλυτο
1st, pl.	ἐλελύκειμεν	ἐλελύμεθα
2nd, pl.	ἐλελύκειτε	ἐλέλυσθε
3rd, pl.	ἐλελύκεισαν	ἐλέλυντο

Imperative Verb Endings

Table 13. Present Imperative

Person, Number	Present, Active	Present, Middle/Passive
2nd, sg.	λῦε	λύου
3rd, sg.	λυέτω	λυέσθω
2nd, pl.	λύετε	λύεσθε
3rd, pl.	λυέτωσαν	λυέσθωσαν

Table 14. First Aorist Imperative

Person, Number	First Aorist, Active	First Aorist, Middle	First Aorist, Passive
2nd, sg.	λῦσον	λῦσαι	λύθητι
3rd, sg.	λυσάτω	λυσάσθω	λυθήτω
2nd, pl.	λύσατε	λύσασθε	λύθητε
3rd, pl.	λυσάτωσαν	λυσάσθωσαν	λυθήτωσαν

Table 15. Second Aorist Imperative

Person, Number	Second Aorist, Active	Second Aorist, Middle	Second Aorist, Passive
2nd, sg.	λίπε	λιποῦ	χάρηθι
3rd, sg.	λιπέτω	λιπέσθω	χαρήτω
2nd, pl.	λίπετε	λίπεσθε	χάρητε
3rd, pl.	λιπέτωσαν	λιπέσθωσαν	χαρήτωσαν

Subjunctive Verb Endings

Table 16. Present Subjunctive

Person, Number	Present, Active	Present, Middle/Passive
1st, sg.	λύω	λύωμαι
2nd, sg.	λύῃς	λύῃ
3rd, sg.	λύῃ	λύηται
1st, pl.	λύωμεν	λυώμεθα
2nd, pl.	λύητε	λύησθε
3rd, pl.	λύωσι(ν)	λύωνται

Table 17. First Aorist Subjunctive

Person, Number	First Aorist, Active	First Aorist, Middle	First Aorist, Passive
1st, sg.	λύσω	λύσωμαι	λυθῶ
2nd, sg.	λύσῃς	λύσῃ	λυθῇς
3rd, sg.	λύσῃ	λύσηται	λυθῇ
1st, pl.	λύσωμεν	λυσώμεθα	λυθῶμεν
2nd, pl.	λύσητε	λύσησθε	λυθῆτε
3rd, pl.	λύσωσι(ν)	λύσωνται	λυθῶσι(ν)

Table 18. Second Aorist Subjunctive

Person, Number	Second Aorist, Active	Second Aorist, Middle	Second Aorist, Passive
1st, sg.	λίπω	λίπωμαι	γραφῶ
2nd, sg.	λίπῃς	λίπῃ	γραφῇς
3rd, sg.	λίπῃ	λίπηται	γραφῇ
1st, pl.	λίπωμεν	λιπώμεθα	γραφῶμεν
2nd, pl.	λίπητε	λίπησθε	γραφῆτε
3rd, pl.	λίπωσι(ν)	λίπωνται	γραφῶσι(ν)

Infinitive Endings

Table 19. Present Infinitive

Present, Active	Present, Middle/Passive
λύειν	λύεσθαι

Table 20. First Aorist Infinitive

First Aorist, Active	First Aorist, Middle	First Aorist, Passive
λῦσαι	λύσασθαι	λυθῆναι

Table 21. Second Aorist Infinitive

Second Aorist, Active	Second Aorist, Middle	Second Aorist, Passive
βαλεῖν	βαλέσθαι	γραφῆναι

Table 22. Perfect Infinitive

Perfect, Active	Perfect, Middle/Passive
λελυκέναι	λελύσθαι

Participle Endings

Table 23. Present Active Participle

Case, Number	Masculine	Feminine	Neuter
nom., sg.	λύων	λύουσα	λῦον
gen., sg.	λύοντος	λυούσης	λύοντος
dat., sg.	λύοντι	λυούσῃ	λύοντι
acc., sg.	λύοντα	λύουσαν	λῦον
nom., pl.	λύοντες	λύουσαι	λύοντα
gen., pl.	λυόντων	λυουσῶν	λυόντων
dat., pl.	λύουσι(ν)	λυούσαις	λύουσι(ν)
acc., pl.	λύοντας	λυούσας	λύοντα

Table 24. Present Middle/Passive Participle

Case, Number	Masculine	Feminine	Neuter
nom., sg.	λυόμενος	λυομένη	λυόμενον
gen., sg.	λυομένου	λυομένης	λυομένου
dat., sg.	λυομένῳ	λυομένη	λυομένῳ
acc., sg.	λυόμενον	λυομένην	λυόμενον
nom., pl.	λυόμενοι	λυόμεναι	λυόμενα
gen., pl.	λυομένων	λυομένων	λυομένων
dat., pl.	λυομένοις	λυομέναις	λυομένοις
acc., pl.	λυομένους	λυομένας	λυόμενα

Table 25. First Aorist Active Participle

Case, Number	Masculine	Feminine	Neuter
nom., sg.	λύσας	λύσασα	λῦσαν
gen., sg.	λύσαντος	λυσάσης	λύσαντος
dat., sg.	λύσαντι	λυσάσῃ	λύσαντι
acc., sg.	λύσαντα	λύσασαν	λῦσαν
nom., pl.	λύσαντες	λύσασαι	λύσαντα
gen., pl.	λυσάντων	λυσασῶν	λυσάντων
dat., pl.	λύσασι(ν)	λυσάσαις	λύσασι(ν)
acc., pl.	λύσαντας	λυσάσας	λύσαντα

Table 26. First Aorist Middle Participle

Case, Number	Masculine	Feminine	Neuter
nom., sg.	λυσάμενος	λυσαμένη	λυσάμενον
gen., sg.	λυσαμένου	λυσαμένης	λυσαμένου
dat., sg.	λυσαμένῳ	λυσαμένη	λυσαμένῳ
acc., sg.	λυσάμενον	λυσαμένην	λυσάμενον
nom., pl.	λυσάμενοι	λυσάμεναι	λυσάμενα
gen., pl.	λυσαμένων	λυσαμένων	λυσαμένων
dat., pl.	λυσαμένοις	λυσαμέναις	λυσαμένοις
acc., pl.	λυσαμένους	λυσαμένας	λυσάμενα

Table 27. First Aorist Passive Participle

Case, Number	Masculine	Feminine	Neuter
nom., sg.	λυθείς	λυθεῖσα	λυθέν
gen., sg.	λυθέντος	λυθείσης	λυθέντος
dat., sg.	λυθέντι	λυθείσῃ	λυθέντι
acc., sg.	λυθέντα	λυθεῖσαν	λυθέν
nom., pl.	λυθέντες	λυθεῖσαι	λυθέντα
gen., pl.	λυθέντων	λυθεισῶν	λυθέντων
dat., pl.	λυθεῖσι(ν)	λυθείσαις	λυθεῖσι(ν)
acc., pl.	λυθέντας	λυθείσας	λυθέντα

Table 28. Second Aorist Active Participle

Case, Number	Masculine	Feminine	Neuter
nom., sg.	ἐλθών	ἐλθοῦσα	ἐλθόν
gen., sg.	ἐλθόντος	ἐλθούσης	ἐλθόντος
dat., sg.	ἐλθόντι	ἐλθούσῃ	ἐλθόντι
acc., sg.	ἐλθόντα	ἐλθοῦσαν	ἐλθόν
nom., pl.	ἐλθόντες	ἐλθοῦσαι	ἐλθόντα
gen., pl.	ἐλθόντων	ἐλθουσῶν	ἐλθόντων
dat., pl.	ἐλθοῦσι(ν)	ἐλθούσαις	ἐλθοῦσι(ν)
acc., pl.	ἐλθόντας	ἐλθούσας	ἐλθόντα

Table 29. Second Aorist Middle Participle

Case, Number	Masculine	Feminine	Neuter
nom., sg.	γενόμενος	γενομένη	γενόμενον
gen., sg.	γενομένου	γενομένης	γενομένου
dat., sg.	γενομένῳ	γενομένῃ	γενομένῳ
acc., sg.	γενόμενον	γενομένην	γενόμενον
nom., pl.	γενόμενοι	γενόμεναι	γενόμενα
gen., pl.	γενομένων	γενομένων	γενομένων
dat., pl.	γενομένοις	γενομέναις	γενομένοις
acc., pl.	γενομένους	γενομένας	γενόμενα

Table 30. Second Aorist Passive Participle

Case, Number	Masculine	Feminine	Neuter
nom., sg.	στραφείς	στραφεῖσα	στραφέν
gen., sg.	στραφέντος	στραφείσης	στραφέντος
dat., sg.	στραφέντι	στραφείσῃ	στραφέντι
acc., sg.	στραφέντα	στραφεῖσαν	στραφέν
nom., pl.	στραφέντες	στραφεῖσαι	στραφέντα
gen., pl.	στραφέντων	στραφεισῶν	στραφέντων
dat., pl.	στραφεῖσι(ν)	στραφείσαις	στραφεῖσι(ν)
acc., pl.	στραφέντας	στραφείσας	στραφέντα

Table 31. Perfect Active Participle

Case, Number	Masculine	Feminine	Neuter
nom., sg.	λελυκώς	λελυκυῖα	λελυκός
gen., sg.	λελυκότος	λελυκυίας	λελυκότος
dat., sg.	λελυκότι	λελυκυίᾳ	λελυκότι
acc., sg.	λελυκότα	λελυκυῖαν	λελυκός
nom., pl.	λελυκότες	λελυκυῖαι	λελυκότα
gen., pl.	λελυκότων	λελυκυιῶν	λελυκότων
dat., pl.	λελυκόσι(ν)	λελυκυίαις	λελυκόσι(ν)
acc., pl.	λελυκότας	λελυκυίας	λελυκότα

Table 32. Perfect Middle/Passive Participle

Case, Number	Masculine	Feminine	Neuter
nom., sg.	λελυμένος	λελυμένη	λελυμένον
gen., sg.	λελυμένου	λελυμένης	λελυμένου
dat., sg.	λελυμένῳ	λελυμένῃ	λελυμένῳ
acc., sg.	λελυμένον	λελυμένην	λελυμένον
nom., pl.	λελυμένοι	λελυμέναι	λελυμένα
gen., pl.	λελυμένων	λελυμένων	λελυμένων
dat., pl.	λελυμένοις	λελυμέναις	λελυμένοις
acc., pl.	λελυμένους	λελυμένας	λελυμένα

Notes

Preface

1. A. T. Robertson, *A Grammar of the Greek New Testament in Light of Historical Research*, 5th ed. (Nashville: Broadman, 1934); William D. Mounce, *Basics of Biblical Greek*, 3rd ed. (Grand Rapids: Zondervan, 2009); Rodney J. Decker, *Reading Koine Greek* (Grand Rapids: Baker Academic, 2014); Daniel B. Wallace, *Greek Grammar beyond the Basics* (Grand Rapids: Zondervan, 1997); Stanley Porter, *Idioms of the Greek New Testament*, 2nd ed. (Sheffield: Sheffield Academic, 1994); Constantine R. Campbell, *Basics of Verbal Aspect in Biblical Greek* (Grand Rapids: Zondervan, 2008); Steven E. Runge, *Discourse Grammar of the Greek New Testament* (Peabody, MA: Hendrickson, 2010). See also the recommended resources in chapter 18, below.

Chapter 2 The Big Picture of Language

1. John Nolland, for example, reflecting on the larger context of what has preceded this section, suggests, "It would appear that Matthew holds that Jesus offered, in part by drawing on the insight of the Prophets, a new depth of insight into what the Law requires over against what he (Matthew) considered to be a general superficiality, a foreshortened perspective, in the reading of the Law" (John Nolland, *Matthew*, New International Greek Testament Commentary [Grand Rapids: Eerdmans, 2005], 219).

Chapter 4 Resources for Navigating the Greek New Testament

1. Frederick W. Danker, Walter Bauer, William F. Arndt, and F. Wilbur Gingrich, *A Greek-English Lexicon of the New Testament and Other Early Christian Literature*, 3rd ed. (Chicago: University of Chicago Press, 2000); Johannes P. Louw and Eugene A. Nida, eds., *Greek-English Lexicon of the New Testament: Based on Semantic Domains*, 2nd ed. (New York: United Bible Societies, 1989).

2. James Strong, *Strong's Exhaustive Concordance of the Bible*, updated ed. (Peabody, MA: Hendrickson, 2009).

3. Cleon L. Rogers Jr. and Cleon L. Rogers III, *New Linguistic and Exegetical Key to the Greek New Testament* (Grand Rapids: Zondervan, 1998).

Chapter 5 Introduction to Greek Verbs and Nominals

1. A growing body of literature argues against the use of the category "deponent." It is used here primarily for pragmatic reasons rather than linguistic ones. For a summary, see Constantine R. Campbell, *Advances in the Study of Greek: New Insights for Reading the New Testament* (Grand Rapids: Zondervan, 2015), 91–104.

Chapter 6 Nominative, Accusative, and Vocative Cases

1. Note that appendix 2 provides ending charts for all of the major parts of speech for those who may be inclined to commit them to memory.

Chapter 9 (Independent) Indicative-Mood Verbs

1. The bracketed word in the Greek text of this passage represents a text-critical question. It has been included in the passage though its originality to the text has been debated. More on this in chapter 15.

2. Constantine R. Campbell, *Basics of Verbal Aspect in Biblical Greek* (Grand Rapids: Zondervan, 2008), 106.

Chapter 13 (Dependent) Greek Participles

1. Though the form αὐτοῦ in this verse looks like the personal pronoun, this is actually an adverb meaning "here."

Chapter 15 Comparing English Translations

1. Daniel B. Wallace, "Dr. Wallace: Earliest Manuscript of the New Testament Discovered?," *DTS Magazine*, February 9, 2012, http://www.dts.edu/read/wallace-new-testament-manscript-first-century/.

2. George Houston, *Inside Roman Libraries: Book Collections and Their Management in Antiquity* (Chapel Hill: University of North Carolina Press, 2014).

3. Daniel B. Wallace, "The Textual Reliability of the New Testament," in *The Reliability of the New Testament: Bart D. Ehrman and Daniel B. Wallace in Dialogue*, ed. Robert B. Stewart (Minneapolis: Fortress, 2011), 35.

4. For a study of the early period of copying, see James R. Royse, *Scribal Habits in Early Greek New Testament Papyri*, New Testament Tools, Studies and Documents 36 (Leiden: Brill, 2008). See also Charles E. Hill and Michael J. Kruger, *The Early Text of the New Testament* (Oxford: Oxford University Press, 2012).

5. Summary data taken from Craig L. Blomberg with Jennifer Foutz Markley, *A Handbook of New Testament Exegesis* (Grand Rapids: Baker Academic, 2010), 9–13.

6. For introductions to the field of textual criticism, see David A. Black, *New Testament Textual Criticism: A Concise Guide* (Grand Rapids: Baker, 1994); Bruce M. Metzger and Bart D. Ehrman, *The Text of the New Testament: Its Transmission, Corruption, and Restoration*, 4th ed. (New York: Oxford University Press, 2005).

7. *The Greek New Testament*, 5th ed. (New York: United Bible Societies, 2014); Barbara Aland et al., eds., *Novum Testamentum Graece*, 28th ed. (Stuttgart: Deutsche Bibelgesellschaft, 2012).

8. Bruce Manning Metzger, *A Textual Commentary on the Greek New Testament: A Companion Volume to the United Bible Societies' Greek New Testament*, 4th rev. ed. (London / New York: United Bible Societies, 1994), 6–7.

9. For a list of the most-used translations, see the findings of the Barna Group's 2013 "State of the Bible" report, accessible at http://www.americanbible.org/uploads /content/State%20of%20the%20Bible%20Report%202013.pdf.

10. National Center for Education Statistics, "National Assessment of Adult Literacy: A Nationally Representative and Continuing Assessment of English Language Literary Skills of American Adults," accessed November 27, 2015, http://nces.ed.gov /naal.

11. See Herbert W. Bateman IV, *Interpreting the General Letters: An Exegetical Handbook* (Grand Rapids: Kregel, 2013), 146–48.

12. For an introductory guide, see Gordon D. Fee and Mark L. Strauss, *How to Choose a Translation for All Its Worth: A Guide to Understanding and Using Bible Versions* (Grand Rapids: Zondervan, 2007).

13. For a theoretical overview of the importance of this valuable process, see Dave Brunn, *One Bible, Many Versions: Are All Translations Created Equal?* (Downers Grove, IL: InterVarsity, 2013).

Chapter 16 Bridging Contexts

1. For a fairly exhaustive rebuttal, see Kevin J. Vanhoozer, *Is There a Meaning in This Text? The Bible, the Reader, and the Morality of Literary Knowledge* (Grand Rapids: Zondervan, 2009).

2. Hard delineations in these areas probably cannot be raised, since the historical, social, and cultural contexts share certain features. These are simply different lenses that help us to focus on relevant aspects of the world of and around the New Testament. For a helpful volume dealing with the major areas of historical, social, and cultural contexts, see Joel B. Green and Lee Martin McDonald, eds., *The World of the New Testament: Cultural, Social, and Historical Contexts* (Grand Rapids: Baker Academic, 2013).

3. For helpful overviews of the period, see Shaye J. D. Cohen, *From the Maccabees to the Mishnah*, 2nd ed. (Louisville: Westminster John Knox, 2006); James C. VanderKam, *An Introduction to Early Judaism* (Grand Rapids: Eerdmans, 2001).

4. For a helpful introduction, see Dietmar Neufeld and Richard E. DeMaris, eds., *Understanding the Social World of the New Testament* (New York: Routledge, 2009).

5. For a helpful study, see Joseph H. Hellerman, *Jesus and the People of God: Reconfiguring Ethnic Identity* (Sheffield: Phoenix Press, 2007).

6. For a recent volume exploring this issue, see Scot McKnight and Joseph B. Modica, eds., *Jesus Is Lord, Caesar Is Not: Evaluating Empire in New Testament Studies* (Downers Grove, IL: IVP Academic, 2013).

7. J. A. Harrill, "Slavery," in *Dictionary of New Testament Background*, ed. Craig A. Evans and Stanley E. Porter (Downers Grove, IL: InterVarsity, 2000), 1126.

8. For a helpful recent introduction to reading the Gospels, see Jonathan T. Pennington, *Reading the Gospels Wisely: A Narrative and Theological Introduction* (Grand Rapids: Baker Academic, 2012).

9. A work's intended outcomes are what scholars sometimes refer to as its "perlocutionary force," that is, what the author intended to accomplish within the audience by writing in the manner in which they did.

10. For a discussion, see R. T. France, *The Gospel of Matthew*, New International Commentary on the New Testament (Grand Rapids: Eerdmans, 2007), 126; I. Howard Marshall, *The Gospel of Luke*, New International Greek Testament Commentary (Grand Rapids: Eerdmans, 1978), 166–67.

11. For an introduction to historical Jesus studies, see Darrell L. Bock, *Studying the Historical Jesus: A Guide to Sources and Methods* (Grand Rapids: Baker Academic, 2002).

12. For an introductory summary, see D. F. Watson, "Chreia/Aphorism," in *Dictionary of Jesus and the Gospels: A Compendium of Contemporary Biblical Scholarship* (Downers Grove, IL: InterVarsity, 1992), 104–6.

13. New Testament scholars often debate the extent to which the Pauline Epistles actually come from Paul himself. Of those questioned, Ephesians, Colossians, and the Pastoral Epistles (1 and 2 Timothy and Titus) are the most commonly doubted to be from Paul directly. There are good reasons to believe Paul used amanuenses (individuals who write on someone's behalf; cf. Rom. 16:22) or collaborated with coauthors and/or editors who may have contributed to what was written. For a discussion of authorship issues in the Pauline corpus, see Stanley E. Porter, *The Pauline Canon* (Leiden: Brill, 2004). For examination of authorship issues for the New Testament as a whole, see Gary M. Burge, Lynn H. Cohick, and Gene L. Green, *The New Testament in Antiquity: A Survey of the New Testament within Its Cultural Contexts* (Grand Rapids: Zondervan, 2009); Luke T. Johnson, *The Writings of the New Testament*, 3rd ed. (Minneapolis: Fortress, 2010).

14. The classic introduction to the topic is John J. Collins, *The Apocalyptic Imagination*, 2nd ed. (Grand Rapids: Eerdmans, 1998).

15. For a study of the different forms that Jesus's teaching materials take, see Robert H. Stein, *The Method and Message of Jesus' Teaching*, rev. ed. (Louisville: Westminster John Knox, 1994).

16. See Ben Witherington III, *The Letters to Philemon, the Colossians, and the Ephesians: A Socio-Rhetorical Commentary on the Captivity Epistles* (Grand Rapids: Eerdmans, 2007), 219–23.

17. See R. Timothy McLay, *The Use of the Septuagint in New Testament Research* (Grand Rapids: Eerdmans, 2003).

18. For examinations of the use of the Old Testament in the New Testament in Paul and the Gospels, see Richard B. Hays, *Echoes of Scripture in the Letters of Paul* (New Haven: Yale University Press, 1993); Hays, *Reading Backwards: Figural Christology in the Fourfold Gospel Witness* (Waco: Baylor University Press, 2014).

19. For an introduction and presentation of three approaches, see Kenneth Berding, Jonathan Lunde, and Stanley N. Gundry, eds., *Three Views on the New Testament Use of the Old Testament* (Grand Rapids: Zondervan, 2008).

20. For an example, see A. Chadwick Thornhill, *The Chosen People: Election, Paul, and Second Temple Judaism* (Downers Grove, IL: IVP Academic, 2015).

21. For an introduction, see Kent L. Yinger, *The New Perspective on Paul: An Introduction* (Eugene, OR: Wipf & Stock, 2011).

22. Grant R. Osborne, *The Hermeneutical Spiral: A Comprehensive Introduction to Biblical Interpretation*, 2nd ed. (Downers Grove, IL: InterVarsity, 2006), 22.

Chapter 17 Word Studies

1. Frederick W. Danker, Walter Bauer, William F. Arndt, and F. Wilbur Gingrich, *A Greek-English Lexicon of the New Testament and Other Early Christian Literature*, 3rd ed. (Chicago: University of Chicago Press, 2000); Johannes P. Louw and Eugene A. Nida, eds., *Greek-English Lexicon of the New Testament: Based on Semantic Domains*, 2nd ed. (New York: United Bible Societies, 1989); Moisés Silva, ed., *New International Dictionary of New Testament Theology and Exegesis*, 2nd ed., 5 vols. (Grand Rapids: Zondervan, 2014); Douglas Mangum, ed., *Lexham Theological Wordbook* (Bellingham, WA: Lexham, 2014).

2. The biases of the *Theological Dictionary of the New Testament* (ed. G. Kittel and G. Friedrich, trans. G. W. Bromiley, 10 vols. [Grand Rapids: Eerdmans, 1964–76]) are, for example, well documented. This does not negate the value of the work in its entirety, but it does mean its insights should be evaluated and not used uncritically. For an examination, see Wayne A. Meeks, "A Nazi New Testament Professor Reads His Bible: The Strange Case of Gerhard Kittel," in *The Idea of Biblical Interpretation: Essays in Honor of James L. Kugel*, ed. Hindy Najman and Judith H. Newman (Leiden: Brill, 2004), 513–44.

3. Henry George Liddell, Robert Scott, and Henry Stuart Jones, *A Greek-English Lexicon*, 9th ed. with rev. supplement (Oxford: Clarendon, 1996); Johan Lust, Erik Eynikel, and Katrin Hauspie, eds., *A Greek-English Lexicon of the Septuagint*, rev. ed. (Stuttgart: Deutsche Bibelgesellschaft, 2003).

4. For an introduction to the debate, see James K. Beilby and Paul Rhodes Eddy, eds., *Justification: Five Views* (Downers Grove, IL: InterVarsity, 2011).

5. Romans 1:17, 32; 2:5, 13, 26; 3:4–5, 10, 20, 21–30; 4:2–6, 9, 11, 13, 22, 25; 5:1, 7, 9, 16–21; 6:7, 13, 16, 18–20; 7:12; 8:4, 10, 30, 33; 9:30–31; 10:3–6, 10; 14:17.

6. Lust, Eynikel, and Hauspie, eds., *Greek-English Lexicon of the Septuagint*.

7. Moisés Silva, ed., *New International Dictionary of New Testament Theology and Exegesis* (Grand Rapids: Zondervan, 2014), 725.

8. BDAG, 249.

9. Louw-Nida, 2:64.

10. For a helpful analysis of the lexical evidence, see Richard K. Moore, "ΔΙΚΑΙΟΣΥΝΗ and Cognates in Paul: The Semantic Gulf between Two Major Lexicons (Bauer-Arndt-Gingrich-Danker and Louw-Nida)," *Colloquium* 30 (1998): 27–43.

11. For an introduction to the role of works at the final judgment, see Alan P. Stanley and Stanley N. Gundry, eds., *Four Views on the Role of Works at the Final Judgment* (Grand Rapids: Zondervan, 2013).

12. For a helpful interpretation, see Simon J. Gathercole, "A Law unto Themselves: The Gentiles in Romans 2.14–15 Revisited," *Journal for the Study of the New Testament* 85 (2002): 27–49.

13. There are a host of exegetical questions in this section that cannot be explored here but that are worth pursuing in the secondary literature.

14. For some recent, and divergent, interpretations, see Michael F. Bird, "Justification as Forensic Declaration and Covenant Membership: A *Via Media* between Reformed and Revisionist Readings of Paul," *Tyndale Bulletin* 57 (2006): 109–30; Douglas A. Campbell, "Beyond Justification in Paul: The Thesis of the Deliverance of God," *Scottish Journal of Theology* 65 (2012): 90–104; F. Gerald Downing, "Justification as Acquittal? A Critical Examination of Judicial Verdicts in Paul's Literary and Actual Contexts," *Catholic Biblical Quarterly* 74 (2012): 298–318; Paula Frederiksen, "Paul's Letter to the Romans, the Ten Commandments, and Pagan 'Justification by Faith,'" *Journal of Biblical Literature* 133 (2014): 801–8; Benjamin J. Ribbens, "Forensic-Retributive Justification in Romans 3:21–26: Paul's Doctrine of Justification in Dialogue with Hebrews," *Catholic Biblical Quarterly* 74 (2012): 548–67; N. T. Wright, "Justification: Yesterday, Today, and Forever," *Journal of the Evangelical Theological Society* 54 (2011): 49–63.

Chapter 18 The Grammar of Theology (Putting It All Together)

1. Grant R. Osborne, *The Hermeneutical Spiral: A Comprehensive Introduction to Biblical Interpretation*, 2nd ed. (Downers Grove, IL: InterVarsity, 2006).

2. Ben Witherington III, *The Rest of Life: Rest, Play, Eating, Studying, Sex from a Kingdom Perspective* (Grand Rapids: Eerdmans, 2012), 111.

3. Craig A. Evans and Stanley E. Porter, eds., *Dictionary of New Testament Background* (Downers Grove, IL: InterVarsity, 2000); John J. Collins and Daniel C. Harlow, eds., *The Eerdmans Dictionary of Early Judaism* (Grand Rapids: Eerdmans, 2010); David Noel Freedman, ed., *Anchor Bible Dictionary*, 6 vols. (New York: Doubleday, 1992); Freedman, ed., *Eerdmans Dictionary of the Bible* (Grand Rapids: Eerdmans, 2000); John D. Barry et al., eds., *Lexham Bible Dictionary* (Bellingham, WA: Lexham, 2015).

4. Craig S. Keener, *IVP Bible Background Commentary: New Testament*, 2nd ed. (Downers Grove, IL: IVP Academic, 2014); C. K. Barrett, ed., *New Testament Background*, rev. ed. (San Francisco: HarperSanFrancisco, 1995); Craig A. Evans, *Ancient Texts for New Testament Studies* (Grand Rapids: Baker Academic, 2011); Joel B. Green and Lee Martin McDonald, eds., *The World of the New Testament: Cultural, Social, and Historical Contexts* (Grand Rapids: Baker Academic, 2013); Everett Ferguson, *Backgrounds of Early Christianity*, 3rd ed. (Grand Rapids: Eerdmans, 2003); Bruce J. Malina, *The New Testament World*, 3rd ed. (Louisville: Westminster John Knox, 2001).

5. William M. Klein, Craig L. Blomberg, and Robert L. Hubbard Jr., *Introduction to Biblical Interpretation*, rev. ed. (Nashville: Nelson, 2004); Darrell L. Bock and Buist M. Fanning, eds., *Interpreting the New Testament Text* (Wheaton: Crossway, 2006); David R. Bauer and Robert A. Traina, *Inductive Bible Study* (Grand Rapids: Baker Academic, 2011); Craig L. Blomberg with Jennifer Foutz Markley, *A Handbook of New Testament Exegesis* (Grand Rapids: Baker Academic, 2010); Richard J. Erickson, *A Beginner's Guide to New Testament Exegesis* (Downers Grove, IL: IVP Academic, 2005).

6. Moisés Silva, *Biblical Words and Their Meaning* (Grand Rapids: Zondervan, 1995); Ben Witherington III, *New Testament Rhetoric* (Eugene, OR: Wipf & Stock, 2009); Joel B. Green, ed., *Hearing the New Testament* (Grand Rapids: Eerdmans, 2010); G. K. Beale and D. A. Carson, eds., *Commentary on the New Testament Use of the Old Testament* (Grand Rapids: Baker Academic, 2007); Gleason L. Archer and Gregory Chirichigno, *Old Testament Quotations in the New Testament* (repr., Eugene, OR: Wipf & Stock, 2005).

7. These questions are adopted and adapted from Klein, Blomberg, and Hubbard, *Introduction to Biblical Interpretation*, 487–98.

8. William D. Mounce, *Basics of Biblical Greek*, 3rd ed. (Grand Rapids: Zondervan, 2009); Rodney J. Decker, *Reading Koine Greek* (Grand Rapids: Baker Academic, 2014); Stanley E. Porter, Jeffrey T. Reed, and Matthew Brook O'Donnell, *Fundamentals of New Testament Greek* (Grand Rapids: Eerdmans, 2010).

9. Daniel B. Wallace, *Greek Grammar beyond the Basics* (Grand Rapids: Zondervan, 1997); Wallace, *The Basics of New Testament Syntax* (Grand Rapids: Zondervan, 2000); Stanley Porter, *Idioms of the Greek New Testament*, 2nd ed. (Sheffield: Sheffield Academic, 1994); Steven E. Runge, *Discourse Grammar of the Greek New Testament* (Peabody, MA: Hendrickson, 2010); David Alan Black, *Linguistics for Students of New Testament Greek*, 2nd ed. (Grand Rapids: Baker Academic, 1995); Constantine R. Campbell, *Basics of Verbal Aspect in Biblical Greek* (Grand Rapids: Zondervan, 2008); Murray Harris, *Prepositions and Theology in the Greek New Testament* (Grand Rapids: Zondervan, 2012).

Glossary of Select Greek Terms

The following glossary includes only those words that were included throughout the book as words to memorize.

ἀγαπάω to love

ἅγιος holy, saint

αἰτέω to ask

ἀκολουθέω to follow

ἀκούω to hear

ἀλλά but, and, yet

ἁμαρτία sin

ἀνά (acc.) up

ἀνήρ man, husband

ἄνθρωπος human, man

ἄξιος worthy

ἀπό from

ἀπόστολος apostle, emissary

αὐτός he, she, it; self, same

γάρ for, because

γίνομαι to be, to exist (deponent)

γινώσκω to know

γλῶσσα tongue, language

γραφή writing, Scripture

γυνή woman, wife

δέ and, but, now

διά (gen.) through; (acc.) on account of

δίκαιος righteous

δοῦλος slave, servant

δῶρον gift

ἐάν if, when

ἑαυτοῦ yourself

ἐγείρω to rise, to wake

ἐγώ I

ἔθνος nation, people

εἰ if, because, that

εἶδον to see

εἰμί to be

εἰς (acc.) into

ἐκ, ἐξ (gen.) out of, from

ἐκεῖνος, ἐκείνη, ἐκεῖνο that; he, she, it

ἐν (dat.) in

ἐπί (gen.) over, on, at the time of; (dat.) on the basis of; (acc.) on, to, against

ἔρχομαι to come, to go

εὑρίσκω to find

ἐχθρός enemy

ζητέω to seek

ἡμεῖς we

θέλω to wish, to desire

θεός God, god

Ἰησοῦς Jesus

ἵνα in order that, so that, that

ἵστημι to stand

καί and, now, also, yet, then

καρπός fruit

κατά (gen.) down from, against; (acc.) according to, throughout, during

κηρύσσω to proclaim, to preach

κύριος a lord, Lord

λαμβάνω to take, to receive

λέγω to speak (aorist: εἶπον)

λόγος word, statement

μετάνοια repentance

μή not, lest

νεκρός dead

νόμος law, Law

ὁ, ἡ, τό the, this one, who

οἶδα to know

ὄνομα name

ὅς, ἥ, ὅ who, which

ὅτε when, as long as

ὅτι that, because

οὐ, οὐκ, οὐχ not

οὐδείς no one

οὖν therefore, thus, indeed, but

οὗτος, αὕτη, τοῦτο this; he, she, it

ὄχλος crowd

παρά (gen.) from; (dat.) with; (acc.) beside

πᾶς all, each, every

πατήρ father

πίστις faith, trust, faithfulness

πνεῦμα spirit, Spirit

ποιέω to do, to make

πορεύομαι to come, to go

πρός to, toward, with

προσεύχομαι to pray

προφήτης prophet, proclaimer

σάρξ flesh, body

σταυρόω to crucify

σύ you (sg.)

σῶμα body

τίς, τί who, what

τις, τι someone, a certain one

ὕδωρ water

ὑμεῖς you (pl.)

ὑπέρ (gen.) for; (acc.) above

ὑπό (gen.) by; (acc.) under

Χριστός Christ, Anointed One

Index of Greek Words

Index of Scripture

Index of Subjects

accent marks, 6–7
accusative. *See* nominal: accusative
adjective, 68–69
  attributive, 68–69
  predicate, 69
  substantival, 69
agency, 36
alphabet, 5–6
analytical lexicon, 32, 44–46
apposition, 49, 53, 56
article, 46–48, 61–64
association, 58
attributive genitive, 54, 56

breathing marks, 6–7

case. *See* nominal: case
cause, 59
clause, 12, 23–25
  dependent, 23–25, 121–23
  independent, 23–24, 121–23
commentaries, 34
compound verb, 58
concordance, 33
conditional sentences, 122–23
conjunction, 25–26
context, 15–76
  canonical, 173–75
  cultural, 159–61

historical, 152–56
intertextual, 169–73
literary, 161–69
social, 156–59

dative. *See* nominal: dative
dative of interest, 57
demonstrative pronoun, 66–67
diagramming, 126–30
direct object, 48
diphthong, 6
discourse analysis, 124–26
double accusative, 48–49

gender. *See* nominal: gender
genitive. *See* nominal: genitive
genre, 161–68
grammatical agreement, 41

imperative mood, 25, 37, 87–92, 95,
    111, 118, 121, 125, 169, 198, 204
indefinite pronoun, 68
indicative mood, 25, 37, 39, 73–87, 92,
    103, 106, 113, 117–18, 121–22, 125,
    127, 169, 188–89, 198, 204
indirect object, 57
infinitive, 17, 20–25, 29, 64, 99–108,
    110, 117, 121–22
interlinear, 30
interrogative pronoun, 67–68

Made in the USA
Coppell, TX
07 September 2024

36951413R00163